Glassy Water
A Novel

By
Philip Gagnon

This book is a work of fiction. Names, characters, places, and incidents are products of the author's imagination or are used fictitiously. Any resemblance to actual events, locales or persons, living or dead, is entirely coincidental.

July 2014

Copyright © 2014 by Philip Gagnon
All rights reserved. This book may not be reproduced in any form, in whole or in part, without written permission from the author.

Printed in the United States of America

Mitzu Publishing Service

MitzuPublishing@aol.com
ISBN-13: 978-0692272930
ISBN-10: 0692272933

Other books by Mitzu Publishing include:

MOM, I NEED YOUR HELP

BEWARE THE THIEF WHO COMES IN A BAGGIE

A GUN IN THE HOUSE

GLASSY WATER
A Novel

by
Philip Gagnon

Chapter 1
Today, October 11

What the..? How in..? Why did..? He would have been more at ease learning how to fly after being pushed naked from the top of a twenty-story building. *Who am I..?*

This was a strange feeling he could not fathom. As his mind gradually focused, he pondered why he blacked out. It was cold, damp, and pressure enveloped every square inch of his body. *John Doe...huh...* had no idea why he felt wrapped-up tighter than a mummy, and as he wished his eyes open in an attempt at seeing, nothing presented itself except a literal void. No part of his body would budge other than his eyelids, and he could only speculate if they were moving.

John worked hard getting his senses about himself but became extremely frustrated when nothing obeyed his commands. Both legs were angled away from his body and both arms were down by his sides, but it was impossible to glean if he was flat on his back or buttocks up. Was he facing those pearly gates on cloud nine with a welcoming committee in Cottonelle white sheets or a fire pit guarded by the lunatic pitchfork toting Lucifer.

He ordered his legs to perform some Fred Astaire moves, but it seemed as if they didn't comprehend very well or were encased in something solid. Attempting to move his arms produced the same result. Badly flustered, John initiated an argument with himself which caused a sneezing fit that began snapping his noggin and created some movement, but he didn't realize it because the crying and tears would come first. The inherent urge to scream and yell high on his list of achievements.

It was useless, like being the cream filling jailed inside a

Twinkie; itself cast aside after losing its bite due to an expiration date. He just could not understand his precarious predicament. At that moment, John figured he was defeated and ready to submit, giving up all hope. But the man knew he wasn't built like that, and even when failure became reality, he always gave it all he could afford. There was no way he imagined himself giving up now, even though it was hopeless envisioning a positive outcome.

He sank so low the thought of making a deal with one of the shady characters from a few paragraphs above came to mind. You know, the bozo with the dinner fork or whatever it was. But no, John would not allow that guy to take credit for what he was about to do. Wait a minute. Wouldn't that mean going backwards? Wasn't it the same bozo referenced in the third paragraph after the story began? An idea by the nut job writing this piece of trash? Definitely won't be going back there. He'll go it alone and man up as no one would be helping if there was nothing in it for them.

With nothing more worth thinking about and time on his hands with no where else to go, John battled to move his arms, legs, and head while rocking himself back and forth. Slowly but honestly, body parts made headway and gained territory. Whatever was encompassing his frame started giving in to the fight, moving away or compacting in some forgiving manner.

He was getting good movement from his arms and continued digging at what was around him. It felt like dirt and leaves and had a composted smell. The increase in movement encouraging enough that John was stronger with every growing moment. Still no light anywhere in his tunnel, but one can dream on while looking for that elusive cream filled snack.

He managed to move himself somewhat and brought both hands in front of his stomach. The dirt on the sides and against his back was soft, but while digging in front of him, the ground may as well have been concrete, and he couldn't gain at all.

Hard as a rock? Well, Einstein figured he was facing down, and using his arms, he tried to push himself up a la Jack Lalanne. He fancied impressing the audience with the same grace and style Jack had. Nope. Even at 96, Jack performed better than anything attempted in this neck of the woods. The push-ups began with a small amount of movement and lots of choice words. The dirt was moving against his back and falling down each side towards his hands. Then he attempted bringing both knees up to his midsection, but only one would make the trip. The other knee was stuck straight and would not be bribed at any level.

John pushed and shoved with all his net worth. With both arms and one leg working together, he huffed and puffed and produced a big push, going up three inches. He maneuvered himself through the rubble to benefit from the added real estate and abused those limbs, trying to pack down the encompassing dirt then gave another effort using every muscle in his arsenal. He found himself breaking free and brought his one thigh close to his belly, pushing himself up and away from the tomb he was beginning to dig. *That's stupid! Dig as in like? Dumb!*

John cleaned his eyes, ears, nose, mouth, and hair of crud. The side of his head felt like it had been hit with a baseball bat. He glanced around with eyeballs that were dancing in *La La Land*, and noticed he was in the middle of the woods with his feet still in the debris he'd just dug his way out of. There was a cast on one leg which explained the immobility. *Why was that on there?*

The ground by his grave was more leaves than dirt, which was why he could breathe and didn't suffocate. The array of branches circling his head must have also let air in. But John did not, and could not know how or why he ended up in that hole.

Off to the right, he saw a white car covered in mud and parked on a dirt road. Another car was behind it. John was too confused to process why they were there, or even where he was.

He started feeling light-headed and famished, his brain taxed beyond a refund. He looked up to get his bearings. The sun was low in the sky, and Einstein figured in a few minutes, he'd be able to tell which way it was moving, letting him know if it was morning or afternoon, and if it was rising in the east or setting in the west, thereby creating a mental compass and the approximate time of day.

Looking at the foliage on the trees gave him a hint of the season. Leaves were starting to color, but they were still mostly on the trees, telling him it would be sometime in early to mid-October. Glancing at his calendar watch would've been easier.

Thinking about that, John remembered he didn't even

know where he was, so it could be a month one way or the other. *Canada or Texas, where is this place?* As he thought of those things and knew they came from some type of education, he realized again he didn't know his name or anything else about himself. Checking his wallet would offer sound guidance.

Beside him, there was another area of disturbed ground. Curious, John leaned over and used his hands to dig into the soft soil. It was not packed at all with leaves and sticks mixed in, making for easy digging. After penetrating the ground a few inches, he detected an odor. A little farther down and with the odor getting real strong, he saw clothing. As he moved the dirt away, he could see a person's belt.

Einstein was back and figured the body couldn't have been there long or the animals would've been doing the excavating. He dug his way up the shirt and a few minutes later came to a throat. He desperately kept working his way up and completely cleared the area around the face but could tell immediately the person was gone. Dead. It was a woman whose skin had turned blue, and there appeared to be bite marks all over the front of her. He checked for signs of life anyway but found none. The doctor in him ever the professional.

John recognized the girl and knew her name, but he didn't immediately realize what it was. A few minutes went by and all of a sudden like a slap upside the head, it came to him sure as a tornado gets upset when stuff enters its path. His name was Jim. Jim Kamae, and the woman lying in the shallow grave beside him was his wife, Sharon. Sharon Kamae. Dead Sharon Kamae.

Jim's heart hammered so hard against his rib cage he freaked out thinking it was a panic attack and his ticker would explode. Tears flowed in rivers over his face. Jim really, more than anything, loved his wife. She was everything to him and his best friend. The reality of it all was overwhelming. Suddenly overcome by emotion, Jim succumbed to the embarrassment of passing out and having his head strike a rock.

Chapter 2
October 5, Six days earlier

"Portland Approach, Floatplane Two Four Two Three Foxtrot," Jim broadcast on the airplane's radio.

"Floatplane Two Four Two Three Foxtrot, Portland. How's everything going?" asked Portland Air Traffic Control friend, Sam.

"Great, Sam, everything's good. I'm approaching my destination and would like to begin my descent down to the lake and terminate the flight following."

"Okay, Jim, I know you've done this a time or two before, but from where I'm sitting it looks pretty dark out there. Would you rather go over to Big Sebago where you have miles of water so you can take it slow and easy?"

"My eyes are well adjusted, and I'm going to power-down all inside lighting while I set up for a glassy water landing on Panther Pond." He planned on having the copilot, who also doubled as his wife, use a special light that would illuminate the gauges he needed to see. It was red and wouldn't affect his vision when he looked outside the plane.

What Jim was doing was not right, but he didn't have a lot of choices, except, as Sam said, to go over to the next lake and take his chances there. The big difference being exactly that. It was a big lake with miles of water to land on. Jim also knew there would be boat traffic on the big lake, so there was a chance someone would call the wardens or police to complain about his landing in the dark.

And a better chance a boat without lights may be on the water that couldn't be seen. He would also have to find a spot to tie up or beach the plane while having to sleep in the seat for the night. Because his wife was with him, he didn't want to put her through all of that.

Jim didn't plan on arriving thirty minutes after sunset but fought a serious headwind all the way home that made the trip a lot longer than planned. They should have left earlier. Ultimately, the blame fell on him because as the "Pilot in Command" it was his responsibility for all aspects of the flight. It was the pilot's job to educate themselves and be sure all the bases were covered so there were no unexpected surprises.

When you encountered unknowns you were supposed to know of, but didn't take the time to educate yourself about before the flight, you were a fool. Pilots who became lazy because they took things for granted were bad foolish pilots, and Jim was one of those now. The liabilities increasing to keep up with his blood pressure.

Yes, he made the same mistake the other day and came out of it without any problems. He was late departing from the camp and arrived back at Panther Pond nineteen minutes after sunset, which was at the edge of being dark but just light enough to see and be seen. A pilot would still have to do a glassy water landing because of the darkness.

Jim dismissed the events of the other day and decided to stay with his initial plan and land on the small lake with one mile of water to use. His reasoning was he'd lived on Panther Pond most of his life. He knew where all the rock piles and sandbars were located and rarely were any boats on the lake after dark. He was familiar with Big Sebago but nowhere near as comfortable. While there were many advantages to using the big lake, there were even more negatives.

To successfully land a seaplane at night you had to use the "Glassy Water Technique." That type of landing was taught to all pilots who wished to achieve their seaplane rating, which was an add-on to the basic pilot's license. You learned and became proficient in all aspects of flying a plane with floats, then you must take a performance test with a "Federally Licensed Instructor," executing and passing whatever maneuvers they would request of you.

Sam canceled the flight following and gave Jim permission to begin his descent. He was at 4500 feet and 128 miles per hour. Jim pulled back on the throttle and pushed the yoke forward still keeping the speed constant.

Changing the radio station away from the Portland Approach frequency and over to the local channel used by pilots, Jim broadcast his location and intentions. Up until he broke off the flight following, air traffic control kept him aware of any other aircraft in his general area. Once he broke it off, he was on his own. He made the transmission over the local 122.8 frequency to alert anyone listening or flying nearby. Yes, people flew at night but used runways with lights to take off and land. Only a misguided fool would try to land in the dark, especially on the water.

At around half a mile out, he began to slow the plane's speed to where the airspeed needle was in the zone that showed it was safe to deploy the flaps. He set the flaps at 20 degrees, reduced the throttle some more, and applied forward pressure on the yoke while adjusting the trim wheel for the horizontal stabilizer, which had to be set properly to allow for stabilized flight.

The plane's speed was set at 64 miles an hour and the rate of descent around 73 feet per minute. The airplane's weight would take on a big role in how easily and quickly the aircraft stabilized for a smooth glide-path. And they had to remain constant, so Jim wanted those numbers held steady before he cleared the trees at the edge of the lake.

Everything mattered when it came to the plane's weight. What was the weight of the remaining fuel, how many seats full, and how much cargo was on board? The heavier the plane, the more power needed to keep the rate of descent and speed stabilized. Having the horizontal stabilizer wheel adjusted properly would also help keeping things on course.

To enhance his vision, Jim turned off the vertical stabilizer strobe light and the wingtip lights. All exterior lighting had been extinguished so the plane no longer had any outside illuminated references. It sounded like games, but in reality, it helped the pilot see better outside the cockpit. With the plane's lights illuminated while trying to land in a black hole with no bottom in sight, it could cut down on the pilot's night vision tremendously and cause distractions.

Next to go were the dashboard lights. Again, to be able to see clearly with visibility at its best, Jim needed his eyes perfectly adjusted to the darkness. As it became darker on the way home, his eyes adjusted naturally. If there had been a full moon without clouds, the visibility would have been much better, but there were only small breaks in the overcast, so the moon was not helping much. If he were landing at a runway with lights, things would be different. But out here in the pitch-black puckies, well, "things... they were... difficult."

As they approached the shoreline of the lake, which was the last threshold before they were over open water, Jim told his wife to keep an eye out for anything on the water, *as if a floating log would have a light on it*, and to keep her special dashboard cockpit flashlight on the gauges he needed to watch. The artificial horizon would be used to keep the plane flying level, the airspeed indicator was needed to verify the airspeed stayed constant, and the vertical speed indicator would be used to make sure the rate of descent remained steady. He lined up with the longest stretch of the lake and had the plane going straight.

Jim could make out both shorelines he was flying parallel to because some of the camps had their lights on, and believed he would be about 80 feet above the trees at the lake's edge. That could be a big problem for him. With it being so dark, Jim was not sure exactly how far above them the plane was. If he was too high, it would take longer to get down to the surface, and he could well run out of space before he landed. And if the plane was too low, he risked running into the treetops.

Using all the references available to him and making small adjustments to keep the airspeed and rate of descent constant, they were on their way down. A controlled approach. Though Jim believed everything was going well, it seemed to take forever to settle on the lake's surface.

Philip Gagnon

He wanted it to happen quickly, but also knew he must be patient for the landing to be successful. A few quick glances at the lights on the camps by the shoreline, and he could tell there was still a long way to go. When the plane cleared the trees at the water's edge, Jim must have been much higher than he needed to be. It was so dark he had guessed wrong, and the plane was nowhere near close to touching down.

The way Jim came in, there would have been plenty of lake in front of him to land on if he'd set up properly and began his descent at 50 to 80 feet above the tree line. But he must have been much higher, since the lights in the homes directly in front of him at the far end of the lake were getting closer and closer, and the plane was not down.

If he could turn the plane a little to the right, there was a large cove that would open up more water and extend the landing area. But that would have been extremely dangerous. If by chance he tried to turn the plane even slightly, and it happened to touch the water at the same time, the aircraft would cartwheel out of control and crash. Jim wasn't sure if he was one inch or twenty feet above the surface, so he couldn't attempt a turn.

Jim then remembered the altimeter setting. On the way home while using flight following and then being turned over from Navy Brunswick to Portland, he was given the local pressure reading of 29.96. He set the pressure number into the altimeter gauge and that gave him an accurate altitude reading for the area. The floats would get wet when the altimeter read 276 because the lake was 276 feet above sea level. He asked Sharon to light up that gauge and saw it read 290. He looked to see if the barometric pressure was set correctly at 29.96 and it was, meaning they still had to settle 14 feet before they touched the water.

Jim thought he had all the information necessary to know where the lake's surface was, but when he glanced outside the cockpit, he couldn't tell. And Jim knew that, but he was getting anxious. The camps and homes with lights on that were in his windshield were now getting uncomfortably close, and he needed to make the decision quickly to abort and go around, or hope he touched down in a matter of seconds. If he didn't land real quick, he would have to apply full power and pull up hard just to miss the homes and surrounding trees.

Approaching them, he could see they were well-lit and clearly tell how fast he was coming at them. The camps provided a good reference for keeping the plane's wings level. Without that reference, Jim's eyes would be stuck to the artificial horizon gauge on the dashboard, and he wouldn't have the freedom he had looking outside the cockpit.

Decision time had come, and Jim was afraid he may have already waited too long. One last look at the altimeter and he read it at 282. That's still 6 feet to go, but he was coming up on the shoreline in front of the plane too fast. Even if he touched down now, he was worried he would run into the land before being able to slow the plane enough to turn on the water. He made the choice to apply full power and go around.

The plane quickly began to climb out, and Jim could tell he was not going to have a lot of room over the treetops. The plane missed them, and by how much he didn't know, but the noise and commotion from the plane's exhaust and prop wash going so close over the roofs of the camps and homes would have shaken those buildings and generated a lot of 911 calls.

Jim's nerves were getting the better of him, and his knees and legs began shaking badly. Sharon was staring at him, and he felt like Superman. She looked like kryptonite. He was real lucky his wife wasn't screaming at him. No one could concentrate or make the right decisions when you were experiencing difficulties while someone was yelling at you. Having a person screaming in the plane was the worst possible situation for a pilot. It would be impossible to think straight.

But Jim had done it before, just not in as much darkness. Back then, it was closer to nineteen minutes after sunset when there was just enough light to safely land the plane.

His mind was racing madly in many directions searching for the right things to do. Knowing his wife was nervous didn't sit well with him. She trusted Jim completely, and he just failed her. Only a complete dummkopf would put his loved ones in a predicament like that. His stupidity on sale to the highest bidder. It was time to grow up and fast.

There was no chance to rethink everything that didn't work or had gone wrong up until then. They were still in the air and hadn't hit anything yet. Just move forward and suffer the humiliation and punishment he would receive later. If they lived to talk about it. He needed to get them somewhere safe.

He apologized to his wife and told her he would take care of everything, really hoping those would not turn out to be his famous last words. She nodded her head to say she understood, and Jim could make out streams of tears on her face. He felt like the worst jerk alive. Such a waste. He had to smarten up and fly the plane, so he could get out of the jam he'd gotten her into. He could only imagine how scared she was right then.

Jim wanted to help calm her, so he explained what he was doing to involve her more in the things that needed to be done. He had her power-up the taillight strobe, the wingtip lights, and the dash lights. He told her they were going to level off at 800 feet and asked that she keep an eye out for any towers or other obstacles they'd need to stay clear of. He was going to slow the aircraft and fly it at 80 miles an hour. The plane would fly 128 miles an hour with floats on and 155 without them. You'd want that speed when you had someplace to go. They had no place to go fast and decisions that needed to be made quick.

The plane was at the preferred altitude and was in slow flight, with flaps at 20 degrees and throttle maintained for the desired speed. It was very loud when flying that close to the ground, but he didn't have a choice. If he went higher, Sam or someone else at Portland Tower would pick him up on radar. Because it was pitch black out now, and he had missed the landing, air traffic control would probably make him fly up to Navy Brunswick.

There, the Navy boys would soak the grass next to the active runway that had lights, and make him do a power-on landing in the foamed or wet grass. He would be under the watchful eye of every flight controller in the region. *How embarrassing. Those professionals would gossip that the arrogance displayed was a testament of his ignorant ways exceeded only by his horrendously ridiculous actions.*

They would surely alert the picture takers for the local papers and camera reporters from the TV stations. "First of all, come and see the clown who's flying at night on floats illegally, and secondly, come and see how the Navy saves the day." And even though they did save the day, every day, for good reasons, and Jim had nothing but the highest respect for all in the armed services, he was hoping to avoid that scenario.

At 800 feet above sea level or 525 feet above the ground, Jim knew the immediate area well enough to avoid most problems. The hills and mountains were not that high locally. The towers were all well-lit. He was not a pilot who had lots of hours under his belt, and not one to go out and fire the beast up so he could bore holes in the sky while trying to log hours and build time. Jim needed someplace to go, so he could feel there was a purpose for doing it. Flying and traveling away from and back to an area helped with the education of the terrain surrounding it. Finding a better landing site was now the focus of his thoughts.

A longer lake was needed, and it would be nice if it was isolated. The idea of using Big Sebago was scary. Too much boat traffic, even at night, among the other issues. Then he remembered a lake to the north that would work perfectly. It was long and narrow with no camps around. Jim had used it many times. While learning to fly floats, he would go up there and do touch and go landings. When performing those, he would usually go to different bodies of water and only do a couple on each one because of the noise. At that particular lake, he did them over and over because there were no houses nearby and nobody ever complained which meant a lot.

They were now headed in that general direction with the lights of the Naples Causeway acting as a guide. The causeway was on the main road with a bridge that separated Long Lake and Brandy Pond. There were many seasonal businesses on the causeway as well as streetlights, so it was well-lit at night. The lake was only five minutes away at normal cruise speed, and a little longer at their current speed. Not too far from home, but far enough out of the way that they wouldn't drive there.

At the altitude and speed they were flying, the landscape was going by fairly fast, and Jim didn't have the lake in sight. The cloud cover was thinning some and allowing the moon to lighten up the terrain. That would really help them a lot, but because they were so low, their forward vision was nothing like it would be if they were up higher. Passing over the Naples Causeway had a calming effect on Jim. They were going in the right direction.

And there it was, in the middle of nowhere with no lights for miles around. He could see the outline of the lake clearly with the help of the moon. He set the plane up on a downwind leg and broadcast their position and intentions over the radio. With the extra moonlight, he could see the treetops better at the edge of the lake but would still keep the altitude on the high side to be safe.

Jim began slowing the aircraft to 70 miles per hour and would slow it to 65 after turning onto the base leg. By the time they turned on final, the plane would be all set for making a glassy water landing. The extra light from the moon didn't help to find the lake's surface, and looking down at the water would be like looking into a mirror. That's not a problem because the runway was plenty long enough no matter how high they started out. Well, within reason. Confidence was coming back to Jim and that was a good thing.

As they turned onto the base leg, Jim made additional adjustments for their approach. When they turned on final, there would be more adjustments necessary because of the turn, but they would be small ones. The plane had flaps deployed 20 degrees, airspeed at 63 miles per hour, and rate of descent at 72 feet per minute. The moonlight outside the plane was good enough that Jim left the wingtip lights on while having Sharon shut down the dash lights and the taillight strobe. That taillight had such a bright pulse when lit that it was very distracting and might cause a visual problem for him when they got down close to the water.

When they turned final and the last small adjustments were made to keep things constant, Jim explained everything he was doing to Sharon in an attempt to keep her involved. They were coming up on the tree line at the water's edge, and he believed they were 70 feet or so above the treetops. The plane was crossing the threshold now, and checking the gauges confirmed everything was holding steady. Until they touched down on the water, Jim would rely heavily on the gauges while only occasionally looking outside the cockpit. It certainly helped that the winds had gone calm, or else keeping everything in check would be a real chore.

The plane was on a smooth path down to its wet landing strip. At what Jim would have guessed to be 50 feet above the water, he could see a light up ahead of them and off to the left in the trees. He pointed for Sharon to see and told her to watch it, but then it was doused. Or gone. *Don't have the luxury of thinking about that now.* Less than a minute later, the plane touched the lake's surface and he chopped the throttle, retracted the flaps to reduce lift, and dropped the water rudders, which were on the back of the floats and steered the plane on the water while at slow speeds. Jim retracted the rudders when flying because they could cause steering issues.

Now that they were down on the water and idling, Jim rotated the plane 360 degrees so they could scan the shoreline around the lake for signs of any lights. Seeing none, they chose to shut the engine down and float in the middle while deciding what to do next. Jim left the wingtip lights on for the time being. Whenever he had flown near the lake, he'd never seen any roads in the area and assumed it must be landlocked with all the land owned by a farmer. He was thinking there weren't any people around for miles.

"Was that a light in the woods or did I imagine it?" Jim asked.

"I never saw anything."

"Must have been a big lightning bug."

Sharon turned to Jim and lied, "I was never worried. I had all the faith in the world you'd get the job done right."

"Ya, sure. I know for a fact you were not at all happy with the situation I'd gotten us into. I'm glad we're okay, but I feel bad it happened. We just need to survive the night, and we'll be back home first thing tomorrow morning."

"Will we sleep in the plane?"

"It's the only place that won't be loaded with mosquitoes," Jim said. "Can I use your cell? I want to call Sam and explain what happened just in case they saw us on radar."

After removing the phone from her purse, Sharon could see there was no service. "Maybe if you climb up on top of the wing you'd get it."

"That won't work. I don't remember ever seeing any cell towers around here. The only way we'll get any service is to go back up in the air. I should've had you call before we came in here. I could've called him on the radio but didn't want to panic anyone about our dilemma. You never know who's listening.

"There was so much to think about as far as getting out of this in one piece that notifying someone else about our problem didn't even come to mind. We're safe for the time being and should try to relax. There's nothing more we can do." Jim turned off the wingtip lights and prayed there would not be another fool who would try to land on the lake tonight.

Chapter 3

Standing on the shore of the lake about the distance of two football fields away from the plane, the three cousins stared out wondering what it would do next.

They spoke amongst themselves in Aruban Papiamento.

"Why is that happening in the dark?" Juan asked.

"It does not make any sense the plane would have any business here," Jose replied, "so these people must have some type of problem to land here at night."

Anncherry added, "We can use some extra money, and that thing reeks of being rich. We should get hold of it and see if we can shake some coin out."

"Might be easier said than done," Jose, the smart one, said. "I have read where these types of people will have a gun or other weapon with them. We have the pistol, but using it at night would echo everywhere. I do not think that noise would be good for us. Then we have the spears we made from the sticks. We would need to be close if we were to be successful, and I do not like the odds. Unless of course…"

"Unless of course what?" Anncherry said. "There cannot be many in that thing. If we surprise them by coming up from behind, we would be in control."

"What I was going to say is we will wait until early morning and then sneak out to them in our canoe. They will hopefully be asleep, and we will quietly board the thing and attack them."

"I like that," Juan said, "and we could climb on the floats from the rear while Anncherry takes care of the boat."

"That will not work," Jose said. "I have been on this kind

of aircraft before back home. While on the water, it will want to sink the back of the floats if the two of us stand on them. The whole plane will move or rock like a big wave has hit the thing, and it would alert the people inside to us being there. No, the only way to board would be on the floats directly at the door to the cabin. The problem with that is we would need to come in from the rear and under the belly. I have seen cables and stabilizer bars on other planes that stretched across from float to float. We would have to climb over the cables and on the bars at the same time so we do not rock the thing. I am not sure where the cables are, so we would have to feel our way around them."

"Let us plan on it then, and in the meantime I will go back to the campsite and gather the spears," Anncherry said. "I will bring the gun also. You two can get the canoe and paddles, then bring them here. We do not want them to see the flashlight, so be careful when you use it. I say we launch at one o'clock in the morning."

Chapter 4

Sometime after midnight on the eastern side of the lake, flashlight beams could be seen moving through the woods. The foliage was still on the trees, but the leaves were changing color because of the cooler temperatures and the shortened amount of sunlight available to them. The lights were 100 feet away from the shore of the lake, so no one was aware of them yet.

As the three game wardens made their way toward the water, they came upon an opening in the woods that may have been a campsite at one time. The trees overhead were like a solid canopy and totally hid the site from above. There were no trails anywhere close to the water, only the old logging roads back 150 feet from the lake. The wardens were responsible for safety and control of all inland waterways but had never been to this one before. It was completely surrounded by private land belonging to one family who never allowed access to anyone.

While the family harvested the trees six years ago, they did not allow any timber cutting within 100 feet of the water's edge. The property had been left in a trust to living family members, and the trust was loaded with restrictions that would guarantee the surviving beneficiaries would not hack the landscape up for profit and ruin what the trustees worked so hard to maintain in its natural beauty while also protecting it from development. A rarity by today's standards.

"Do you think this campsite is just people camping out, or do you get the feeling they were here a few days?" Warden Smith said. "Look at the edges where the ground has all been freshly turned over. I'd bet that's where trash that wouldn't burn is buried. You can tell by all the wood ash that's left on top of the fresh turned dirt that someone burned a lot of lumber in the fire pit. At least they were smart enough to dispose of the ash where it wouldn't start a forest fire."

"Yeah, this doesn't make sense," Warden Chopay said. "I know the family who owns this land, and they wouldn't want campers settling here. For these people to have fires, they would've had them only at night so the smoke couldn't be seen during the day, and they'd need to use the logging roads for access. One of the owners has a small plane she uses to fly over the property a few times a week looking for trespassers. There's so much land it may be tough to spot something like this from above. And the logging roads have the foliage above them hiding their existence. Unless they were on foot, they'd never find this."

"Right," agreed Warden Truit. "I know the owners well enough, and all of the men in the family would rather watch football on TV while drinking beer than to ever hike this land."

Glancing around the campsite, Warden Chopay saw what looked like freshly turned ground covered with leaves and pine needles. It looked obvious to him somebody had covered that spot with more care than that given to other areas. After using his boot to move the leaves away, he kicked at the ground to turn up the surface. There was nothing but dirt.

He used the heel of his boot to go deeper, and at eight inches down came upon a layer of plastic. He kicked at the dirt to open the hole up more and saw the plastic appeared to be covering rocks. It was hard to tell because there was so much moisture on the bottom side of the plastic.

"This site will be worth looking into further," Warden Smith said. "Maybe when we get some spare time during daylight hours we can bring some gear in and probe some more. I can ask the owners for permission, but we should get out to the water and see if we can find the plane."

Just then they heard the sound of a shrill scream coming from Warden Chopay. "My God, I'm gonna puke! I broke the plastic, and the odor is making me sick!" He backed away from the small hole he made in the ground.

The other wardens aimed their flashlights at the oversized

divot from eight feet away. Warden Truit moved back farther. "I can smell it over here. I can't believe the animals haven't found it yet. That's the worst garbage I've ever smelled."

Warden Smith worked in the woods for 26 years and had seen it all. "I don't think that's trash. Trash can smell bad but not that foul. It's either a dead animal or something else that once roamed the land. I don't think it's been there long."

"We need to check on the plane," Warden Truit said. "Should we split up and one of us stay here, or do what we were sent to do and deal with this later?"

"We stay together," Warden Smith stated. "This deserves more attention, but we need to check to see if the plane landed on the lake and if the occupants are okay. We can move this ahead of our other duties tomorrow and come back with the necessary tools. We really need the daylight."

"We have to fill the hole back in, and even then the animals might get a whiff and dig it up," Warden Chopay said. "They're probably lining up and licking their chops as we speak. I'll grab some sticks and see if I can put the plastic back in place. Maybe if we throw some wood ash on the plastic and then re-bury it, that would help kill the scent."

"Let's do that and get moving so we can report back in," Warden Smith said. Glancing at his watch he noticed the time was 12:48.

The three of them gathered wood ash to throw on the plastic and sticks to move the dirt back in the hole. None of them wanted to get close to the odor. Like cigarette smoke that would cling to your clothes, they didn't want to give the stink a chance to stick to them.

After working together for five minutes, they considered the job done as best as possible and headed for the lake. The moon was bright and made for good visibility. The brush was very dense in some spots making it tough to penetrate.

Once the wardens were at the water's edge, the thick vegetation made it difficult to see up or down the lake, but the view straight across was good. They made their way along the shoreline until they found a large rock out beyond the bushes that would give a good look around the lake.

Warden Smith went out on the rock and saw the plane. It was up the lake some distance sitting still, and he could see it clearly. He removed the flashlight from his belt clip and was going to point it at the plane when he detected a small boat on the water. It looked to be moving towards the aircraft.

It was one o'clock in the morning, and this was private property that had been camped on recently. Though the campers did clean up after themselves, there was the unknown buried stuff in the ground. Had they used up all the space available to them around the campsite and moved to another spot? Maybe they were going out to see if they could help the plane in some way or perhaps it was a drug deal going down. Reaching back towards shore, he asked for the binoculars and Warden Truit handed them over.

"What have you got?" Warden Truit asked.

"The plane and a small boat headed towards it. Give me a second to sort it out." Looking through the binoculars revealed nothing moving in or around the aircraft. The boat was a couple hundred feet from the plane and closing. There were three people in what looked like a canoe.

Both the plane and boat were a quarter mile or more away from the rock. No way for the boaters to understand him if he were to yell something. He informed the other two wardens of the situation and suggested they make their way up the shoreline in the direction of the plane. The brush was heaviest at the shore, so it would be easier to move back in about 100 feet and go from there. The wardens were on the move.

Chapter 5

From the cockpit of the plane, Sharon spotted a boat coming towards them. She nudged Jim who was awake but trying to rest his eyes.

"Can you pass me the binoculars?" he said. "They're in the glove box." Jim looked through the binoculars and was not comfortable with the view. "Two guys paddling a canoe with a girl in the middle. They're all wearing glasses and look a little familiar to me."

"You think you know them?" Sharon asked.

"They're looking just like a group Sam and I ran into at Richard's," Jim said. "Not really people you'd write home about. I can't guess what they're doing out here at this time of the morning, but I would bet they're up to no good. They handle themselves pretty well and had a gun last time I saw them. We're not staying here to see what they want."

Normally, before a pilot would fire up a small plane, the area around the aircraft would be visually scanned to make sure no one was nearby. Then with a door or window open, the pilot would yell, "Clear!" before shutting the door or window and starting it up. No time for that. The boat was less than 100 feet away and closing quickly. Power-up and move out fast as possible.

The plane started moving and Jim hoped the prop wash would blow them around and head the boat back the way it came. It did just that and nearly capsized the canoe. The cousins looked like panic-stricken tourist about to be taken under by a huge wave. They knew the water was cold because all three had taken sponge baths in it.

Getting swamped this far from shore would not be good. It was a narrow lake but still almost a mile wide. A long swim with clothes and shoes on, so they paddled and did everything possible to keep the canoe from tipping over. The amount of air whipping by them and moving the boat was amazing. It was pure luck they did not capsize.

The plane was on step, flaps extended, and water rudders retracted. Looking off to the left side, Jim could see flashlights at the shoreline aimed in his direction. More bad news and time to leave. Without much weight on board, the plane was light and broke from the water quickly. The only lights Jim had on were the dash lights, and now that they were away from the lake, he had Sharon power-up the radio, wingtip lights, and the rear strobe light. Jim made a call on frequency 122.8 to alert anyone in the area of his location.

Then he asked Sharon to get Sam on the cell so he could speak with him. After a minute, Sam was talking to Jim from the tower at the airport. He stayed well past his shift because he was worried about their ordeal. He'd been trying to reach them on the tower radio and cell phone but had gotten no response and assumed they'd turned the radio off on the approach at the first lake. Sam picked them back up on radar when they'd left that lake and watched until they disappeared from the screen. When the plane didn't become airborne again, he hoped they'd landed but wanted to be sure they hadn't crashed and were indeed safe.

"Sorry, Sam," Jim said. "My cell phone had a dead battery, so I left it at home. We have Sharon's with us."

Sam had alerted the wardens that a plane was landing in a very dangerous environment, in an unoccupied and unlit area, and may have crashed. The warden service said they would dispatch some of their men, but they were on another life-threatening call at that time. They'd go there as soon as they could. The service could bring in wardens from another division, but they'd have a few hours travel time, and the local wardens would hopefully be freed up before then.

"The problem is we have no way to communicate with the wardens," Sam said. "We've got two different cell numbers but

Glassy Water

get no response on either one."

"There's no cell service in the area," Jim said, "so if you called the wardens, the lights coming from the woods must have been theirs." He then told Sam about his visitors.

"That's why you're up again. What are your plans now?"

"I wish there was a plan. If there was a way to contact the wardens and find out the coast is clear, we'll go back in and land. The lake is perfectly sized for a night landing. No rocks or sandbars either. I'd be afraid to go over to Sebago because of the rocks. This is the only spot that will work for us tonight. Our fuel is a little low too. We'll get some altitude and slow flight until we can figure things out."

"I'll call the warden service and see what they have to say about the issues we're having. And I'll try the wardens' cell phones again. Give me a few minutes, and I'll get back to you."

"Okay, Sam, thanks."

The sky was really beautiful when flying at night. The cloud cover was thinning more as time went on, and at 1:20 in the morning, all was quiet with the stars shining brightly. After seven minutes, the cell rang and Sharon handed it to Jim. It was Sam.

"The warden service usually has mobile radio contact with its people, but the radio went dead on the previous call they were on. There is a radio in the truck, but they're on foot. They were informed their men entered the woods on a logging road and that's the last communication they had. The service suggests you go back in and make contact with their people. They should be easy to spot with all three being dressed alike because they're in uniform. Shine your headlights on them." The plane had a set of headlights in the front of the wing.

"That sounds good, but we wouldn't be able to make out anything if they're shining flashlights at us," Jim said. "We can go back in but can't come out again until daylight because of our fuel situation. We need to be sure there's enough to get us home. The other thing is we can't talk to you once the plane gets down low. I'm guessing we'll lose you somewhere at treetop level. It would be nice to know our friends aren't waiting for us to return. I'll bet they're camping in the woods next to the lake."

"I think you have to plan on them being there," Sam said. "Somehow, you need to hook up with the wardens. I wish there was a way I could help more."

"You've done everything you could, Sam. Sharon and I want to thank you. We're heading down now. Hopefully, I'll call you tomorrow after we've left. Go home and sleep. You can't do anything else."

"Be safe, bye."

"We will, goodnight."

Jim was going to make the same approach he did earlier. He made the call on the local channel and stated his location and intention. Believe it or not, people were out flying at all hours of the night. Especially when the weather was perfect for it. One requirement you must fulfill before getting your pilot's license was to have a number of hours flying at night along with nighttime takeoffs and landings at different airports. You needed to show you were capable of finding your way around in the dark.

Next, they turned and entered the downwind leg. Speed was below 80, flaps extended to 20 degrees, and they were again flying parallel to the length of the lake. The plane continued past the end of the water for about 500 yards and then turned onto the base leg. Speed was at 65, and Jim was trying to get his rate of descent set. It was time to turn on final, and he asked Sharon to turn off the taillight strobe and the dash lights. He was not sure why, but decided leaving the wingtip lights on was the right thing to do. *As if it mattered in the middle of nowhere.*

Visibility was perfect, and they were at 64 miles per hour with a rate of descent at 70 feet per minute and steady. A nice controlled power-on landing with a fixed rate of descent in the middle of the night. Jim actually liked that part. Made it look like he knew what he was doing. Sharon had her flashlight on and was helping with the gauges. The trees could be seen easily, and they were only a minute from touching down.

Flashlights at the shore to the left caught Sharon's eye. At the same instant, they touched down on the lake's surface. Jim chopped the power, retracted the flaps, and dropped the water rudders. The plane was idling as they made a complete circle trying to see what they could. No boat on the water and only a couple of flashlights off to the one side. Jim went that way.

Around 40 feet from land and still idling, he had Sharon steer the plane with the water rudders and stepped out on the float. Jim hoped it was the wardens and not the other group. He remembered the one guy had a gun, and if it was them, they were in trouble. But it was the area just above where they saw the lights when taking off, and the troublemakers were out in the canoe, so it should be the wardens. Jim yelled and asked them to shut off their flashlights. They did, and with Jim's light he could see they were in uniform. He told Sharon to kill the engine and shut everything down.

Now, the plane was dead in the water. The wardens wanted to know if they were okay, and what was going on. Jim briefed them as best he could after apologizing repeatedly for the noise and 911 calls from homeowners on Panther Pond. The wardens told him he would be receiving at least one citation for disturbing the peace.

"We saw the boat with people in it," Warden Smith said. "There was no way for us to know if they were with you or not. And after you left, they must have seen our lights because they disappeared on the other side of the lake. We actually went to our vehicle on a logging road and called dispatch, and they told us you'd be back, so we returned. What are your plans for the rest of the night?"

"We'll stay with the plane and hope our friends don't show up," Jim said. "If they do, we'll run the plane up to the other end of the lake and stay clear of them. We have to save fuel so there will be enough for an early morning takeoff. If they're watching us now, they can see we have company, and that should keep them from coming over. We'll float 200 feet from this shoreline. Thank you for checking on us."

"You're welcome. We have other business here later today, so we'll be back then and check to be sure you're gone." The warden didn't offer to tell them what business, and Jim didn't think it was his place to ask. They said their goodbyes and the wardens left.

Philip Gagnon

The rest of the night was without incident, and they departed at first light. While tying the plane to the dock, Jim promised his lovely wife he would never let that happen again.

"Uh huh," Sharon responded. "We'll see. So what are you doing today?"

"I have to take a generator to the camp. It's a special order, so I need to wait for it to arrive here. But I'll be home very early. No night flying tonight."

Sharon hoped she would never be a witness to anything like that ever again.

Later in the afternoon, a local news station reported the Maine Warden Service had discovered human remains in an area of woods in the town of Naples near the shore of one of its lakes. "It is an active investigation and no other information is available at this time."

Chapter 6
October 3, Two days earlier

Portland, Maine, Jetport. Students in class for a seaplane rating.

The teacher, Mr. Coombs, was speaking;

"This is the hardest part of flying a seaplane because you have to execute good judgment and rely more heavily on your gauges. Your instincts will tell you to look outside the plane because you were trained as a Visual Flight Rules Pilot. You can't tell where the surface of the lake is in a glassy water situation. I cannot impress upon you people enough how serious you must take this. If you don't do it by the book, you could literally drive the plane into the water and die.

"The reason for a glassy water landing is so you can safely land your seaplane on a lake's surface that resembles that of a mirror. A body of water with no winds to turn up the surface gives off the effect of looking in a mirror when looking down on it. What you're really looking at is a reflection of the sky. In shallow water, you're looking at the bottom, and at times a combination of both. It is impossible to determine where the surface of the lake is.

"There are a few ways to cheat this condition, but these can also cause you legal problems if you're not careful, and you could be considered reckless. Let's say you pick out a boat or raft on the lake and decide to use it as a surface reference. For this to work you'd have to land close to the marker, and that is usually a source of the problems I just mentioned, as most people will freak out when the sky-monster looks like it'll hit them or something

Philip Gagnon

on the water. That's the easiest way to get in trouble and reported. Probably a situation you want to avoid.

"Before you can even attempt a glassy water landing, there are a number of things you must do to set up for your approach. Let's pretend we're flying in a Cessna 180, which a few of you own. We have slowed the aircraft so we can deploy 20 degrees of flaps. The 20 degrees should give us the proper nose attitude at the preferred approach speed. Our usual approach speed is 70 miles per hour, but with this plane we want 65 in a glassy water situation.

"We'll have set maximum propeller pitch in case we need full power on abort. Then we'll need to have a reasonable rate of descent and a starting point. A 70 to 80 feet per minute rate of descent would be acceptable, but remember the faster you drop, the more you increase the chance you'll bounce off the water when you hit, and then because your rate of descent and speed has changed, you may as well abort, apply full power, and go around to try again with less of a rate of descent.

"Experienced float pilots can feel the aircraft sink out from under them and will add more power while allowing the plane to settle back down on the lake's surface. I don't recommend doing this until you're confident enough with this type of landing. You can't just nose the plane over to achieve your rate of descent. You'll drive it into the lake and crash. Go around and be safe.

"We have our speed set, flaps deployed, rate of descent set, and with the slower speed and 20 degrees of flaps, we should have a good nose-up attitude. Obviously, you'll have to make some adjustments to the throttle and nose pitch to keep everything on the level. Having the horizontal stabilizer trim wheel set properly will help too.

"Our beginning reference point will be the trees or a building at the edge of the lake we're approaching. As you're coming in over them, you know where the tops of the trees are. We're going to clear them at say 75 feet, but if you were landing on a small pond you would need to be lower. The lower you start out, the quicker you're on the water.

Glassy Water

"Try sticking with trees if you come in low, as homeowners become nervous because of the noise. And remember the old saying that goes, '5 inches or 50 feet, all that matters is we missed them.' That's really just a joke, and let's make sure it stays that way. Always allow plenty of room.

"Now that we've cleared the threshold and there's nothing but glassy water in front of us, we must keep our rate of descent and speed steady, which means we'll have to keep an eye on those gauges while also using the distant shoreline to keep the plane straight and level. Once you touch the surface, you want to chop the power and retract the flaps so you stay down. If you bounce, you go around. Any questions?"

Jim's hand went up.

"Yes, Jim?"

"There's a lot to it, but practice will make the landing easier. I wanted to ask for everyone's benefit if most aircraft handle differently due to additional circumstances such as how hot it is, weight, size, or type of plane. I mean, not all seaplanes will handle the same way, right?"

"Yes, there are many things that will make planes different, and because of these issues, you'll want to practice in ideal conditions with little added weight to get comfortable and confident with your aircraft. If you're flying a 172 on floats, you can't compare it to the 180. They are not the same in weight and have different power units with the 172 having a fixed pitch prop, and the 180 a variable pitch prop. The 180 has a 230 horsepower engine, and you need a special sign off for any aircraft over 200 horsepower. It requires extra training.

"There are a lot of smaller aircraft with floats on them that will have trouble getting off the water on a calm, very hot day. Some of them are underpowered to begin with because of the extra weight and drag of the floats. But when you have full fuel tanks, maximum passengers, and cargo weight to the max, you're going to need perfect conditions for it to get off the lake, if it gets off at all. You've all been educated on density altitude and understand the effects it has on flying.

"Your aircraft is a completely different machine with just

you in it; fuel tanks that are only a quarter full, and no cargo on board. Compare the light 180 with the heavy 180. Full fuel tanks, all four seats used, useful cargo load to the limit, and on floats it wants to fall out of the sky like an inverted rocket.

"On a glassy water landing, you'll need considerably more power to maintain a descent of 75 feet a minute. But that's why we preach practice, practice, practice, so much and tell you to begin with the lighter plane and slowly work your way up to your full weight. Going from a light load to full weight is as different as night and day. Thanks for the question, Jim, and we're out of time for today. I'll see all of you next week."

While all the students were leaving the room, Jim walked over to a longtime friend of his, Sam Arends. Sam worked as a flight controller at the jetport and considered it real good duty. Very rarely did it get too busy, so there wasn't much pressure. He's the same age as Jim, but Sam felt at forty-two he was late arriving on the scene as a pilot. He had been flying for two years and was now getting involved with float flying because Jim recently bought a Cessna 180 with floats.

At 6 foot 3, 225 pounds, Sam carried himself well. A large man with the shoulders of a football player, people usually moved aside when he approached them. Jim was a different bird altogether. At 6 feet and 165 pounds, he looked mean as the devil but was the nicest person you'd ever want to meet and would take the shirt off his back if he thought it would help you out.

Jim was so nice he was also an easy target to take advantage of. He'd had some good friends in the past that would help themselves to things he owned without even thinking of giving them back. Money included. Sam was the only person he considered a friend now, and he trusted him dearly. It was the end of the day, and Jim wanted a beer.

"Have you got time to suck one down with me?" Jim asked.

Sam knew that sucking one down with Jim never actually meant just one. At times, it would be one dozen. Jim liked his brew and handled it well. In his younger days, he would get arrogant, but the years had mellowed him out. Sam also felt if he ever was in a fight he'd want Jim on his side because he fought harder than a cornered animal and never gave up. Both men were in good physical shape, and Sam had nothing but the highest respect for Jim.

"Sure, but I can only have one or two," Sam said. "I'm on an early morning shift tomorrow."

"Great. When are you back to your regular shift?"

"Day after tomorrow. We're back at full strength then."

"Can I drive your car to Richard's?" Jim asked.

Sam had a 1966 Chevelle SS396 that Jim drooled over. The car was in mint condition with only 23000 original miles. His father bought her new and left it to Sam when he passed on. You could see her coming from miles away. The candy apple red color really stood out. Jim would be the pilot when they visited the local bars, but never if they were going to drink much. That car didn't get touched then.

Richard's was named after an acquaintance of theirs who lived in town. He was always working in the kitchen or the bar that was attached to his restaurant. They admired him for his honesty and how hard he worked. He was of Chinese descent and married to an American woman.

He played a mean game of Liar's Poker because while the drinks and beers were flowing, Richard, always with his apron on so it appeared he had to work, was the only sober one in the bunch. While the rest of the players were operating without the benefit of a full working brain, Richard would routinely clean house. And his friends didn't mind because he was always giving them free drinks and food. They really liked him.

As Sam and Jim were arriving at the bar, they could see there was a commotion of some type taking place outside and to the right of the building. It looked like three girls arguing and a fourth one on the ground. No one else was around. As the men exited the car, the girls were screaming at each other, but that's all.

Sam and Jim went over to the girl lying on the grass to see if she was all right. She seemed to be laughing with both hands over her mouth. She was a petite girl dressed nicely in jeans and a collared shirt. A pair of sunglasses were on the ground next to her head. Both eyes were like road maps, so the men figured she was drunk.

She saw them and quickly got up, grabbed her sunglasses, and charged the other three girls, none of whom were as small as she was. The petite beauty had all three on the ground in a matter of seconds and punched each one and then kicked them repeatedly. The guys were stunned since it all happened so fast. The girls on the ground were all in defensive positions, with knees up to their stomachs and hands covering their faces.

The attacker was moving like lightning, and then she turned towards the parking lot and took off running. She was gone just like that. Sam and Jim were scratching their heads when they turned their attention back to the other girls on the ground. After helping them get up they made sure nobody was injured. Sam and Jim didn't know any of them.

"What just happened here?" Jim asked.

"We met her up on a back road just north of Naples," the tall blonde girl said. "We were on our way home to Massachusetts after staying at a friend's home for the week when our car broke down. We had no cell signal to call for help, and that witch came by and offered us a ride."

Two of the girls got in the back seat while the tall blonde was at the driver's window talking, and even though the woman had sunglasses on, they slid down her nose revealing bloodshot eyes. While being questioned about drinking, the lady screamed something about making fun of her eyes and then drove off with the passenger door slamming shut.

Confused, the blonde girl started running after the car before hearing another vehicle approach from behind. She turned and tried to flag it down. The car stopped and the driver reached back and pushed the rear door open. She jumped in and began blurting out her problem, only to have the guy in the passenger seat turn to her. As he turned his head, he hit the headrest on the back of the seat and knocked his sunglasses off. He had dark skin and bloodshot eyes. She glanced at the rearview mirror and could see the driver had sunglasses on too, but couldn't tell if he was drinking or not.

Probably would have been smarter to think things through before getting in with a couple of drunks. Dude in the passenger seat told her they were after the driver of the Mustang that should have passed by a few minutes earlier.

"He spoke with an accent of some type," the blonde said, "and I also noticed he didn't contract his words."

"Contract his words?" Sam asked.

"Yeah. You know, like the contraction of two words shortened to one. He will is he'll, I am is I'm, and so on. He didn't do that. Now that I think of it, he spoke more of a foreign English.

"Funny thing was they didn't sound drunk and seemed to be driving responsibly. I couldn't detect any alcohol odor either, but then I thought it could be pills or other drugs."

Driving into town the men indicated they knew where their friend would be. The Mustang was parked at a bar with nobody in it. The blonde got out of the car when it stopped and shut the door. The two dudes took off down an alleyway on the left side of the building.

"I heard some voices that sounded like my friends yelling on the other side. I ran over to them and just got here when you showed up. Red eyes was already on the ground, and I thought you were with them and let her beat us up."

"But why was she on the ground laughing?" Jim asked.

One of the other girls spoke of their ride to town with her. As they were driving, red eyes was making all kinds of threats against them, and they couldn't understand why. They told her the cops would be called, and she basically dared them to. She drove like a Tasmanian Devil on cocaine. The two girls didn't think anyone was capable of driving the way she did. They were hoping the cops would pull her over, but no such luck.

"When she parked her car out front, both of us were out of the backseat fast. Not knowing where we were, we saw the tables with umbrellas and headed towards them.

"After we'd made the corner and saw nobody at the tables, we didn't want to continue down towards the back, so we turned

Philip Gagnon

around, and I ran smack into her. Nancy showed up then and was yelling at us like the whole thing was our fault for getting in the car. Then you two showed up and you know the rest."

From the corner of his eye, Jim saw something and turned to see a black car with chrome wheels sitting at the back of the building in an alley. There were three people in the car, and they were staring at Jim's group.

When they saw Jim looking at them, the three got out and started towards them. Running. It was two guys with the girl they had seen many minutes before on the ground going crazy. Jim told the girls to go out through the parking lot, into the restaurant, and call the police.

Sam was saying this was not a problem because the two of them weren't part of it. Jim really wanted to believe he was right, but his nerves were saying it was not a good spot to be in. Both men stood there because they thought the people charging them were, for some reason, after the girls. At five feet away, the two guys stopped while the girl went airborne with a look on her face resembling a hungry piranha and then drove the heel of one foot into Jim's solar plexus and the other heel into Sam's at the same time.

Both men hit the ground like bags of cement and couldn't breathe. She had knocked the wind out of them and was now at Jim's face screaming, pulling his hair, and trying to gouge his eyes out. At least that's what it felt like to him. Everything was happening so fast. She abruptly left Jim, went to Sam, and began mauling him.

Out of one eye that worked, Jim could see the other two guys looking towards the inside of the restaurant, and then they both headed for the door. At the same time, he heard the girl on Sam scream and saw she was flipped over with her hands to her throat. One of her man friends drew a handgun and pointed it at Sam saying, "Bo Ta Morto!" Sam was close enough that he whipped his foot and hit the gunman on the side of the knee.

A siren coming from a police vehicle had all three of them running for their car in the alley. They were away in seconds and out of sight even faster. Jim knew that getting their license plate number would have been good, but he and Sam were still on the ground, just now getting their normal breathing back and checking to see if anything was broken.

The policeman arrived and shouted for them to stay down with both hands over their heads. Richard and the girls came out then and explained what happened. Not that Sam and Jim hadn't been yelling their side of the story the entire time. The officer then said they could get up. As they stood on wobbly legs, they looked up and down the road for the black car and gave him the description.

For the next half hour, they told the officer all the details he asked for and the best physical identifications they could provide. With no beer in them yet, it should have been easy to nail their appearances down, but everything happened so quickly, a lot of it was a blur. The car, however, was easy to describe being black with chrome wheels, which was the first thing the officer called out on the radio.

The girls had been looking for crazy red-eyed girl's car, but it was gone. Those people were no amateurs. Even if they hadn't planned the attack, their tracks were well covered. One thing all the girls agreed on was those people did not appear drunk or otherwise impaired. But two of the three had bad red eyes, and the third had glasses on, so his eyes couldn't be seen. Sam and Jim saw the eyes of the girl and believed she was straight because of how accurate she had been.

"Are you suggesting they were wearing the glasses to hide their eyes?" the officer asked and thought cows would fly before any of the morons figured out what was happening. Unbelievable a little girl could kick the snot out of them.

"In my opinion, yes," the blonde girl replied. "Like when the guy knocked them off when his face hit the seat rest, he looked uncomfortable and awkward trying to get them back on quickly while turning from me at the same time. Now that I think of it, he brought his hand up to shield his eyes away from me. It was like he was embarrassed."

Jim explained the trio came from the area of "Thompson's Point" on the other side of Naples, which was what the girls had told them. The officer assured everyone they would find the trio and then left while shaking his head.

Sam had had enough and was thinking of leaving, but Jim needed a long neck. The men entered the bar, and Jim asked Richard for two cold ones. Sam could fend for himself. They watched the girls get in the cab they called for after arranging to have their car hauled.

Good luck to them, Jim thought. They didn't appear any worse for the wear after the beating they had taken. The beauty of being young.

Jim, on the other hand, had bruises and hurts all over, which was why he could wait no longer for his liquid medication. As soon as they arrived, he ordered another. No one was going to deny this boy his pain meds. As much as Jim did drink, one would think he was in pain all the time. *Not really, but sometimes it seemed that way. The only thing missing; a funnel.*

As the men were sitting there reliving the good old times of an hour ago, it hit Jim about the words the guy with the gun said to Sam.

"It didn't come to me until just now, but he said, 'You're dead.'"

"It did strike me as strange, but then again, so didn't the whole situation."

"But he said it in Papiamento."

"Regardless of what lingo it was in, that's how I understood it. Gun in your face is an international language."

"Yeah, I get it," Jim said, "but why was he speaking in Papiamento?"

"Papiamento?" Sam said. "As in a foreign tongue spoken in a country like Aruba type Papiamento?"

Not the language of many islands, and each one had its own dialect. Jim and Sharon had lived in Aruba on and off for five years. Even though Jim and his friends spoke often it was usually about flying. During the years they owned property there, Jim had taken to learning Papiamento as a second language.

"I did it because even though most of the people there were fluent in English, they would converse in their language between themselves, even when it was your question or situation they were discussing in front of you. I wanted to know what they were saying. It took more than three years to talk comfortably, and even then they had their own slang that was hard to pick up. So you would learn to speak properly and then have to relearn the slang if you wanted a chance to even begin understanding what they were saying.

"I wish I'd learned it at a younger age. It's much easier to learn when you start out young. If you attended school in Aruba, you would have to be fluent in four languages just to graduate from high school."

"I can't believe that," Sam said. "My head would explode trying to learn so much. How can they possibly do it?"

"They start them very early on in life," Jim said, "and you have to understand they live on a very small island in a very big world. Most, if not all of them, will leave the island for some reason or another during their lifetime, and they're aware that to survive in this world only speaking the language of Papiamento would be difficult. So from an early age, they're taught to become fluent in Papiamento, Dutch, Spanish, and English.

"Because they begin at such a young age, it's second nature to them, and like I said, you're not going to graduate without being fluent in each language. They obviously carry an accent with them, but they can go almost anywhere and survive, talking with locals as if they're one of them."

"Unbelievable to just think about it," Sam said. "You wonder how they keep it all straight."

"It's as natural to them as walking is to us," Jim continued. "Did you know the Dutch have a hand in what happens in Aruba? The Dutch lay claim to the island, although a lot of Arubans recently pushed for but later voted against, complete independence without Dutch influence. I think they really hate each other, the Arubans and the Dutch.

"But what I was getting at is because of the support and help of the Dutch, every Aruban high school graduate can attend college in the Netherlands. So you can see the need for extra languages. The Dutch also educate their kids to speak multiple languages early on. They're big on education."

"Why do the Arubans and the Dutch hate each other?" Sam asked.

"I was an outsider but had both Aruban and Dutch neighbors who were beer drinkers and liked to talk," Jim said, "and I was there enough to see for myself how things worked. This is only my opinion, but they did not trust each other. The Dutch think the island is theirs to use as they see fit, but the Arubans know it's their island, and the Dutch are invited guest.

"Had the Arubans voted for independence, they would have lost most of the funding and help provided by the Dutch. The Dutch have a Marine base and a sizable Marine presence on the island and none of that may have changed. But without an influence in politics and lack of a voice in other government policies, the Dutch felt the Arubans would drown themselves in a short period of time. The Arubans valued the Dutch money which was badly needed and appreciated. Amsterdam assumed the vote for independence would get shot down. In reality, things were a little rough around the edges."

"A gun to your head an hour ago and now you're planning a vacation," Richard said as he joined his friends. "I couldn't help overhearing your conversation, and I'd like to talk more about the island, but these people who were here with guns scare me. They might come back and do who knows what. They were definitely whacked. I didn't come to America for that."

"We don't like it either," Sam said, "but that kind of violence is everywhere. People are brain dead to act out like that. The law will get them, and they'll get the usual slap on the wrist. Our system is too lenient with most people who commit crimes, and they end up being career criminals. We'll never win that battle.

"I wouldn't expect our gun-toting friends to come back around here again. They were smart and covered their tracks well. That and the fact they, well at least the one guy, spoke a foreign language. If they're from another country, they really do fear our prison system. I'm sure they'll hide until things cool down and then relocate to a place where they're not wanted and watched out for."

This was all being said for everyone's benefit including Sam's, who was definitely scared but could only hope he never saw them again.

"I hope you're right," Richard said. "I don't want to dwell on it, but this is hard to let go. So, Aruba you say," he continued, hoping to brighten the mood back up. "Did you know the Chinese have a large population on the island? I have a cousin who owns a grocery store there with his family. I've never been to the island but someday would like to go."

There was indeed a large population of Chinese on Aruba and from what experiences Jim had they were the hardest working and most honest people you would ever have the pleasure of dealing with. Most of the larger warehouses and grocery stores were owned and operated by them. Their restaurants were over the top good.

Some smaller convenience stores they operated were scattered around the island that offered food and hardware. It was completely amazing to see how many useful items they could fit in any size building and keep it orderly. You could find almost anything you needed at those locations. And they had good prices.

Jim and Sharon bought a home in the neighborhood named Wayaca Residence in November of 2006 and the island experienced heavy thunderstorms shortly after they closed the deal that flooded most areas. Their home was spared damage but the flood waters were within inches of entering the home. Some of the low lying developments had three feet of standing water when the storm was at its worst.

The realtor they dealt with when purchasing the home became a friend, and they occasionally went to dinner or a club with him and his girlfriend. He was aware of the uneasiness caused by the flooding shortly after they got the home, and told them of a vacant lot at the northeast section of the island in Kurimiau that's on a hill.

There were not many hills you could build on, but if you secured an elevated lot on one of them, the flooding should not be a concern. Erosion was a problem which became obvious when they went and viewed the land. Heavy rains created deep gouges in the ground and some of the roads were in terrible shape. Jim and Sharon thought they could divert runoff away from the lot because no other parcels had been developed next to it. They liked the spot plus it had views of the cruise ship terminal, some ocean front hotels, and the sunset.

That night, they went out with their realtor friend, Paul. He had taken the liberty of drawing up a purchase agreement for the property and wanted to explain how the land was held in the system compared to the property the Kamaes just bought.

A local program was developed to encourage economic development for those families low on income and had the government awarding a native Aruban a lot of land free of charge for him or her to build on. The land was actually a leased lot for a period of 60 years with rights of renewal, and the legal term used to convey the property was called 'Economic Rights.' Some people built a home completely and lived there, some built a little here and there as they could afford, and some tried to sell the land for profit.

What he failed to mention was that a leased lot acquired through the giveaway option could be sold twice without any restrictions, but the third owner would be required to build and had less than a year to do so. The lot had been sold twice, and the Kamaes would have been the third owner but were not made aware of that fact until the day of the closing.

All legal work concerning real estate on the island was handled by notaries, which were law offices filled with lawyers who actually do the work. They thought they were in good hands legally and repeatedly questioned Paul of any problems that may arise. Being a lifelong resident and real Aruban, they took him at his word. He assured them it was as straight forward as any other deal and the purchase and sale agreement was signed.

The home they bought in Wayaca Residence was on freehold property land which was the same as fee simple ownership back home in the states. Leased lots usually came with annual fees due to the government in addition to property taxes, so that was different from what they were used to.

Jim and Sharon continued their friendship and soon gave money to Paul for paying the phone, water, and electric bills when they were not around. It was a service he provided for other absentee homeowners as well. That's what he told them anyway.

Somehow the notary office handling the transfer and sale made an error and wanted to return the deposit to the Kamaes claiming it wasn't necessary on a land lease. Paul was asked to deal with it while they were away and the funds ended up in his bank account. As time went by and repairs were performed at the home in Wayaca, Paul used those funds to pay for them.

A closing was scheduled for the land, but Jim and Sharon could not be there for it. They had to leave the island the same day and the flight was an early one to Miami. Their flights were booked six weeks before so Sharon could keep an important doctor's appointment. It just happened to be that the closing was scheduled the same day. The funds were transferred to the notary the day before and the closing would be at ten o'clock in the morning. They gave 'Power of Attorney' to Paul so he could sign for them in their absence.

The Kamaes had bought and sold a few homes and usually had the closing documents a day early to review. They checked the computer before leaving the house that morning to see if the closing documents had been e-mailed. They hadn't been, so they couldn't check again until they were in Miami.

Once they arrived in Miami, the documents were viewed and the problem of building within one year was seen. Because it wasn't ten o'clock yet, the notary handling the transaction was called to cancel the deal, but she was in a meeting and would have to get back to him. She did call back at just after ten and Jim told her not to close the deal. She said it was already done as everyone had shown up early, signed, and finalized the sale.

"I complained," Jim said, "but it didn't help."

"You set yourself up to fail," Sam said.

When buying property in a foreign country, take nothing for granted. Because Jim and Sharon had the experience with Wayaca and both deals had been completed by lawyers, they felt comfortable with the transaction. Trusting Paul was a big mistake and not doing the due diligence necessary an even bigger one. There was no one to blame but themselves.

Their broker friend must have known they wouldn't notice any problems until the day of the transfer. Just get the buyers to the closing and everyone would see that everything was explained completely. Then they figure you're in love with the land and will work through the issues.

Jim and Sharon never saw their friend again, and he still had thousands of dollars of their money in his account to cover work they wanted done at the house in Wayaca. In exchanging e-mails, he always said he'd pay them back, but he never did. Jim kept trying to catch up with him whenever they were there but could never find him.

"How's that possible?" Sam said. "Didn't you know where he lived or worked?"

"He had a real estate office but closed it up and was living with a woman. Then she kicked him out. The best information I ever got was he'd been living with one of his children, but it never led me to find him. I passed him once when I was leaving our house in Wayaca, but after I got turned around, he was gone. I never saw the guy again. We ended up borrowing money and building a house on the hill."

"Now after a few beers, I feel a little loose lipped, so I'll tell you something I've never told anyone before," Jim continued, "and I'd appreciate you guys not repeating it. Can I trust the two of you to keep my secret?"

Both Sam and Richard nodded yes.

There were many sleazy areas in Aruba, and Jim went on a mission to find someone who would beat up his broker friend. While having a few beers with one of his Dutch neighbors, he was told some good stories that had Jim on the edge of his seat. They were very believable, so he let it slip about his situation. As usual, the neighbor was full of ideas. He knew some people and would make a few inquiries for Jim.

The Dutch neighbor set him up with a girl at a bar in San Nicholas called Charlie's. He told Jim she was a 'kind of pimp' for a group of men, and for the right price she would discreetly

Glassy Water

handle the circumstances without knowing his name. What eventually happened was the neighbor took care of everything, and he didn't need to be involved. They wanted the broker friend's name, a picture, and the money to pay for the job that needed to be done. Jim thought long and hard about the problems that would come back on him, but that jerk really put it to them, and he didn't think he could be connected to the situation.

The due diligence that should have been done on the land would now be done correctly. Jim asked the neighbor what they would do to him, and was told, 'Anything you want.' That, 'They do it all the time.' And that, 'Money drives the sinners to perform any task needed.' Jim suggested they break a leg and was told, 'Consider it done, but if you want worse damage, that would be no problem either, but the money must be paid in advance.' Jim didn't have to consider it because at the age of fifty-two, his ex-friend would be devastated with a broken leg.

"What you asked for was more trouble," Sam said.

"You're right. But I was determined and wanted to know if it could look like an accident and he told me they had a job to do and would not care how it got done or looked. So I asked if something worse could happen to the guy, and he told me they guarantee the broken limb, but all other damage was out of their control. It depended on how much he fought back."

A few days later, Jim read in the daily paper, Diario, there had been a local man beaten, and he'd suffered a broken leg in the scuffle. They gave his name and age. There was no mention of it in the papers that were published in English, probably because they wanted as little bad information as possible available to the tourists, and the Diario was in Papiamento, which Jim always picked up at Ling and Sons' supermarket.

"For the last year we were there on and off, Sharon was having problems with her back and stomach, and the long flight to the island was becoming a problem for her. We thought about renting the houses and coming back in the future but decided instead to market them for sale. My neighbor had a Dutch realtor he used when selling his properties, so I went to him and listed both of our properties to sell for less money than what the realtor said they were worth because we wanted fast sales."

"Smartest thing you've done so far," Sam said.

The night after Jim read the article in the Diario, a car arrived at his home, and three men came to the door. The one who did the talking was a fair-skinned man, and the other two were dark-skinned. It was dark out and they had sunglasses on. He was asked if he wanted a quote on a new swimming pool, and Jim told them no, he wasn't interested. The fair skinned man then asked about any other work that might be available to them, and was told there was none he knew of.

After an uncomfortable pause, the man went on to say he knew Jim was interested in hiring them for something similar to the work they had just done for him. At a loss for words and fearing brown stains would appear on his underwear, Jim stuttered, "What work? I haven't hired anyone for anything."

"Not directly," the man said, "but you paid to break Paul's leg and unless you continue to grease the wheel you set in motion with 1000 florins right this minute, we will take our information and loyalty to the cops. Get us the money now!"

Jim didn't have that much on him and told them he would have to go and get it from the Aruba Bank ATM. The bank was not far from the house and he wanted to be rid of those men. The man told Jim to get in their car so they could make the trip. He shouted back in the house to Sharon that he'd be right back and quickly locked and shut the door.

After the short drive to the bank, they kindly helped Jim out of the car with a push, and he proceeded to withdraw the funds. As the machine was spitting out the florins, the door to the ATM booth opened, and the two dark-skinned men joined him. They wanted to know what his balance was and were aware the machine gave a receipt after the withdrawal showing the transaction and the remaining amount in the account.

One of the men grabbed the receipt from where it exited the machine and noticing there was a balance of more than two thousand florins, demanded Jim take out all of it. He tried but got a warning that said the amount withdrawn so far today was the maximum allowed in twenty-four hours. The men saw the issue on the screen and insisted meeting again the next night at the same time. He would have agreed to anything because the Kamaes were leaving early in the morning, but he wasn't going to tell them that.

The three thieves peeled out of the bank parking lot and headed towards town while a nervous Jim stood there picking his nose. They were going in the opposite direction and that's a relief. The roads between the bank and Wayaca Residence were well-lit, so he didn't mind walking and headed home.

He apologized to Sharon for the abrupt departure and made up a lie about a neighbor needing a quick hand. She had no knowledge of any of the shenanigans concerning Paul and intended to keep it that way.

"The next morning we caught our flight without a problem," Jim continued, "and I have more stories for another time, but it's getting late for Sam, and we should get going."

"Two o'clock will be coming early," Sam said.

The men squared up with Richard and went out to Sam's car, which he was going to drive this time. He took Jim back to his vehicle and then went home.

After getting in his car to head home, Jim began to think of his blood alcohol content. He had six beers at the bar over a period of about two hours.

From what he remembered, the body gained two points of alcohol for every 12-ounce beer you drank and lost two points naturally per hour. Doing a quick calculation meant he was around point 08 which was the legal limit. Jim was aware it could be a point or two either way, so all the more reason to be extra careful. When he was younger, he never cared about the math. He just tried not to get caught.

Jim made it home without incident, had dinner, spoke with his wife for a while, and then went to bed. It proved a restless night while he lay awake and thought of what had happened that day. *Why did the guy speak a dialect of a foreign language I understood?*

Chapter 7
September 28, The Beginning of the Payback

Oranjestad, Aruba

"You look good for a guy who had his leg broke in a mugging," Alex said.

"Well, you know how it is in this neck of the woods," Paul said. "Money buys everything."

"I think it is like that everywhere in the world."

"It is, but here, we Arubans are all connected by blood."

"Do you mean to tell me the thugs you paid off were your brothers and cousins?"

"No, nothing like that. We share a common cause, and that is to empty the pockets of every foreigner who touches our soil. Some get enjoyment for their money and do not mind leaving without a dime. Others leave their money here for various reasons, but it is our duty to keep as much as we can on the island. We do not want to be thought of as an island of thieves, and we are only serving a common good that will help our secluded economy. They do not teach us these things in school. You learn them on the street as you grow up."

A conversation between Alex Aagnet and Paul Balluwe was taking place after Paul had paid the attackers not to break his leg or otherwise hurt him, as they had been ordered to do for an American. Paul also paid the newspaper, "Diario" -*pronounced Dee Ah Reo*- to print a false story for him.

Paul knew money did indeed speak volumes above any and all activities on the island. You could buy anything you needed, and finding people with the goods was not difficult. Law enforcement was practically non-existent, and you had to literally

Glassy Water

run into them to even get a look. There were homes on the island in such remote spots, that if you were to call and report a crime, it would probably take the police half a day to find them.

And do not get him started on the Dutch Marines. They were on the island for R&R more than anything else. Those people were not allowed to get involved in domestic issues concerning law enforcement. Paul assumed the marines were only on the island training for a day the Russians, in co-hoots with the Venezuelan government, decided they wanted a ready-to-go oil refinery. Aruba just happened to have one, and Venezuela was only fifteen miles away.

Paul was aware there were as many immigrants on the island as there were Arubans. Venezuelans, Ecuadorians, Peruvians, Chileans, Chinese, and countless other nationalities on the island who were looking to work and live the good life. Some legally, most not so.

More than anything else though, Paul loved Aruba. It was a country of its own. Owned and operated by the Arubans with the help of the Dutch. When it came to political issues, the Dutch had considerable influence, and sometimes he thought the island would be far better off if complete Dutch policy was implemented and made law. But it pretty much ended there.

For decades, the Dutch had made inroads infiltrating government and monetary decisions. All legal documents on the island were written in Dutch, even though the official language of Aruba was Papiamento. The Dutch had a legal claim to the island that dated to 1629. Recently, a more hands-off policy of sink or swim was more appropriate in describing their interest in helping the Arubans with 'One Happy Island'.

The Arubans did not like to be taken advantage of either. Just ask Paul Balluwe. So what if he managed to keep a few thousand American dollars from an American loser he was acquainted with. He had done that to others as well. That did not give them the right to order any part of his body broken. He knew everyone who was involved, and they would be made to pay.

The name of every player involved had been put on a list. Paul's countrymen would not charge him but a small amount to do his will. Most of his blood brothers were foreigners, and they understood what could be had with money. And that bought loyalty. Paul's money would acquire the goods he needed and all the rights he deemed his. Regardless of the type of merchandise. Human or otherwise. Those people would pay for what they wished on him.

Paul hated most people. He would be the first to tell you how well he knew his fellow Arubans, and that he loved them all, but at the same time, if he could find his mother's checkbook, properly forge her name, and drain her account for his benefit, he would do it in a heartbeat. *Two faced.*

But he hated foreigners more. Especially the Americans and the Dutch. They were all fakes. They went to church on Sunday to confess their sins committed in the previous week, so they could begin the new week with a clean slate. If they did not let the sins pile up too high, then no one would know of them. And God was the most forgiving. You could do the worst act in the world and end up condemned by all of mankind, but God would still forgive you. And that should be all that mattered.

It should all come down to me. What was best for me? Paul believed all Americans were that way. They were all brought up to believe they were the best, and the entire universe was theirs to use the way they saw fit. And that the whole world owed them. Those Americans were like oil and water. They did not mix well with anything. They believed they could go anywhere on earth and fit in, and most all foreigners would make them feel that way, but the truth was, if it was not for their money, they would not be welcome at all.

Paul was a shark. He was a real estate salesman and self-described consultant. He smoked Marlboro cigarettes and drank Budweiser beer. Like all Arubans, he enjoyed everything the Americans produced. They drank their milk, ate their poultry, used their paper products, and consumed every edible item made in America. They somehow managed to get the best fruit America had to offer. When the Americans were screaming bloody murder at the tobacco companies for causing cancer, Paul believed they would shut the companies down, so he bought 257 cartons of his

Glassy Water

favorite Marlboros. He liked to plan ahead.

And so it came to be that he would send three of his cousins to America to break a leg of the American that had ordered his leg broken. An eye for an eye. He would finance the entire trip with the money kept from the American. That was how things were recycled in Aruba.

The American had put some funds in Paul's account to pay for services he would need in the future. More money became available when the American had put a deposit on a vacant lot belonging to Paul's nephew, and the notary made an error and wanted to return the money. The foolish American asked if the funds could be put in his newly trusted Aruban friend's account. "Provide the bank information and it will be done," replied the notary.

It does take a little money and costs more than a little to transfer dollars to the Island of Aruba. Most of the time, it involved numerous banks, and they all generate a fee. Then at the end of the line, in Aruba, you have to pay and convert it to their currency, the florin. Once the money was there, and depending on what you were using it for; in this case a long-term real estate holding, it was cost effective to leave it there. The charges to take it back off the island were costly. You had to pay a sizable fee to the government to take your money off the island. That was probably why the American wanted to leave his money there.

Paul's funding could not have come easier. He had won his American friends' trust while guzzling beers with them and sharing friendly stories. It took almost a year of being nice, but the money began with small amounts to pay things like electric and phone bills. He did not plan on it turning out the way it did but hit the lotto on that one. His other clients usually only gave him enough to cover bills monthly.

His cousins were a rowdy bunch and were his two nephews and a niece, the children of a sister. But Paul would always refer to the trio as "The Cousins" because he liked the sound of it. The cousins had tried to live in Amsterdam but were thrown out because they were incapable of working and had no money. Stealing from the Dutch was not easy, and that was the only work they knew. The Dutch were also very smart with their money and investments. Not at all loose like the Americans.

Uncle Paul had promised them a job that would take the trio to America. The three siblings had all been there before at different times, and with money in their pockets. There should not be any problems going as a trio on vacation. They would be flying to New York and then drive to Maine, the location of their target. Uncle Paul had all the goods and specifics, and the work was right up the cousins' alley.

The boys were good fighters and all would protect each other. The girl was a demon. The three of them had done the same deed for a brother of Paul's and were surprisingly successful. Their mouths were like wire traps, and none of them would ever tell a soul of what they were up to, or who else might be involved. Paul had only found out what the trio had done when his brother told him while completely drunk at the rum festival a few months before.

While they were all good looking kids, they did have a bad case of bloodshot eyes that had been passed to them from their father. They learned to live with the disability the hard way, with kids making fun of them growing up, and they responded by beating them to a pulp. Word circulated quickly on the small island that they were not to be messed with. Of course, there was always someone bigger who had to show he was the boss and would make fun of them. He, too, was dispatched to the ground by their smart street fighting. That bully became their best friend. *Funny how those things turn out.*

At Uncle Paul's home, the cousins were given their assignment. While Paul had some information, there was much more required to know about their target. Enter the internet. It was just completely amazing the things you could find out about people on the internet. Paul had two sons who were close to their father. Neither was very bright, but both were ambitious.

They, along with their father, had started many businesses that failed. If Dad could find the bucks to supply them for a business venture, they were all game. It did not matter even if someone else close to them had tried the same business and went bankrupt. That would not mean anything to them, and they did not learn from the mistakes of others. Those fools had to find out for themselves that the Aruban people would not buy their junk or use their services. Not your average business professionals. Amsterdam college graduates, but always Aruban.

One of the sons was proficient on the computer and smarter with the internet. One nephew, Jose, was also talented with the computer. There was very little available over the web in Aruba. But if you looked elsewhere, the information was unbelievable. Most of America spilled its guts on the internet. Social media was becoming a normal reality. There were cities and towns that exposed every detail of your financial and professional life for anyone to see. If it was considered public information, it would be out there to be viewed.

Some cities did not allow such a wide open policy. Public outcry over how much they owed in taxes, and when they paid them, put pressure on what to expose and what not to. Some cities even had blown up pictures of your house at the assessor's page on their website, along with the price you paid for the property. A lot of people felt their rights had been trashed.

But because of the information available on the internet from anywhere in the world, gladly exposed for all to see, people needing information for targets of interest easily found what they needed at their fingertips. In the comfort of their living room while swilling Budweisers or Balashis, the cousins could formulate a plan of action and know exactly what the home of the target looked like. Of course, that would only be if the town he lived in put that information over the net.

That would definitely save some time on surveillance. If the idiots who were responsible for putting the information on the web were ever to be the victims of such planning and found out it was because of what they believed in, they would surely do what they could to eliminate the data and protect the privacy of individuals. Themselves first.

Just because somebody was making a plan to attack you and do bodily harm should not be a factor though, should it? Most of those dreams never panned out, and the better thought was you watched too much TV. Why would anyone in their right mind plan anything negative from what they found on the internet? That was like suggesting there may be unstable minds amongst us.

We all know anyone capable of such an unkindly act had been taken care of in advance. With today's technology, we could see beforehand who the criminals were and what they were thinking. Was that not right? Maybe not. We would just go back to watching TV and see how it all ended up. That was what they did in Aruba.

A plan had taken shape, and verbal agreements made. The big "Cheese Doodle," Uncle Paul, had booked the flights and would send them on their way. Travel lightly and then buy what was necessary in New York. A weapon of choice had already been arranged for, so after arriving in New York and grabbing the rental car, they would drive to a 7-Eleven on Long Island and buy the gun. Make the call to a number and the time to meet would be given. The cousins were to see a gentleman who would be in a red VW Karmann Ghia parked at the south end of the store on the other side of a dumpster.

That, at first, became a problem for the three cousins. None of them knew what a Karmann Ghia was or looked like. They were assured that getting to the right 7-Eleven and then finding a red car next to the dumpster would relieve them of the problem. And if the guy had a gun to sell? *"Wah-lah."*

All that was left was going to the bank and getting dollars for the three cousins. They saw it as a real vacation and vowed to enjoy themselves. Nothing was more fun than knowing what it was you would be doing to unsuspecting people. Especially Americans, who were no better than the worst termites on earth.

The group was to meet that night one last time before the trio departed Aruba. They gathered at a motel adjacent to a rotary on the main road to the city. At the Talk of the Town, the three cousins met with Uncle Paul and his two sons. All had beers in front of them and laughter could be heard from their group. They noisily discussed the details of their little mission and made sure everybody was on board with no unanswered questions.

Glassy Water

The rowdy cousins were pumped to go and juiced enough on Balashis to know everything already. Paul wanted them to wear their sunglasses at all times, which was not a problem because they went to bed with them on. It was a funny thing their night vision was better with sunglasses on.

While the three of them were considered fluent in English, they all cheated their way through the class and lacked some of the basic skills required to speak it properly. Paul hoped that would not cause them any problems.

After three hours at the bar and their money gone, the group had to leave. They were kicked out after the tab was shorted, and no tip was left. Their party only got away because of promises made by Paul to return tomorrow and square up. That was not going to happen. Give them a chance of skipping out and not coming clean on the tab, and you would never see them again.

The Talk of the Town was a motel, restaurant, and bar. Over the years, it had its share of ups and downs and was shuttered a couple of times so it could be updated. The place bordered a roundabout that acted as a slingshot for cars going into town. The Talk was at the edge of the roundabout, and the front of the building was close to the road. A sidewalk out front was all that separated the two. Vehicles would shoot out of the rotary and fly by. It was an unsafe location at best.

Out on the sidewalk in front of the Talk, Paul and his group were saying their goodbyes when they heard a scream from the parking area across the street. It was getting dark, and it looked as if a woman was being attacked. Paul's computer literate son, with his liquid courage urging him on, thought he would intervene and fix the problem. With the speed of a superhero, he darted across the street to save the day.

Only he did not quite make it. Everyone watched in horror as he was struck by a car and run over. They saw it and heard it. "Whack! Thump! Splat!" The driver of the vehicle slammed on the brakes and came to a stop. He did not see anything and had no idea what just happened. Thankfully, the beer between his legs did not spill, but it made him mad that he had to stop, so he swore profusely. That would have made a mess of the rental car. He was leaving in the morning returning home to Holland and did not need any extra work. It was bad enough he had to fill the tank with petrol somewhere.

There was nothing in front of the car, so he backed up to see what he could. All the other vehicles were passing him on the left and blowing their horns while flashing hand signals his way. He backed up quickly and went over what felt like speed bumps; "Thump Splat, Thump Splat." The sounds of people screaming and horns blaring were thundering in his ears.

No one was going to treat him like a common person, so he rolled the window down, and using his own hand signal technique, produced his middle finger and flashed his IQ back at them all. It was total chaos. "What a bunch of idiots!" he yelled. Something could be seen in front of his car, like maybe a dead animal, but he did not know what it was. With his mind racing, he made a decision then and there, which was helped along by the 12 pack of beer he just drank, to clear out in case the cops came.

He shifted into forward, and while still flashing hand signals using the one finger that showed his age, the car began moving. Just as he stepped on the throttle and checked his sideview mirror for traffic, two other idiots jumped in front of his car, waving their arms. Not having the time to be social, he kept the pedal to the metal, looking over his shoulder and trying to get into a traffic opening he spotted.

"Eyes on the road at all times," he told himself as another set of speed bumps were hit. "Whack! Whack! Thump! Splatter! Thump! Splat!" With all the traffic blowing by on his left, it was no wonder the speed bumps were installed to try and slow them down. "Idiots! What are they thinking?" he screamed. He kept the gas matted and joined the line of traffic headed into town, happy to be on his way.

The woman across the street was screaming at her child for going to the bathroom in his pants before they were to go and eat at the Talk. "What a mess!" she cried. How was she going to deal with his soiled pants? After thinking for a few seconds, she popped the trunk open and told the little brat to get in or else. He did, and she slammed the trunk lid down. The traffic was going wild for some reason. She decided to leave and come back another time.

The cousins stood there alone with their mouths open and growing dryer by the second. They were not stupid. The trio knew dead people when they saw them. There was a plane to catch early tomorrow, and nothing could be done to help their uncle or cousins. Getting tied up with the cops would mean a long night. They decided to leave before anyone could place them there. The bartender was too stupid to remember their faces. The choice was made to head for another bar. One of the cousins just remembered he had their mother's visa card.

The next morning they made their flight to New York. *Vacation time.*

Chapter 8
New York, September 29

Everybody in New York was so helpful. And it seemed genuine. Arubans in America on vacation. It just was not the same as back home. These people did not act like they wanted to empty your pockets every time you reached into them. They wanted you to spread the wealth. And it was kind of chilly. So cold the cousins bought winter coats, gloves, and hats at the local Goodwill store.

An excellent tip received from the car rental girl. Your money goes a long way at those stores. The cousins felt like they were shopping at Macy's or something. But you could definitely see there were some quality issues with some of the store's merchandise. Some things had rips and tears in them. Those items should all be in a special bin called "Seconds." The defective items do not belong with all the new stuff. The trio got what they needed and were on their way.

After finding a phone booth outside the Goodwill store, a call was made to arrange for the weapon pickup. The person who answered questioned them about the location of the meet, and his vehicle type and color. When he was convinced they were the cousins, he gave them a time.

All was going well now. They had acquired the weapon and were ready to travel the roads to Maine. Not wanting to drive at night, it was decided to wait until the following day, so the entire trip could be made during daylight hours. There was no reason to risk getting lost in the dark.

The nightlife in New York was different than anything they had ever experienced back home. After suffering the loss of

Glassy Water

their family members last night, the trio discussed going to bed early at the hotel where they had gotten a room and stashed their stuff. But being young, they knew their cousins and uncle would have wanted them to party and forget about their demise. So be it. *Tonight will be party in New York night.*

At first, the cousins agreed it would be better to take the car and check some clubs out. That was a mistake. Before they knew it, the signs overhead were welcoming them to New Jersey. They kept getting stuck in lines of traffic they could not get out of. There was a measurable amount of yelling inside the car.

Three drivers, but only one steering wheel. Arms were flying, and anyone watching had to laugh. It was exactly what you expected people to act like when they were lost in unforgiving traffic. While following a line of cars off the roadway and then up to a stoplight, the trio managed to get on the expressway in the reverse direction so they could go back to where they came from. Thankfully, there were three of them to remember the way.

The cousins were not always in agreement though, with the yelling continuing until the airport and rental car signs were seen. Not wanting to take a chance getting tied up in traffic again, the trio exited into the airport to start over at the rental car location where the car was picked up. Still not all on the same page, they ended up circling the airport three times because they were in the wrong lanes to make the correct exit.

Complaints were made there was not enough notice from when the sign came in view to when they were at the exit. The third time was a charm. The problem now was they were at the rental car drop off. Tempers flared. The yelling persisted. Awful names were called out. Insults were hurled.

Only after a half hour of help from an elderly rental car worker did the trio get to the proper side where the cars were picked up and driven off the lot. When at that location, they pulled the map out which was given to them by the rental car girl and used it to get back to familiar territory.

There was none. Two minutes of driving and they were lost. It became necessary to pull over and gather their thoughts, but they found themselves again stuck in a line of traffic that did not allow much room between their bumpers and the ones in front of or behind them. The yelling was back. There were votes that a new driver was needed. Punches were thrown.

For some unknown reason, the lane to the right of them opened up. After a quick look to be sure no cars were in the way, the choice was made to take the spot. Too late. As they began to move over, a horn blared and sign language became the mode of communication. IQs were flashed. Not to be outdone, the cousins flashed theirs back like a choir singing in perfect harmony.

The trio's car was brought back in its lane fast and waited for the next opening. A traffic light was ahead, and it looked to be a chance that would put them in the lane for a right turn and off the road. They took it and pulled into a gas station lot.

It took some time checking the map to figure out how to get back to the hotel. Once it was certain of how to get there, the girl needed to pee before the trip was made. Just the thought of her having to go made the boys need to go. The three of them went into the station, which was also a mini-mart, and found the restrooms.

The cousins were not the cleanest people on earth but knew filth when exposed to it. The restrooms were terrible. The seat in the ladies' room was covered with human waste. The girl had to straddle the rim with the seat up. There was no toilet paper, just some used paper towels in the wastebasket. She would not stoop that low. A little dribble in the shorts would never hurt anybody.

The men's room was not much better. The floor in front of the urinal was drenched with pee. You had to stand in the pee to use the thing. There were flies all over the place. The toilet was an even riskier option, as it had multiple colors of different coatings on it. It appeared no one had cleaned the restroom in quite a while. The brothers washed their hands, but with no soap or paper towels to dry them, it did not help much.

When the two of them went out and looked for their sister, they noticed the "Out of Order" signs on both bathroom doors. Their eyes must have been adjusted to the bright sunlight outside,

Glassy Water

and when they came in with their shades on it made it hard to read the small writing. Signs no bigger than a small matchbook cover.

The cousins decided to pass on buying anything from the mini-mart, and when they went outside their ride was gone. The three of them walked around the building, then up and down the street looking for it. Their car was not there. Realizing it must have been stolen, the trio went back to the mini store and called the rental car joint. They did not know who else to call.

Well, it turned out the car place took care of everything, but the cousins had to meet with a police person and answer some questions. That person was on the way while another car was being sent from the rental lot out to them. Some extra charges had to be settled, and the cousins had to keep their cash, so the mother's visa card was used to settle up with the rental agency. The insurance turned out to be very expensive.

The police person with the questions had come and gone, and while waiting for the new car to arrive, one of the cousins pointed to a flatbed truck with a car sitting on the back of it. The car was identical to the one they lost except that one was missing all the tires, the glass was all gone, and who knew what else was stripped off it.

They were smart enough to know that tons of those type cars were on the road, and there was no way that was the one they had lost. The new car was pulling in the lot with an elderly gentleman driving; the same one that had been so kind to them earlier. He had them jump in and would drive to the agency's lot. Once there, he got out and let them have the car. *Sweet,* thought the cousins.

It was still early by the time they arrived back at the hotel. The decision was made to park the car and walk. A Wendy's nearby made an excellent choice for dinner. The three of them wanted the fried chicken like they had at the Wendy's in Noord back home. It was the best. But in New York, the restaurant did not have the fried chicken dinner. So they all settled for triple burgers with cheese and extra large everything. It was all gone in six minutes. *Young appetites.*

Philip Gagnon

The time had arrived for some brews, and there was no shortage of places to grab them. Young thirsts in need of hydration. Not having to be fussy and not wanting to walk a long distance, they settled on the first bar they came to. It was called, "The Creepy Crawler."

The "Creepy" was a basement business. Upon entering through the front doors, it became obvious the establishment was loaded with people who smoked. When the doors opened, the smoke rolled out from the top of the doorway, so the cousins figured it for a smoker's club. *Cool.*

Making their way to the bar was a challenge, as the people had their chairs in the middle of the aisles the trio needed to walk through. The smoke, along with their sunglasses, made for poor visibility, but they could see enough to tell everyone was in black leather gear with policeman hats on. *Maybe a costume party? Even more cool.*

Sitting at the bar they ordered three Buds. The bartender told them it was a private club, and only members were allowed. No problem. The three cousins got up to leave but were confronted by two of the club's members who nicely told them to sit back down and have a beer. The bartender was told to get their Buds.

"Please relax and enjoy your drinks," the larger man said. "Are you here because you wish to join our club?"

The computer literate cousin, Jose, replied, "No, we are only passing through. But this is a special club, yes?"

"Don't mix words with me, boy. Are you interested in joining or just drinking?" He looked to be getting upset.

"Just drinking, thanks."

The large man put his face in Jose's face and said, "Them beers are twenty bucks apiece for non-members, two bucks for members. You gonna join, yes?"

"Sorry, but we have to leave for Maine tomorrow. We were only hoping for a few beers."

"Pay the barkeep and finish your beers! Then get out!"

"OK."

The three cousins quickly slugged their beers and got up

to leave. When they turned to go, the door was blocked by a bunch of leather-clad men. The large man who had talked to them before was in front of the leather.

"If you want out you must pay to go," the large man said. "Empty your pockets and give us all your jewelry."

Truth be told, the sixty bucks for the beers cleaned them out. There were about eight dollars left between them. The rest of their money was back at the hotel. A couple of cheap Bozo watches and two rings was it for jewelry.

The cousins did what they were told and handed everything over. They were getting mad. All three of them.

"That's it? That's all you got?" asked the large man.

"Yeah, that is it," Jose mocked, "and the twenty-dollar beers took all our cash. We are not much on jewelry either. Costs too much."

"Don't you dare insult me! Give us all your money or you pay with skin!"

"That is all we have! You took it all!"

The large man had heard enough. This was his house, and they weren't invited. He hadn't had the time to kick some tail lately, and the girl would bring some good money on the street. He charged at them.

While sitting at the bar enjoying her beer for the three seconds she had to enjoy it, Anncherry saw a hallway that began where the bar ended and it had an exit sign over the door. That was the back of the building. Everyone was in front of them at the entrance. A quick look told her no one was near the hall. The barkeep was behind the bar and the path to the door was clear.

She drop kicked the large man between the legs. There was a collective "Ohhhh" from the leather group. All of them knew that must have smarted. The large man doubled over and fell to the floor. Anncherry told Jose and Juan to follow her. She bolted to the hallway and saw the barkeep was moving to get in her way. After allowing herself a nice kick to his neck, he fell on the floor also. Her brothers were at her side when she was standing over him. The leather group was sounding like a bunch of cowpoke on the warpath and approaching. The trio headed for the back door with leather group coming their way.

Anncherry, Jose, and Juan reached the door but could not get it open. The metal bar securing the handle could not be seen from where they were seated. The leather group was closing the gap fast. It was a narrow hall, so only two people could stand side by side.

That was a gift for the cousins who began fighting with a vengeance. The men in the leather group appeared soft. They were falling like flies that had been sprayed with insect killer. It was like they were so full of beer and smoke they could barely fight. Groin kicks and chest punches were delivered free of charge by the cousins. Landing the punches on leather made it easy on the knuckles. They could do it all day.

It was not long before they made their way back to the end of the bar. The cousins were stepping over bodies to continue their assault. Being sober had never paid so many dividends. Their drunk competitors were no match for them. And the funny thing was that after the leather went down, they stayed down. Like they were all dead.

The last of the leather hit the floor, and the cousins looked at each other with tremendous satisfaction. Not one of them stirred. Computer cousin, Jose, went behind the bar and grabbed three long necks. It was time to get their sixty-eight bucks worth of beer.

Anncherry walked over to the large man and reached in his pocket for the jewelry and money. He did not move, but there were lots of moans and groans to be heard. The cousins could even hear a few snores and then other sounds accompanied by foul-smelling odors. *These guys must have started drinking at six in the morning!*

Not wanting to outdo their welcome, they grabbed another twelve beers while Juan cleaned out the cash register. The cousins had their money's worth and would now leave. They wanted to grab wallets from each piece of leather on the floor but figured it would take too much time. Plus the place was beginning to smell. It was time to head back to the hotel and relax.

So be it. In the morning, the trio would leave for Maine.

Vacation was over.

But not so fast.

The NYPD didn't like anyone getting away with a crime. Whoever had done the damage at the "Creepy" bar would have been left alone except for the fact that it was a robbery. Just because the clientele had been beat up didn't really bother the cops. They were a troublesome lot, and many complaints had been lodged against them in recent years. Other than the hangovers the men were suffering from, you couldn't tell they'd been taken advantage of. And that was too bad because they surely had it coming.

But someone had taken all the money from the cash register, and they would find the criminals. The recollections given by all the leather varied quite a bit. It was obvious to the cops these individuals were not seeing very clearly when the perps showed up and then enjoyed themselves at the expense of all the leather.

The descriptions given by the police pretenders were not much help. Collectively, they painted a picture of three monkeys who wore sunglasses and were going to Maine the next day.

The usual reports were made and the cops left ever so thankful for the fresh air. They didn't have much to go on. One item of interest was somebody had mentioned that the trio had walked to the bar and were staying nearby. It wasn't much, but sometimes it didn't take a lot. The police began canvassing local hotels in search of a threesome that included two males and a female, who all had sunglasses on and resembled monkeys.

Early the next morning, and with a new shift on for the police, they arrived at the correct hotel and found a room had been given to a threesome of interest. The clerk on duty confirmed the customers had sunglasses on but checked out fifteen minutes earlier.

Due to the fact he had the phone in his ear taking a reservation at the same time as checking them out, he gave no effort to really get a good look at them. He was useless for any kind of description other than the glasses. The names of the three were taken but could easily be false ones. However, it was a place to start.

Chapter 9

The cousins spent a good part of their evening studying maps on how to get to the interstate. From where they were it was quite simple. The trio left early in hopes of avoiding any rush-hour congestion. Back home in Aruba, the traffic on the main roads in the morning would come to a halt because there were so many cars on the motorway from the San Nicholas area to the city of Oranjestad. Twenty years ago, there was reasonable traffic, but the population almost doubled and there were too many vehicles on the island.

Not getting caught up in any stalled traffic would help their cause. The police would be looking for them. They had the fake IDs they used at the hotel, so that should help if the cops showed up there.

Traffic was good for them early on. Theirs was not the only car on the road, and there were numerous other vehicles so they could stay behind them in line and not get looked at for speeding. The cousins thought that would be the only way for them to attract attention.

And maybe getting into a fender bender. After passing two collisions that morning, it became a concern. The three of them had multiple accidents back home, but when the car was rented, nobody ever asked for any history. They could only guess the insurance companies back home did not communicate with those here in the U.S.

Thinking back, there was no way the trio would have gotten what was considered a reasonable insurance rate for a vehicle if the car rental people had an accident profile on any of them. Well that was just too bad. And the cousins were not going to offer anything up. Holding to the agreement of keeping their mouths shut, no information would be forthcoming from them.

Police cars seemed to be everywhere, and they hoped that was normal. Having spent time in the jail back home, the three of them knew it would not be the same here in America. The police here did not mess around, and for the first time in their lives, the cousins actually felt guilty about what had been done last night. A discussion was being had so they could wash their hands of the guilt.

How could the trio have known it was a private club? Maybe the smoke should have warned them. Computer wiz, Jose, had read somewhere on the internet that smoking in public places was banned in most all of America. The only way around it was to have a private club that was closed to the public. And even then the lawmakers wanted to close that loophole. Guess he should have remembered that last night. Jose would have suggested going elsewhere.

But the large man tried to rob them and started the whole debacle. It was like the bar patrons hoped some people would enter the place so they could cause some trouble. Then the men would not let them leave without giving up all their valuables. And even after that, there was no telling if the trio could have left. Surely if the police stopped the cousins, and their side of the story could be told, the cops would understand.

Well, that lifted any weight that was on their shoulders. They were now free of any crimes committed by way of discussion. All would be forgiven, and the cousins knew they were not stupid. If someone did not understand, that person would just have to ask, and the trio would tell them, "We are not stupid! We know what is going on here!" *And so on.*

Usually, you can tell those kinds of people from ten miles away. Their arrogance became completely transparent when their mouths spit out words before their brains coordinated them. Their ignorance was surpassed only by the fact that their stupidity allowed them to attempt communication on the same level as dead flies.

At the same time, those people would look down on you

as if they owned your soul. Puff out their chest and create an air of authority. If only they could see how they really did stick out in a crowd. People like that never did grow up or realize the mistakes that had been made. They kept chugging forward, stepping over all the debris and chaos that was created and never looked back. "Why bother, it is behind us now, and who cares anyhow?"

The cousins had those types of head knocking talks often. It was why the three of them stayed together. They were attached at the hip and without each other all would be lost. Especially now that Uncle Paul was gone. He was the only family member who treated them fairly. Uncle Paul's brother used them once and paid them well, but for some reason wanted nothing to do with them afterward.

The trio believed that in helping their uncle, they would become closer to him and be like one big family. It also helped that he had lots of money. They wanted to be close to that, and who does not dream of some easy cash from a family member. Well, the three were paid for the job and then thrown aside. The other uncle would not even look their way when they saw each other out around town. If the cousins had real hearts, they would have been broken. But they did not and could not have cared less.

"We will be in Maine in seven hours or so," Jose said. "I looked at all the roads on the internet and the going looks good. There were a few cautions about travel through areas of Massachusetts, but that was it."

"Good," Anncherry said. "I will follow the maps as best I can, so we know where we are."

The trip was uneventful until they arrived in the eastern part of Massachusetts. A helicopter had flown low while passing over them, and then they came upon traffic that was at a complete stop on the highway. There was an exit from the highway just before the stopped traffic.

"This does not look good," Juan said. "It may have nothing to do with us, but we do not want to chance that. I think we should exit here and try to keep moving."

"I will see if I can figure out a way around this,"

Anncherry said. "If we get off and then go left at the end of the ramp, that will take us north. Let us start with that and give me a few minutes to decide what is next."

Juan did as he was told and made a serious effort to watch his speed. They had not gotten far before they had cops on their tail.

"Do not turn around, but there is a cop car behind us," Juan said. The two other cousins immediately turned around to catch the view. *Must be a dumb human reaction.* That was when the lights and siren came on, so Juan smashed the gas pedal to the floor. It was a good thing there were three of them to help with the driving. If they could keep the yelling down a little, some of the instructions might have been heard.

They came to a light that was red and without slowing down blew right through it. The cop car slowed and then had to stop and crawl through the intersection. There was not much traffic, but the cops had to play it safe. *Gee, that was too bad.* They had to be careful, and that would cost them. The cousins had good separation between the vehicles.

"If we stay straight on this road, they will block us in," Anncherry said. "The map shows a road up ahead that will go over to another main drag that will take us back to the freeway. We should take the next right, follow it to the next road, and go right again. It is right there where that car is turning in front of us! Take that right!"

Juan did, and then they found themselves behind the other car that turned in front of them, so it was passed without any loss of speed. Looking back, Jose could see they still had a good lead on the police. Another light was ahead.

"Go right at the light!" Anncherry screamed. The colors of the lights never entered the conversation. Every light was green to them. Again, and with the luck of something, their car made a clean transition without running anybody else off the road. Juan continued on and encountered another light that was green and then could see the overpass up ahead. The traffic on the highway was going the opposite direction they wanted to go in, so the trio figured the traffic was held up before the on-ramp. There was a

Glassy Water

light where they needed to make the turn, but it did not matter. Juan zoomed through and up on the wide-open highway thinking how smart he was to have made it back unscathed.

The thought did not last long. Coming up the same ramp were three cop cars with lights and sirens going.

"We have to get off again!" Anncherry screamed. "Same thing! Down the ramp and then left! I will see what I can find on the map!"

The map was not going to help get them out of trouble. But they knew their chances were better on side roads. The light at the end of the ramp was red and cleared without incident. Driving fast as the car would go, they stayed straight through another green light. The map showed a road coming up that went directly over to another one and then back to the highway. Juan took the right, but at the next main road, he went left instead of heading back towards the highway. The cousins knew they had to keep the cops guessing.

"We have to ditch the car!" Anncherry yelled.

"We do not even know where we are!" cried Juan. "Can you keep track of our location with the map?"

"I will do what I can. We have to ditch this rig."

"I know. We heard you. We also need to get rid of the police. And we need to do that quickly. Are there any side roads up ahead that look interesting? Like maybe a place to get lost without being seen or found?"

"Give me a minute," Anncherry said. "Wait. I think I have something. We can go left up ahead and then double back on the main drag, then a fast left and right that will go east for miles. It looks like it ends up back on another road that connects to the freeway. Take your next left and then go in and make the first right."

"OK," Juan said. "We get to the first right and then you tell me what is next."

The turns were made at a high rate of speed, and the cousins still had good separation from the cops.

After they made the right, Anncherry said, "Stay on this road until it comes back to the main drag. Then make a left and then a quick right. That road goes on for a long ways."

The cousins were very lucky traffic was not heavy. As they moved ahead through the street lights, Juan only had to slow once to avoid a collision. The police could no longer be seen behind them. A quick turn off the main route took them east on a back road of some kind. Now that the cops were off their tail, the trio knew they had to concentrate on changing cars.

The road they were on had many homes at the beginning, but the number of houses thinned out as the travel took them farther east. After five minutes, the homes were getting few and far between. They had not passed a car since turning onto the road. The cousins began to slow down and looked for any opportunity that would present itself. One driveway that was interesting went deep in the woods, and no house could be seen through the trees. The trio decided to drive in and see what it led to. It was paved and very narrow, so it had to be a driveway for a house.

"I looked when we turned in and still no police," Anncherry said. "How are we going to handle our entrance when we get to the house?"

"Not sure," Jose quipped. "Maybe we could play you as being sick. We need to locate all the phones and make sure no calls are made. There may also be a problem with what has been put out over the TV. I say we lose the sunglasses and tell them a skunk fumed us the other day, and the reaction irritated our eyes so badly that we are having a poor time seeing. So far, no one has seen us without our glasses on. Anncherry should drive in and look to be alone."

Juan stopped the car and got in the back with Jose so both of them could crouch down in the seat.

Continuing on the pavement, it eventually turned to dirt, but there was no sign of any buildings. The driveway had a horseshoe turn in it and then an entrance that led to a house. Junk cars were strewn around, and there were fences that held livestock like cows and horses. No animals could be seen, but it had the smell of a farm. A dog sitting on the front porch of the house alerted its owner to the cousins' arrival. Anncherry stayed a fair distance from the house so the boys in the backseat could remain hidden. She parked the car and got out.

It was time for her acting career to begin. She had been in a few plays while at school back home in Aruba but had not done well. Anncherry did not like seeing the boys in her class get all the good parts. She ended up fighting with most of them during the play and was quickly cast aside in favor of other classmates who could get along better with each other.

The dog was still barking, and she started his way. The actress was limping badly.

"What a pretty boy," Anncherry said. "Such a good boy."

The dog did not appear overly aggressive, so she continued her way to the porch. An older man opened the door. He had long hair and a longer beard, all salt and pepper colored. And a gut that resembled a 55-gallon drum.

"Can I help you?" he asked.

"I am sorry to bother you, but I hit an animal out at the end of your driveway and did not know what I should do. I got out to check on the poor thing and tripped and twisted my ankle. I just wanted to be sure it was not an animal that belonged to you."

The man told his dog it was okay and that he was a good boy.

"Come on in, and we'll have a look at that ankle."

"Thank you." She gingerly made her way to the front porch, but when she got close to the dog, he growled at her.

His owner scolded him and apologized. "Sorry, we don't get much in the way of visitors. Sampson's just jealous of how pretty you are. He won't be no bother. Come right on in."

When she entered the house, she could see and smell why he had no one come around. The town dump had it all over this place. There were towels draped over every window, and the few lights that were lit put more shine on the subject than she really needed. There was no sign of a TV or telephone, so she asked if he lived alone.

"Just Sampson and me. And of course, we have some cattle out in the back."

"The battery in my phone is dead," Anncherry fibbed.

"Would you have one I could use to call my mother and tell her why I will be late?"

"Nope, nothing like that here," replied the farmer. "I have all I need in the world right here with me. Don't have no reason for a phone."

"That sounds lonely. Do you have any way to get to town?"

"Sure, it's not all caveman-like. I have a car in the barn over there. Would you like an ace bandage to wrap your ankle in?"

"Yes, that would help me a lot."

He left the room, and she went to the front door and yelled for her brothers. They quickly made their way to the door and then into the entry room. The dog was not happy. His owner was not either. He made an appearance back in the room with a shotgun in hand and said, "I heard you do the yelling and thought something was up. I know how to use this weapon, and I'm not afraid to fire it either."

"Please, sir, we mean no disrespect," Anncherry begged. "What I said was true about hitting the animal. I told my brothers to keep their heads down in the car so we would not scare you. I called them in so they could meet you."

"Honey, I may look dumb and sometimes I play it well, but I ain't falling for that line of crap from anyone."

"I am sorry. We will get in our car and leave."

"That's just what you're going to do, and you will not come back. Is that understood? I've got some old ammo I'm dying to use up."

"Yes, we understand." With that said, she motioned for her brothers to about face and leave. The three of them got in the car and drove back out towards the paved road. On the way, she told them what she found out. They were going to hide by the end of his driveway and see if he left. If the farmer did not leave, the trio would go back in and hit him that night. It was time for a new car and the farmer had one in the barn. The cousins had to figure out how to keep him from getting to town or a neighbor's house to let the cops know his car was stolen. The farmer may have to be killed to keep his mouth shut.

The rest of the day went by slowly, and the cousins on occasion got out to stretch their legs. There was no traffic to speak of, and their car had been backed in the woods far enough so it could not be seen anyway. Just after sunset, it was decided the time was right.

If the farmer thought they would return for any reason, he would think it would be in the wee hours of the morning. Their thinking was he would not expect them to show up early that evening. The trio then drove to the horseshoe turn and backed into the brush as far as possible. Satisfied the car was hidden well enough from view, the gear they brought was removed, and the three of them began walking in the direction of the house. Jose removed the gun from the bag it was in.

"What about the dog?" Anncherry asked.

"What do you think?" Jose responded.

"I love animals. Can we lock him in a room without hurting him? Please?"

"Let us see how it all works out. We love animals too."

The house came into view and all was quiet. A light on the front porch was lit, but the house appeared dark. They went around it completely but could not find anyplace that offered a view inside. The dog had not become aware of them yet. Juan went to the barn to see if the car was in there, but it was gone. The farmer and the dog had left. Using their flashlight, the trio followed the tire tracks to another dirt path that left the farm on the other side from the one they drove in on.

That was not in the game plan. Who gave him permission to leave and take the new wheels they needed? The trio went back to their car and got it back on the driveway. After putting the two bags of gear back in the trunk, it was driven out to the road.

The cousins went east again and found another home that sat well back from the road. It was still early in the evening, so time was on their side, but it was also necessary to be concerned about having the headlights seen. Shutting them off, they turned into the drive and went about halfway up. They left the car there and got out.

Heading towards the house, the decision was made to do another walk around to see what presented itself. And that was only if there was no dog. If any barking could be heard they would move to the next home until one was found without a dog. That kind of attention was something the cousins could do without.

The home before them now was very small with windows that were not covered. There was only one light on inside at the front end of the place and a newer looking car sat in the driveway. Sneaking around the sides of the building and looking in the windows revealed very little.

Lights were out in all the rooms that had windows. The home did not look like the farm they had just come from. No other buildings could be seen on the property and so far no signs of any animals. Making their way around the front, they crouched down low and moved toward the one window that was showing light.

At the front of the home was a very small room, and in one corner sat an old man in a wheelchair. His head was tilted to the side, and drool could be seen running from his mouth. The smallest TV the cousins had ever seen was in the opposite corner showing nothing but ant-wars. Only a few old pieces of furniture were in the room.

"Can we check the car for keys and maybe just leave?" Anncherry said. "I do not want any part of hurting this poor soul."

"Since when would you care?" Jose said. "We do not have a choice. If we take the car and leave him to tell, we will not get far. And what if there is anyone else here also? If he is by himself, this would be easy for us, and we may be doing him a favor."

Juan did not like it either. "I agree with Anncherry. Let us move on to something else."

"No way. I am telling you this is perfect for us. Most other homes will have dogs, and if he is home alone it will work nicely."

Juan changed his mind. "I will go and see if the keys are anywhere in the car. Should we go through the front door after that?"

"Yes. Are you with us, Anncherry?"

"I guess so. Let us get it done with."

After a few minutes, Juan returned but did not find the keys.

"We are going up to the door and knock," Jose said. "If anyone else is inside, that should get them to answer. We tell them we are broke down and need to use a phone."

They climbed the steps, and Jose rapped on the door. There was no sound from the TV. The only thing they could hear was a muffled, "Hello? Who's there?"

After waiting what seemed like fifteen seconds, Jose tried the doorknob and found it was unlocked. He pushed the door open and the three of them entered the tiny living room.

"Hello!" was what they were greeted with from the old man in the wheelchair. It was barely audible. He had not so much as moved a millimeter.

Anncherry began with a soft voice, "Sir, we are sorry to bother you, but we broke down and need to use a phone to call for help."

"Take whatever you need." The old man could barely speak. "I don't need anything anymore."

"Are you here alone?" Jose asked.

"I am all alone. No family, no nothing."

"Is that your car out front?"

"Yes, but I haven't used it in three months. Not since I got really bad. You want the car?"

"Only to borrow so we can get some help. Do you have the keys?"

"Yes, on the hook behind you. You take my car, but can you do me a favor?"

"Anything you need," Jose offered.

"I have an old gun in the backroom. Please get it and end my misery. I can't stand the pain anymore, and I got no more drugs."

Jose and Juan were both nodding their heads up and down. It was unusual to get such a request. Anncherry was not thrilled, but it was the old man's idea.

Philip Gagnon

Jose spoke up. "I think we can be of help. Can you excuse us while we discuss it outside?"

"Don't worry about me hearing nothing. It won't matter none."

"OK. If we say something you do not like, just let us know." *As if it would matter.*

The poor old man couldn't even nod his head. A little more spit ran down his chin, and he said, "Okay."

The cousins already knew what they were going to do. It would be Jose who thought of taking the old man out in the woods behind the house, and doing him there after a hole was dug and he was in it. No body parts to clean up; just a pit to fill back in and then made inconspicuous.

"We will dig a grave out in the back and line it with some of his bed sheets," Jose began. "We put him in the hole and then suffocate him with a plastic bag. Less mess and no noise."

The old man didn't like it. The sound of his voice getting more distant every time he tried to talk. "I don't wanna freeze to death. Just shoot me here in my chair and be done with it. I wanna die with the heat on. Shoot me now!" It had to be 90 degrees in the room.

It would take some smooth talking from Anncherry and her soothing voice to convince him their plan would be best. Why should he be very selfish and unfair to make such a mess of the house that they would then have to clean up? At the urging of her brothers, she had convinced the old man that being put in a grave was the proper thing to do. And afterward, they would have a special service for him while praying for his soul. *Sure they will!*

The old man agreed but was not one to believe in baloney of this kind. If there wasn't something in it for him, he would have tried to make more of a stink. The only thing he cared about was ending the pain. It was eating him from the inside out, and getting worse by the hour. *Do it now!*

"Can you at least knock me out first?" asked Grandpa.

"We will do you that favor," Jose replied. "Are there any pills you could take that would help?"

"Only sleeping pills. But I guess I could take a bunch."

Glassy Water

"Let us try that. Anncherry will get them for you."

Jose wanted to know about some tools they would need. "Is there a shovel and rake somewhere?"

"Always was out back against the house."

Juan was in a bedroom grabbing sheets. He took them from the bed with their odors and stains, then balled them up to take outside. There was a comforter on a rocking chair so he took that also. He went to the front door and left to help Jose.

Anncherry gave the old man a fistful of pills to take and wash down with a beer she found in the refrigerator.

"I am going out to see if I can help them," she said.

"Don't be long," the old man said. "I've been ready a while."

Anncherry found her brothers in the woods behind the house. The boys were taking turns trying to dig the hole.

"The ground is full of rocks," Juan said. "This is going to take a little bit."

"I have an idea," Jose said. "Anncherry should go back in and see if he has a will. He said he has no family or anybody else. She should make a will and leave everything to us. He would sign the thing. He wants out badly."

"I like it," Juan said. "After we are done with the business in Maine, we can come back and sell this place. And if anyone ever does find the old man buried out here, an autopsy should show he stopped breathing and died naturally. We could say he disappeared and had not been seen in a while. They would have no way to know who buried him, and like he said, he has nobody. So there would not be anybody who would know the truth except for us. And we will never talk."

"We think very much alike," Anncherry said. "You just managed to say it first. I will go back and work it up."

Looking down at the hole that was started, Jose said, "Take your time. We will be the better part of an hour before we are ready to bring him out. And see if you can find a plastic bag while you are in there. One without holes in it would work best."

"Really, you think?" joked Anncherry, and they all began laughing. It was going to be a good day for the cousins. They could all feel it. Inheritance without obligation was well known as the best source of free stuff. The cousins never had anything given to them before.

Anncherry returned to the house and went in through the front door. The old man was exactly as she left him.

"It will not be long now," she said. "They have a few rocks to deal with but are moving right along."

The old man did not answer. Moving across the room and closer to him, it became obvious something was wrong. She had not noticed before, but his chest was not moving when he was breathing. And his tongue was hanging out the side of his mouth. The spittle had dried up. A doctor was not required to figure out he needed to breathe to live. Anncherry put her hand under his nose to see if there was any air coming or going.

She knew that feeling for a pulse would also tell if a person was living or not. Because there was nothing that showed he was alive, there was no way for her to be sure, so she slapped him. He did not move or make a sound, so she slapped him harder and got the same result. Anncherry turned to go back out through the door to tell her brothers the old man had died. Her testing was conclusive.

While approaching her brothers working the hole, she could tell they were struggling with the rocks. She let them know about the old man.

"He is dead. He was dead when I went in."

The brothers stopped what they were doing and stared at her.

"That was after you had him sign the will, right?" Jose asked.

"No, he was dead when I went in. No conversation, no nothing. He was not breathing, and his tongue was hanging out."

"Then why do we need this hole?" Juan said. "We can just stick him in the basement, or we can put him in the trunk and dump him somewhere."

Jose was shaking his head. "That will not work, none of it. I know the digging is hard, but we have to bury him and hope nobody finds the body or realizes he is even dead. We need time

Glassy Water

on our side to keep the police off our tail. And maybe when the time comes to pass back through here, we can take claim to this place. It was us who were the last to see him alive, and he said he has no one else, so we will become his family."

"As I said, we think alike," agreed Anncherry. "Look at the inheritance we just made. We now have a car that is ours and the house with everything in it. But we need to get him out quick. The place smells bad enough."

"OK," Jose said. "Let us bring him here now and while we are finishing the hole, you can clean up some in there and get a meal ready for us in our new home."

The trio walked back towards the house, nodding their heads in agreement. It took all three of them to wheel the old man out to the front lawn. They put down a blanket and dumped him from the chair onto it. He was very light, like all skin and bones. With a blanket wrapped around the body, they carried him into the woods to where the grave was being made. He was dropped on the ground, and the brothers took turns digging again.

Juan was out of the hole while Jose was digging. "See what you can find for plastic sheets that we can cover him with," Jose said. Juan headed for the house.

When he went in, he saw Anncherry with a can of Black Label beer up to her lips.

"What do you have there?" Juan asked.

"There is a ton of the stuff down in the basement. I brought some up and put them in the freezer. They will be nice and cold when you are ready for one. The old man had a lot of canned food stocked up too, so we will not go hungry tonight."

"I want one of those beers right now. And make it four. I will take them out so me and Jose can stay lubricated. See if you can find a plastic sheet while you are working around the house. I will be right back to grab it."

"OK."

Juan went into the woods and found Jose sitting on the ground taking another break. "Look what Anncherry dug up." Juan handed a brew to Jose.

"Christmas comes early this year," Jose said, popping the

lid and downing his. "I cannot think of a better gift."

"The price is definitely right," Juan said as he set his beer down and jumped in the hole. "This is a very nice gift."

The work began to slow as they talked and swilled their beers. They both chose to take a break and grab another beer at the house. Maybe some chow too. Then a few more brews and back to work. Amazing how forward the brain thinks when it already decided it was time to relax. The brothers may come out in the woods tonight, but no bets were being placed on getting the hole dug.

Anncherry had done a quick and efficient job of cleaning the house. She had found a box of large trash bags and went around throwing everything in them. They were taken to the back door and thrown out. When the brothers came in, she was mopping the floors with a mixture of bleach and water. It had done wonders with the odors that were there earlier.

Jose was impressed and said, "I think it is time for you to relax and have a beer. I will buy us all a round." That was an ongoing family joke because none of the cousins liked to buy rounds of beers. They were brought up to expect the drinks to be bought for them.

"What do you think of our new home?" Anncherry said. "I have been working all day to make it nice and dinner is on the stove."

Juan made his way to retrieve beers for all from the freezer and said, "You have done a fine job. Come and let us sit in the living room and enjoy a beer."

"Then the hole is done?"

"Not yet but soon enough," Jose said. "The rush is no longer with the old man dead. We will finish it in due time. The digging is very tough. Many rocks."

"Then we will take the time to eat. You men have worked so hard today. Drink your beers and relax. After I am done with this one, we will have dinner."

Time sure did fly by when you were relaxing. Especially when you were relaxing with beers. After two more each, they went to the basement to view their inheritance. There were four cases of beer, enough for a couple nights. Glancing around the basement they saw more inheritance.

Garbage. Bags of it. Covered with bugs and maggots and who knows what else. The brothers found a bulkhead, and while enjoying more beers tossed all the garbage bags out in the yard. No way there was going to be trash in their place.

The trio ate cans of beans and chicken noodle soup while drinking more beer. Estimates had been made on how long it would take to finish the hole. The little TV was checked for any signs of receiving a signal and Jose ended up throwing the thing out in the yard with the other trash.

The cousins were going to get a 60-inch flat panel to hang on the wall. Back home, they had a 32-inch TV and that was not big enough. All the walls needed fresh paint first. Plush carpeting on the floors was a must for their feet to be cozy and comfortable. Then brand new furniture brought in, and the place would be their castle. The beers were tasting good and sliding down better.

There was a small couch and not much more for furniture. It looked like it came from the local dump, but tonight the cousins did not care. They found blankets, covered the couch and made the bed. There were more comforters in a closet for whoever was going to sleep on the floor. The beers were flowing nicely and soon all thoughts of doing any work vanished. It was time to do some serious drinking. The other stuff would wait until tomorrow. And that was if they wanted to get out of bed. The three of them may sleep late.

"These are the best brews I have ever had," Juan said. "We should stay here and call this home. Drink beer all day and sleep at night. My kind of life."

Anncherry agreed. "We do not owe anything to anybody. Uncle Paul is dead and that finishes that. I could stay here."

Now the beers were talking.

"You are both right," Jose added. "But you know a promise was made, and we are going to keep it. In Uncle Paul's memory, it has to be done. After that, we come back here and enjoy. There should always be ten cases of beer left here. We should never go without."

Philip Gagnon

So as the beers were drank and the evening rolled on, one by one the cousins passed out. Anncherry was smart enough to pass out in the bed. The other two had no complaints about the sleeping arrangements. They did not get a chance to vote and had to take what they got. The snoring suggested all were happy for the night.

Chapter 10

The next morning, the cousins awoke at the same time and not one of them was hungover. They found a badly needed toothbrush that looked like it had been used recently to clean toilet bowls instead of teeth. All three of them closed their eyes and made do with it, each checking afterward to be sure none of the brown from the toothbrush was left on their teeth.

The toilet was brown and so was the bathtub. It looked as if both should have been white. Anncherry had not had time to perform her magic in the bathroom. They all knew it would get better and chose to skip the shower that morning.

Breakfast had been served and Anncherry was calling to them. The brothers arrived at the table and saw plates with canned fruit on them and cans of beer for juice.

"Everything in the house that could be ate or drank is in a can," she said. "The old man had enough stock in here to last him a year."

"Not enough beer for a year," Juan said. "He could not have stretched those four cases that far."

Jose was laughing. "If the old boot drank one beer, he would have stayed drunk for three weeks. That is a year's worth."

Light conversation followed and duties decided. Anncherry would hit the bathroom and the boys would finish up out in the woods. The problem was once they started drinking, it was hard for any one of them to stop. Pickled for the day, primed for the night, this would be their delight. *No one's fools these cousins.*

With smiles on their faces and brewskis in hand, the boys went out the door and into the woods. When they were within

Philip Gagnon

fifty feet of the hole, their mouths dropped open. The blankets they had wrapped the old man in were thrown off to the side, and his body could not be seen.

The boys wandered around in circles for what seemed a half hour trying to locate the corpse but had no luck. There was nothing nearby that would have left any kind of a clue. Their beers long gone, the brothers figured an animal must have made away with the old man for dinner. There would be no foul play on their part, so they went back to the house.

Once inside, they filled Anncherry in about the goings on and grabbed another beer. The hole would be filled back in and hid best as possible. The trio would then get together and think about what to do next while wetting their whistles.

Lunchtime came, and it was more soup and then canned fruit. And beer. All healthy choices. They were down to two cases of beer and nervous that would not be enough to make the entire evening. The afternoon discussions were all about whether there was enough beer to last the night or not. It was finally decided they did not want to chance running short and would head to the store. Jose remembered there was a quick-mart at the closest intersection.

The decision was made to go now, rather than later, and maybe even get some real food while they were out. Juan found the keys to their new wheels, and the three of them went out to it. They were unable to lock the doors to the house because they had not found the keys yet. The store run would just be going up the road a short distance and coming right back.

The car was a 2005 Chevy Impala that was black and beautiful. For some reason, the old man put chrome wheels on her and they looked good. The hood was popped so the oil could be checked because the cousins wanted their new wheels to last. She was in excellent condition with only 5200 miles on the odometer. The car had not been washed in years, so the trio wanted to clean her before they showed it off in town. They found what was needed to wash her, did the job, and were on the road in a half hour.

The mini-mart had the basics, which was perfect for them.

Glassy Water

There were very few customers, so that would make a quick shopping experience. Jose pocketed the toothbrushes they needed and paid for the beer and six ready-made sandwiches. Thankfully, Anncherry had noticed they were low on toilet paper. "To prove you are a man you must wipe it with your hand." *Gee, the things they did back home in Aruba.* So she got some of that also.

Back in the car, beers were passed around, and the trio headed home. Juan drove very slowly once the car came to the dirt section of the driveway near the house. They did not want to get Black Beauty dirty. After unloading the goods from the store, the cousins sat on the front steps to enjoy a beer. Or two.

An hour went by and all was right with them when they heard first, then saw a car coming on their property. The nerve of some people. They should have gotten "No Trespassing" signs while out at the store.

The trespassing car pulled up beside their new car and got dust all over it. Needless to say, the cousins were not impressed.

The car's only occupant, a man the same age as the cousins got out and asked, "Who are you?"

A smart-aleck who was intruding on their land and just sprayed their new car with dust had no right to be asking questions. Well lubricated and ready with superior vocabulary, Jose, the smart one, was going to deal with him.

"You are on private property, and you should get in your car and leave now before we come over and make you leave."

"This is my grandfather's property, and I have every right being here."

The cousins were surprised by that because the old man said he had no family. No one period.

"If he was your grandfather, he is not anymore, and we own the place now," Jose said.

"You're speaking in the past tense as if he's gone," the grandson said. "What do you mean by that?"

"Just what it sounds like. They took him away dead, and we own the house."

"When did he die?"

Jose was not liking the conversation, and a plan was

formulating in his head.

"A while back. How long has it been since you saw him?"

"At least three months. I wanted to get him supplies. He hated when anyone just showed up and didn't want any help. I came by every few months and tried to get him stuff he needed."

"Well he is gone, and we are sorry for that," Jose offered. "Why not come in and have a beer with us? We can fill you in on what we know."

The grandson was confused but agreed. He wanted to know when Grandpa died and how the three of them ended up buying the house. But more than anything, he wanted to know where his grandfather was buried so he could visit the grave. He followed the cousins into the house.

He didn't recognize any of the few furnishings in the house because most were rearranged and all had been covered with blankets. He did know about the food and beer because he helped his grandpa get it. They were drinking his Black Label. He agreed to have a beer with them, and then Jose was asking questions.

"Did you know about any other things your grandfather owned?"

"I thought I knew everything. He had his car and this house. He didn't share a lot of information with us, but over the years, I was led to believe that was all he owned."

"Then the camp he owns up in the State of Maine is news to you?"

"I've never heard anything about that. I was told he'd spent time up there when he was a young man, but that's the only connection to Maine I ever knew of."

"He told us of the camp before he died," Jose lied. "He asked us to help because he felt so ill, and we stayed to assist him so he could get by every day. It got to the point where he could not feed himself or go to the bathroom without help. He begged us to stay, and we were with him for two months, caring for his needs every hour of the day. Doing what we could to keep him comfortable and making sure he ate well. We were like family at the end, and I know it looks like we did it because he was close to death, but that was not the case at all. He begged for our help, and we felt he definitely needed it. Everything we did, we did for him." *Applause please.*

The grandson opened his second beer and said, "When I last saw him, he seemed fine. I mean very old but able to move around the house okay, and he said he was eating and everything else was good. When I left, I had no reason to think I would never see him again."

"He told us he went downhill quickly," Jose went on. "He was suffering badly when we first saw him, and he continued to get worse. He is much better off where he is now, God rest his soul. We pray for him every day." *Really?!*

Well, thought the grandson, who was drinking his beer on an empty stomach and was already feeling a buzz. *These folks certainly seem as if they cared.* He wanted to ask the one nagging question that was bothering him, which was "How did you come to meet the old boy?" but he couldn't quite think of how to say it without sounding disrespectful. And if the house did belong to them, he couldn't very well insult them in their own home.

"Do you know where he's buried?" the grandson asked.

"He was not buried," Jose replied. "After he died, an ambulance showed up and took him away. But he did tell us before he died that he wanted to be cremated."

That was how it happened back home in Aruba when Jose's father died. Why would it be any different here?

"Then I guess we should have a toast to Grandpa," the grandson suggested, "and as you said earlier, 'God Rest His Soul!'" He punctuated the statement by raising a closed fist.

The cousins did the same, and all took a long haul off of Grandpa's Black Label beer.

Now that they were all close and friendly, the rest of the day was spent downing Grandpa's beers and checking out the grandson's car.

Not a regular car, but a Mustang GT500 with all the goodies. After polishing off the first case of beer, they took turns driving it out to the road and then inland away from any traffic. They did not want to get pulled over while drinking. The car had a loud exhaust and would get some looks as it was. After driving it back and forth for an hour, the car was pulled back into the driveway and parked where it was before. The four of them spent the next hour sitting in the car with the radio blaring and tossing down beers.

The grandson was beginning to nod off time and again. He told them earlier he needed to eat, but they had purposely not fed him so he would pass out. Then the cousins could formulate their latest plan.

They all agreed to go back in the house and relax. The grandson was given the couch to sit on because he would hopefully fall asleep. And he did. He hit the couch and was gone.

The cousins went back out to the Mustang with more beers and knocked heads.

Juan was the first to speak. "I say we finish digging the hole and stick him in it."

"That was my thought at first also," Jose said, "but I do not think we should leave his body here and risk having it found. So far, we have nothing bad here that would link us to problems with this place. We do need to quiet him at some point, but I think we should take him to Maine with us."

"Do you think he would go along with that?" Anncherry asked.

Jose nodded his head. "I do not think it would take much to get him to go. We all jump in Grandpa's car and head to camp. We make him think it will be his. Did anyone see any papers in the house with Gramp's signature on them?"

"I found a box of old checks he had signed," Anncherry said. "His signature should be easy to duplicate. It looks exactly like the scribble you would see from a doctor. And I think I know where you are going with this. You want some documents written up with the old man's stamp on them, right?"

"Right," Jose agreed. "We need a will giving us the house and car. And we can add something in it that gives everything else to his grandson. If he gets nosy tomorrow, we can show him the paperwork and convince him it was what the old man wanted. We can paint a picture of a cabin on the lake based on what the old man told us and get up there and then quiet him. Maine has very few people and lots of woods. And the people who are up there are denser than the bark on trees. I read that in a story on the computer once."

"I will get the paperwork done right off," Anncherry said. "What can we do with his car? I was hoping to keep it."

"You mean keep it here at your new home in America?" Juan said. "I like that idea."

"That would be nice, and the price is right, but I do not think it would be good for us to have a trail that could be started here," Jose said. "No, I think we will have him drive it partway to Maine, and then he can park it. There are parking places beside the highways for leaving cars long-term. We will tell him that after leaving Maine, there will be business for us to handle down in Rhode Island, and on the way, he can pick up his car so he can return home."

"But I thought we were going to tie up all the loose ends concerning Grandpa," Anncherry protested.

"We are," Jose said. "He is only going to be told those things to keep him on our side. He will stay with us until it is decided we do not need him anymore, and then he will be disposed of, which will be Grandpa's last link."

"Then it is settled," Anncherry said. "We leave for Maine tomorrow. The copy of the will giving us this house will be left here on the counter. If anyone should have a reason to enter the house, they should see the will and read it saying the house and car were given to us. And we bring the will that gives his grandson the waterfront camp with us to keep him happy until we are done with him."

"Let us have a beer to celebrate, and then hit the sack," Juan said. "We should leave early in the morning to beat the traffic."

"I will just need fifteen minutes to get the papers done."

And to that they drank another three beers each before falling asleep. The boys anyway. Anncherry still had work to do.

Chapter 11

The boys woke up at 4:30 the next morning to the sound of someone choking. The grandson was barfing in the kitchen sink. Only he was not barfing but dry heaving. Badly. It was hard to barf when there were no solids in your stomach.

"Not much of a drinker our boy there," Juan stated. "I think we should give him some food to make him feel better."

"I will have Anncherry look after him," Jose said, and he went and woke her. He explained what needed to be done.

It took more than a few hours, but the grandson rebounded. If the four of them were not going on such a long trip, they would have begun on the beers right then and there. But because the drive took them to populated areas, they were going to wait a little while before their first one. An hour anyway.

After the cousins' gear was put in the Impala, the house was secured and they drove off. Anncherry was with the grandson in the Mustang, and the brothers were in Black Beauty. Anncherry was told to play stupid and pretend she knew nothing. She would have no problem with that as it came naturally. Besides, three on one would be easier to handle. If the grandson should ask any troublesome questions, the cousins' three heads would be better equipped to tell the lie.

Two hours into the drive, they found a "Park and Ride" parking lot next to the highway. Both cars pulled in, and it would be a good and safe place to leave the Mustang. Anncherry had smoke coming from her ears thinking how they could keep the car with them for the rest of the trip. There were visions of driving it by herself. She thought she could handle it even though the last time she had driven ended in an accident with many fatalities.

After a brief conversation with her brothers, the choice was made to bring it along.

Their destination was now Windham, Maine, where the four of them would grab two motel rooms and then plan the work that needed to be done after getting the grandson drunker. When they got to the motel, the cousins would give the grandson some story to explain the stop. There, he would be shown the grandfather's paper leaving him the waterfront camp. Anncherry had come up with the town of Naples as its location, and she told the grandson that. She found the name on a map the night before and saw it was a little north of where their work was. Jose had also mentioned the town by name before.

One thing about this neck of the woods that made planning the trip easier was the towns of Windham, Raymond, and Naples had only one major artery through them. Everything you needed was on the main route. The streets that branched off from it for the most part took you to large parcels of land with homes. You may have found an occasional store off the beaten path but that was it. The business community was all situated along or close to Roosevelt Trail, or Route 302.

The cousins had known in advance where they would be staying. Because that job had been dealt with ahead of time, they started the beer drinking earlier than planned. Anncherry and the grandson were pounding them too. It would turn out that planning ahead may have been wise but showing up at the motel half in the bag was not.

The thing with the small town motels was that usually, more often than not, the owner or a close family member would be manning the check-in desk when you arrived. Surprisingly, a lot of people paid with cash. A lot of cash in the till could lead to bad ideas, and you could only trust close family to handle the money responsibly.

At the same time, those family members were responsible for anyone who would be allowed to rent at the motel and were educated about who and who not to let stay. One person, or any number of people who had been drinking, and it showed in their attitude, were not welcome to stay. The owners didn't even want them on their property, but unfortunately, one never knew when they would show up.

Today, a group of four would arrive at the Chickadee Motel on Roosevelt Trail in Windham, and it was obvious they were drinking. The owner's daughter was in charge at the front desk, and the three cousins had tried coming through the door at the same time. There was a fourth person still out in one of the cars. The trio tripped and stumbled towards the receptionist giving away their inebriation.

Because it was a girl at the desk, the cousins deferred to Anncherry for performing their business.

"We would like two rooms please," Anncherry spat with barley, yeast, and hops spewing from her lips as she spoke. She never liked being polite but felt it would be best to start that way.

The standard response was to tell unwanted guests there were no rooms available. But the girl was intimidated, so the three drunks were told to wait while she got somebody else who would help them. The room that was through the door behind her was the living room of their house, and she would not have to go far to find help. In fact, she just knocked on the door and her father was out to the desk in thirty seconds. He quickly evaluated the environment and delivered the prepared statement after flicking the switch beside the desk.

"Sorry, we're booked and have no more rooms available. My daughter is only here to help those guests that already have rooms."

Well, thought the cousins. *Does that not beat all?*

"Guess we should have called ahead," Anncherry slurred. "Sorry for bothering you."

"That's no problem at all. Sorry we couldn't have been of help. We do have our 'No Vacancy' light on." *Perfect execution and delivery.* The daughter just saw first hand a pro at work.

The threesome went out to the parking lot. The brothers climbed into their trusty Black Limo while Anncherry got in her new Mustang. *It really looked neat, this car,* she thought. Both vehicles got back on Roosevelt Trail and traveled to the next motel where the rooms would be rented. Or so they hoped.

See, these were small towns, and the owners of all the motels knew each other. So it was only natural for the owner of the Chickadee to call his friends and warn them of what was coming their way. He watched which direction they went in and began with the closest motel. He had them all on speed dial, and they would be in debt to him for helping keep the trash out of their establishments. "No Vacancy" signs were lit up at every motel they came to.

What a busy place, thought the cousins.

The grandson had a great idea. He didn't know why he hadn't thought of it before. "Let's continue on to my cabin and stay there." *What a brilliant intellect!!*

Anncherry knew her brothers hoped for more time to formulate a plan.

"But we do not know if anyone is there. Your grandfather never mentioned if it was used or vacant."

"If it's my place, you let me worry about that. How far is it to Naples? I've heard the name but don't know where it is."

"Not sure, but I could hazard a guess and say maybe an hour from here."

"Well, let's go. We can stop and get some food and then head up there."

The beer was fogging the edges of her brain, and Anncherry could not think fast enough. "Let us see if we can find a store first."

She had the grandson pass her brothers and then pulled into a large parking lot.

The huge BigMart sign in Windham sat out at the road's edge next to a Burger King restaurant. They needed to feed the tummy first, so both cars pulled into the restaurant, and the occupants grabbed some chow. It had a sobering effect none of the cousins liked, but they would make up for that. Jose was on his laptop checking his e-mail, amongst other things.

After the meal, they drove to the BigMart parking lot and left their cars. The grandson was convinced he was the one who should go and get the groceries. The other three would get towels, toothbrushes, soap, and anything else that would make the stay at his camp comfortable. Soon as he was gone shopping the cousins knocked heads.

Jose was the first to speak. "With all the motels full, we will need a tent and three sleeping bags. Also a cooler to keep our food in. I hoped to delay this one more day, but now we cannot. Let us keep him drunk, and after he is asleep we quiet him. Everything else needed to do the job was brought from the house and already in the trunk."

"Do you know where we are going?" Juan asked.

"Back at the restaurant, I spent some time googling an area in Naples. I found a remote place with a lake and no homes nearby. What makes it perfect is I did not see any roads to the lake. So the land must be privately owned. All areas near the water had nothing for miles. We just need a good spot to park the cars, and we can hide out there. It would serve our purpose better than any motel because we can come and go without the worry of someone watching us all the time."

"Camping under the stars has always been a dream for me," Anncherry said. "How far will that be from our job in Raymond?"

"It is like a thirty-minute drive which is perfect," Jose said. "Far enough away but not too far."

"Let us get our gear and then meet out front," Anncherry said. "I will go and find our friend while you two grab the goods. I will keep him near me."

The cousins split up to go about their business. Once the brothers had the supplies that were needed, they went to the front of the store. Anncherry was near a checkout lane with the grandson and got in line when she saw her brothers. Jose and Juan fell in behind them.

The line moved fast, and soon they were back at the cars. The brothers tossed the gear in the trunk and got in.

The grandson was still a little tipsy, and a fresh round of brewskis was passed around. He was turning out to be quite the drinker like he was celebrating something.

"I saw you had three sleeping bags," the grandson said. "How will that work?"

Anncherry anticipated the question and said, "That was all they had left. Hopefully, we will not even need them if your camp has some beds in it. And if there are no beds and we need to use the sleeping bags, me and you will share one."

"I'll drink to that!" the grandson exclaimed. And because he was thinking of her in a sleeping bag with him, he smiled the rest of the way.

When they got to the causeway in Naples, it was lit with streetlights but otherwise empty. The stores and restaurants that lined the main road were deserted. The Naples Causeway, located at the base of Long Lake and the tip of Brandy Pond, was a seasonal destination for tourist in the summer. In the fall, you would get leaf-peepers who would travel through the area by the busload, but there was nothing open for them to stop and patronize. Those people only cared about getting an eye full of foliage anyway and were not keen on leaving much money behind.

After the causeway, the Impala made a left on Route 114 with the Mustang close behind. The road went through no man's land but eventually ended up running parallel to the shore of Sebago Lake and then later, into Gorham village. That was a long ways away.

Jose had spent some time when back home in Aruba studying up on the wooded and uninhabited spaces of Maine. He learned logging was the main event in the state. There were more logging roads in Maine than public roads. He was counting on that information to help them penetrate and hide in the woods. You could easily tell a logging road that was in use now as compared to one that had been abandoned long ago.

The grandson was celebrating wildly by himself but was getting antsy. "Do you know which road the camp is on?" he asked.

"No," Anncherry said. "This area is as new to us as it is to you. Your grandfather told us how to get to it, but he had not been to it in many years. So we may make a few wrong turns first, but we will find it."

What they wanted to find was the best and most remote

place for them to enter the woods, and then go in and check it out for their needs. The grandson could keep dreaming about some camp that never was.

The fourth road they turned onto was very interesting. It began as a left turn off Route 114, and after half a mile curved back out to the main road. They had not seen a house in five minutes and no traffic to speak of. And that was on the main route. The circular shortcut looked like an area where logging trucks would have entered to load their goods for transport.

Jose was aware the tractor-trailers went deep in the woods to wherever the trees were stacked, so they could be loaded and hauled away. Some of the logging roads were big as a paved highway. That was what he had seen on the internet. But here, they were like tunnels through the woods, where the tree canopies had grown together above the road and gave it a "tunnel effect."

No one made a sound except for the slurping of brewskis as they turned towards the perfect tunnel. Before they entered, Jose got out so he could check and be sure a logging road existed beyond the brush that had grown over the beginning, partially concealing it. They could drive the cars through the brush and after they were on the logging road, get out, go back, and toss the brush around to conceal their entrance. *Outstanding!*

It was like heaven. None of the cars' occupants had ever seen or dreamed of being in such a beautiful place. Never even saw anything like it on the tube. Absolutely breathtaking. Until they came upon the "No Trespassing" signs, and they looked to be everywhere. Jose remembered reading about that and thought it was good. "Private Property." Should not have to worry about anybody bothering them there.

Jose was sure they were close to the lake he checked out and figured the signs would have been all around it. Huge parcels of land owned by farmers who managed them as tree farms for tax benefits and profit of the timber. Those farmers would never see or set foot on 95 percent of the property in their lifetimes. It was not like a cattle farm where you would throw on your cowboy hat and ride Trigger around to keep an eye on your flock. These were tree farms and heavily forested. The farmers had areas cut off every so often in a form of management. And financial gain.

Heaven on earth was an accurate description of the terrain they were passing over. No smells from pollution; no trash cast about by human pigs; no junk cars left to rot. Other than the old logging roads, there was no sign of any human activity that would have spoiled the beauty of the land. At least not until the cousins arrived on it.

The headlights of the car gave the illusion of an endless tunnel. The canopy above the road was thick and lush. It was almost as if it was built by humans. And it was because people with heavy equipment had built the logging roads, but nature took over after that and the years were good to the effects left behind. "Heaven on Earth."

The woods were thick on both sides of the road, and Jose knew the water would be off to their right side. He wanted to get a bearing on what part of the lake they were at. They stopped and got out of the cars.

"Let us walk over to the water," Jose said. "We need to see where we are."

The grandson was all smiles. The camp was no longer on his mind.

Jose locked the Impala and turned to go. You never walked away from a car in Aruba without locking the doors.

"I forgot," Juan said. "I need the flashlight. Can you open the trunk?"

Jose did as Juan wanted and then relocked the car.

"Is that really necessary?" Juan said, more trying to be a wisecracker than anything else. "It is not like we are in the big city or anything."

"Just force of habit," Jose replied. "Better safe than sorry."

Anncherry could not pass on a dig. "You mean like the time back home when you left Mom's car unlocked with all the Christmas gifts in it and then went into a nightclub? What happened to all those gifts when you came out?"

"Ha Ha, very funny. How did I know you two would have just left our favorite hangout and saw me drive up. I did lock the car, but you two wiseguys knew where Mom had the hidden key under her bumper. I cannot forget the look on her face when I told her all the gifts were stolen. Then I saw them under the tree. She never did forgive any of us for that little joke you pulled."

"We had planned that for a week," Juan said. "We were hoping Mom would slap you silly when you told her, and she never even knew we had the gifts. Good old Mom never did pay much attention to the details."

A smiling and quite drunk grandson was happy being part of this little bit of nostalgia. Everything in fun, just like family. And they like him.

Jose led the way in the direction of the lake. The brush was thick and at times tough to penetrate. He was not going to mention the camp unless the grandson asked. Once a site was found that suited the cousins' needs, Jose would tell him they were lost and would have to camp out for the night. Keeping him drunk was the plan.

At the water's edge, the brush was very thick and the sky dark. Jose guessed they were a quarter of the way down the lake. Terrific. They would drive deeper into the woods and then look for the perfect site. A place to park the cars away from the logging road and then a spot to build a campsite.

Back at the cars, a new round of brewskis was passed around, and then they all got in and continued along. Down the tunnel of never-ending delight.

When they were at what Jose estimated to be halfway down the lake and well deep in the woods, the Impala crawled along with the Mustang behind it to see if they could find a place to hide the cars. Jose did not expect anyone to pass by, but he wanted to play it safe. A perfect spot presented itself on the left side of the road, and all four got out of the cars to inspect the "Garage" as Jose would come to call it.

After a quick inspection, the gear was unloaded, and then the cars were backed in side by side. When they finally stopped, the vehicles were barely visible from the road. Hearing the branches scratching the paint job broke their hearts, but they knew it had to be done. The cousins would have them buffed and waxed when their mission was complete. The doors were locked, and the drivers made their way back to the logging trail. The grandson could be seen scratching his head.

While walking back to the logging road, Jose saw an old canoe that he and Juan would come back for later. It might be nice to use it out on the water doing some spearfishing like they did back home.

They chose to camp close to the water for obvious reasons. It would be quick access to bathe and get water needed for other things. A small clearing was found, and they saw there was no shortage of firewood. A fire was to be built while the campsite was organized, but first, the four of them would relax and swill some beer.

The grandson was lost but still happy. "Are we far from the camp?"

"Not sure," Jose said. "I think it is nearby, but there are so many side roads. It would be easier to look for it in the daylight."

"I can feel it," the grandson said. "I'm close to home." Then he smiled and winked at Anncherry, who was looking the other way.

Closer than you know, thought Juan as more beers were passed around.

Jose whispered to Anncherry, "Take him for a walk back on the road and plow the beers to him. We are going to do some digging, so give us an hour."

No problem for Anncherry. The Aruban math scholar quickly ran the numbers through her head and figured they would need six beers. Oh, wait, and then times two. It took a few seconds to count the number on her fingers. She put the right amount of beers in a bag and then motioned for her new boyfriend to come with her. Together they were out of sight in fifteen seconds.

Remembering the battle they had with the hole back in Massachusetts, both hoped it would not be a repeat event. After carefully scouting the terrain for the best location to dig a grave, it became obvious there was no good spot. Kicking at the surface and hoping to find a sandy area like the digging they did on the beach as kids back home, the brothers settled for the best flat surface they could find. One push of the spade into the earth and that was all it took.

"How about we tie some rocks to his legs and throw him in the lake," Juan suggested. "It worked for us back home when we threw the guy's body in the ocean. I do not want to spend the entire night digging this hole. I want to drink beer and relax."

"We run the risk of his body being seen in the water," Jose said. "We have to bury him. But I tell you what we can do. Let me start the digging while you go find Anncherry and bring them both back. I do not know why this did not come to me before, but we will have him help dig the hole."

"Well, I like the idea but your thinking is flawed. He is not going to help dig his own grave. I guarantee it." Sometimes Juan thought his brother was really dumb.

"I understand why you would not be able to see the big picture. That pea-sized brain of yours just cannot process such information. We tell him the hole is so we can go to the bathroom and bury our trash. The only problem will be if he can know which end of the shovel to use. So you best hurry and grab them before Anncherry feeds him full of beer."

"I always knew you were the smart one. I will be right back."

Jose was thinking how smart he was, and that all of his smartness called for a break. When the three of them returned, he was still leaning on the shovel, drinking more beer. The hole had not been started yet, so he told Juan to begin and took Anncherry to the side where he explained what was going on.

"The hole is going to be hard, and we were hoping for some help."

"I know. Juan told me the dirt was rocky again, and the two of you needed help for a trash pit. Or was it a bathroom pit?"

"Either or," Jose said. "As long as we can get him to help and make him think it is necessary. Any help will go a long way."

They went back to the ditch Juan was laboring over and found he was exerting more energy shouting swear words than he was digging. But he had gotten a good start on the hole.

"Take a break, Juan. Grab a brew and cool those vocal cords off. You are up next." Jose indicated to the grandson. "You got a name?"

Just like his grandfather, the spittle running down the side of his chin was like a river running endlessly. When he spoke, a wad of spit came out with the word.

"Chuck," he said, but it sounded like anything but Chuck. More like "Tuck," "Duck," "Puck," or "Muck." So as not to confuse the boy, Jose settled on "Uck." He doubted "Uck" would know the difference.

The grandson was a little unsteady but was in the right ditch moving the dirt and rocks in the right direction. More beers were passed around, and the cousins were going to set up the tent. It took twenty minutes and a few choice words, but they got it done. Juan had given the grandson a break in the pit.

After grabbing another brew, he walked over to the tent.

"Awful small for four of us," Chuck said, dribble and spit flying everywhere.

"More than enough room for this foursome," Anncherry fibbed. "Me and you will not take up much space. The sooner you get the pit dug, the faster we get to try it out."

The fact that they would have been stacked like sardines in a can never mattered again to Chuck. The smile was back, and he told Juan to vacate the trench. Time for some fresh muscle.

The cousins sat and watched with delight as Chuck dug his own grave. It would be a long time before they would be able to do better than this stunt. *They were geniuses.*

After a while, a look of concern came across Anncherry's face. "We do not need him sweating out all the beer," she said. "Someone give him a break."

Jose went over and tried to give Chuck a rest, but he became upset. Chuck wanted to get the job done, and anyone that got near him would have to answer to his fists.

Anncherry was no stranger when it came to dealing with those who were recently rewarded with some liquid courage. The sound of her soft voice was all Chuck needed to hear, and he was out of the hole like a bullet from a gun. He was sweating profusely and had his chest stuck out like a strutting pregnant peacock. He sauntered over towards Anncherry and tripped on a rock that had been taken from the pit.

Chuck fell forward and then onto another pile of rocks that had been removed from the pit. His head struck the rocks with such force there was an audible "Crack!" The cousins could not believe their luck. If he was not dead, it would not take too much to get him there. They approached his limp body to check on him. He then began flopping around like a fish out of water. That lasted for twenty seconds or so. He had blood, and lots of it, flowing from the side of his mouth and out of a gash on his head. The cousins made no effort to stop the flow.

"Inconsiderate bum could have fallen closer to the hole!" blasted Juan. He threw a shovel load of dirt at Chuck.

Juan climbed over his body and grabbed a beer. He showed no concern for Chuck. Neither did the others. *Heartless!*

"We should leave him alone and let him drip dry," Anncherry suggested.

"It would be better for us to get him in the hole right away," Jose said. "Less mess to clean up."

The cousins nodded in agreement and took long pulls on their beers. Jose jumped in the trench and had it ready in two minutes. They rolled Chuck in a blanket and threw him in the hole. The three of them then put the rocks back in beginning with the ones he bled on. Using the shovel, Juan scraped the blood off the ground and put it in also.

They had some layered plastic that was draped over the rocks and body. Then they threw dirt on top of it all. The mess was cleaned up in less than a half hour, and the trio decided to cover it with leaves and branches in the morning. They sat down and all had a toast to "Uck." Then it was off to bed.

Chapter 12

The next morning came early, not that it was the plan. The cousins wanted to sleep until noon, but there was no escaping the sound of an airplane flying close by. It was not possible they could have been found that quickly. The trio bounced out of their tent and could hear the noise coming from the direction of the lake. Jose had read that the police used airplanes on floats to access remote areas. They moved towards the shoreline to see what was going on.

The plane making the noise was off the water's surface and lifting into the air. They could see where it made waves when it was on the lake. The three of them watched as it circled out over the woods, and then came back in to land again. The plane touched the water and then the engine was gunned, and it lifted off the lake and gained altitude.

Jose knew the plane was doing touch and go's, so he explained it for the other two. "The pilot is practicing takeoffs and landings. It is a common thing to do, so you can land the plane with confidence. I read that it is always done at airports, but I never thought of them doing it on the water. The pilot even counts how many were done and adds it as an entry into a logbook when finished for the day."

"I cannot believe how loud it is," Anncherry said. "My ears are pulsing. Good thing there are no homes close by. The noise would drive them crazy."

"I think that is why they are using this lake," Jose said. "Because there is no one around. I imagine there would be a lot of people complaining if they did it much on a lake with many houses."

Philip Gagnon

The plane gained altitude and kept going straight. The pilot must be done for now.

The cousins went back to the campsite and busied themselves with the chores ahead of them. After throwing leaves and branches on the pit and then getting something to eat, the trio took turns down at the water to brush their teeth and cleanup. Then it was time to sit and knock heads. They had a job to do.

Chapter 13
Three days later

It was Thursday, October 6th, and Jim Kamae had just done some touch and go's on a few different lakes in his beloved Cessna 180. He tried to do some of those every day while getting used to his equipment. The plane was new to him, and he was still working on his comfort zone. He didn't have a floatplane rating because there were a few more classes to finish up. But that didn't keep him grounded. It was his aircraft, and he could take her out whenever he wanted. And he did, all the time. Not legally mind you because the rating was needed first, but you just do not get caught.

Jim was in a league of his own after successfully landing his plane in the dark on the lake. He had done it three times and both of last night's performances were still fresh in his mind. It was not an ordeal to brag about because he knew his luck would eventually run out, and his landing would not end up successful. And then seeing those people in the middle of the night still sent shivers down his spine. He did not ever want to be put in that situation again.

His plane had a 230 horsepower engine and was considered a workhorse in its day. The last 180s were built in 1981, and going forward they would steadily increase in value. There were more powerful planes on floats, but the 180 was ideal for coming out of small ponds because of its relatively light weight and strong performing motor.

A number of floatplanes were based at the lake Jim lived on, and most of those planes were smaller and a lot quieter. When Jim first bought his plane, he gave no thought to the fact it would be five times louder than the smaller ones. He would blow out of the cove where his house was located, and then up and away. The plane would then be brought around for a few touch and go's and back to the dock for some more waxing. It was his baby.

But the complaints about the loud noise began to trickle in. No one wanted to deny him his fun, but at the same time, he had to respect their right to peace and quiet.

From then on, and in an effort to keep the peace, Jim would taxi his plane out to the middle of the lake and do his takeoff run from there. Whenever it was possible, he would take off at cruise power which cut the noise down a lot. Cruise power was less engine RPMs, and the variable pitched prop was feathered back from maximum pitch. Those two settings at less than full power resulted in much less noise on takeoff.

Of course, that was if you could get away with it. If the plane was heavy with fuel, gear, and passengers, the aircraft would not leave the lake's surface without both control knobs jammed into the dashboard for full power. The more weight you had, the more power you needed, and the longer the takeoff run would be. That created about the worst possible noise, and in return, wreaked havoc on the peace and quiet.

The smaller planes were lighter, usually only carried two people at most, and did not carry as much fuel. They also had a fixed pitch prop that was usually best designed for float flying. Those planes were capable of making the noise of a loud boat, and soon the complainers discovered the difference and questioned why anyone needed something so much noisier.

While Jim was doing his best to keep everyone happy by trying to lower the noise of his plane, there was a neighbor who also had a 180 on floats, and who couldn't have cared less what anyone else thought. As far as that neighbor was concerned, he had just as much right as anybody else to use the lake, and no laws were being broken. His house was in the same cove as Jim's, and he would blast out of it parallel to the shoreline the camps were on. That would also be the exhaust side of the engine that at full power, and with the propeller whipping up the air volume and increasing the exhaust noise by fifty times, it would literally

Glassy Water

shake the windows of the camps. *Now that was very loud.*

Complaints were constant but usually fell short of being heard by that neighbor. His mother and father were the first to build and settle in their camp at the cove. Both parents were in their 80s and held the respect of all the other neighbors. While everyone wanted to hang their son by his neck from the nearest telephone pole, they were also afraid of insulting his parents. So Jim was the recipient of most of the anger. His relationship with the other owner of the 180 was strained at best, so he couldn't act as a conduit and channel the information to him.

Jim was out today doing some touch and go's before he flew over to Downeast Maine. His aunt had a camp on East Grand Lake and needed a generator brought up. Driving to the camp would have taken more than four hours one way. The 180 on floats would do the trip in one hour and ten minutes at 128 miles an hour cruise speed. On wheels and without the drag of the floats, the 180 was capable of 155 miles an hour cruise.

In the winter, they planned on plowing a runway on the lake in front of the camp and use it as long as the ice was safe. The same would be done at Jim's home on Panther Pond in Raymond. There were only a few months a year when the plane had to be kept at the airport. When the floats were changed over to wheels, or wheels to floats, the plane would remain at the airport until the ice was safe in the winter, or melted in the spring. There was no better convenience than having your airplane sitting close to your yard if you flew a lot.

Back at his dock on Panther Pond, Jim topped off the gas tanks while waiting for the generator to be delivered to his house. As soon as it arrived and was loaded into the right side passenger seat of the plane, he prepared to leave. His aunt had to have it at the camp and hooked up to the water pump today. She had friends who were going to use the camp for a week and knew they wouldn't be happy without water.

It was not a big generator like the ones that powered whole houses, but a small and compact one perfect to run a single application. His aunt desperately wanted to make the trip up in the plane but couldn't get out of an all-day conference she was involved in. Jim didn't mind going and enjoyed doing things for others.

People were always asking for rides or to be taken somewhere so they could view something from the air. The beauty of Maine was there were bodies of water to land a floatplane on almost everywhere. And most people were used to them landing and taking off. They never seemed to mind if you came in and then left for a long time.

One of the problems that came with owning your own plane was the cost associated with it. The insurance was expensive and even more so for a seaplane. For some reason, leaving a seaplane at a dock or mooring was frowned upon by insurance companies, and the chance of it sinking to the bottom was not an uncommon thought.

Then you had repairs, and the minimum cost for any repair to a plane was around $1000. Take it in for the plugs to be changed, get a bill for $1000. It didn't matter what the repair was, you could plan on writing all your checks beginning with a number in the thousands.

Gas was another huge expense. No one who wanted a ride or asked you to fly something somewhere would offer to pay for gas. The Cessna 180 Skywagon on floats would use between 13 and 15 gallons per hour. More than that if all you were doing was touch and go's. The smaller planes used quite a bit less gas while the cost to insure and maintain them was also more reasonable. But they were still expensive. So as you can see, deep pockets were necessary to own any flying machine.

To be a safe pilot, Jim called for a weather briefing and forecast for the areas he would be flying through. Okay, he watched The Weather Channel to get the latest update. He didn't file a flight plan either because he would be departing outside of controlled airspace and had all the phone numbers he needed on speed dial if an emergency occurred. That was not what you were taught to do when obtaining your pilot's license, but some guys

Glassy Water

became comfortable with a system they developed and as long as rules were followed, no harm was done.

Jim checked his floats for water and after pumping them dry was ready to leave. The plane was untied and pushed away from the dock, and because the winds were light today, he could do it by himself. When the wind was blowing pretty good, two people were needed for that. Even with their sleek design and while sitting in the water, floatplanes without power act like kites in the wind without a string.

Idling out to the middle of the lake took a little more than eight minutes. Once out there, Jim aimed the plane into the direction the wind was coming from. Then he reached down and pulled the water rudder cable up and locked it in place. He had deployed 20 degrees of flaps, had the horizontal stabilizer adjustment wheel set for takeoff, and eased the throttle in until it was adjusted to cruise power. He then rolled the prop pitch knob back to where it matched the cruise power setting.

The control yoke was pulled back as he brought the plane's floats up on step. While moving forward through the water and gaining speed, the yoke would be pushed forward to a neutral position so the plane would skim across the surface. He would also roll the horizontal elevator adjustment wheel back to balance the pressure on the yoke.

With a light wind and the plane headed directly into it, he slowly pulled back on the yoke when at the right speed and was free of the water. He would climb to 5500 feet and maintain a heading of Zero Eight Six degrees. Jim had made the trip many times and knew the terrain by heart. Should the wind pick up and begin to blow him off course, he'd correct his heading to compensate for the wind. There was also a "Loran" with waypoints plugged into it that would help keep the plane on course.

Most people thought flying was easy, and it is. But there were numerous rules that must be followed on any flight trip. Jim chose an altitude of 5500 feet because once you were 3000 feet above ground level or AGL, flight separation rules apply. If you were flying a magnetic course of between 0 degrees and 179

Philip Gagnon

degrees, the rule says you fly at odd-numbered thousands beginning at 3000 feet and add 500 feet. Meaning 3500, 5500, 7500. If your direction was between 180 degrees and 359 degrees, then you would fly at even-numbered thousands beginning at 4000 feet and add 500 feet. Meaning 4500, 6500, 8500.

VFR, or Visual Flight Rules, were a "see and be seen" principle. The person flying the plane was the "Pilot in Command" and was responsible for all aspects of the flight. Visibility must be clear enough to "see and be seen." You always need to be aware of any aircraft around you and do what needs to be done to keep a safe distance from them.

Although Jim wanted to fly at 5500 feet and the rules allow it, he'd be asking for flight following from air traffic controllers, or ATC, and at times would fly at a different altitude when the controller instructed him to do so. If he didn't ask for flight following, he would have to stay well clear of controlled airspace around major airports.

The most direct route to his aunt's camp would take Jim directly through controlled airspace. He'd be watched by Portland ATC first, then they would hand him over to Navy Brunswick, or "Brunswick Naval Air Station," when he approached their airspace, and then over to Bangor ATC.

"Portland Tower, Two Four Two Three Foxtrot," Jim broadcast over the radio. His friend, Sam, was off duty and was going to make the trip today but instead ended up having to take his mother to a doctor.

"Two Four Two Three Foxtrot, Portland," responded ATC.

"Portland, Two Four Two Three Foxtrot is a Cessna 180 floatplane departing Panther Pond, twenty miles northeast your location, climbing to and maintaining 5500 feet on a heading of Zero Eight Six, destination East Grand Lake, requesting flight following."

"Roger, Two Three Foxtrot, squawk One Niner Five Six and 'ident.'"

"Two Three Foxtrot One Niner Five Six and 'ident' now."

The plane was equipped with a transponder that easily allowed for its signature to be picked up on radar by ATC. The

Glassy Water

ident button was only used when you were told to do so by the controller. It helped them identify your aircraft.

"Two Three Foxtrot, have your position nineteen miles northeast of PWM passing through 3800 feet. Climb to and maintain 5500, stay on your current heading. Pressure is Two Niner Niner Six."

"Two Three Foxtrot, climb to and maintain 5500 on current heading, Two Niner Niner Six," Jim replied. In the old days, just keying the mike would have worked as a response to ATC, but for decades now a pilot would repeat the instructions given by ATC, thereby making sure they were received correctly.

It was a special feeling being alone up high in the sky. Being in command of your own ship was a thrill of its own. The sights that could be seen as you scanned the landscape and kept watch for other air traffic were completely stunning. It was a front-row seat to the best game in town, not to mention the beauty of it all.

Glancing to the southeast, the ocean, along with all the islands that were hugging coastal Maine, made for grand viewing. Looking to the west and inland, there were many mountains including the White Mountains of New Hampshire that filled the window you were peering through. The top of Mount Washington already had snow on it. When you were flying over closer to the mountain itself, you got a nice aerial view of the weather post that sat near the top. *Got to be one of the colder places to hang out at.*

A voice over the radio demanded Jim's attention.

"Two Three Foxtrot, Portland."

"Two Three Foxtrot," Jim said.

"Two Three Foxtrot, you have traffic at your eleven o'clock, one mile out at 8500. He will be passing over you."

"Roger, Portland, Two Three Foxtrot has the traffic."

Jim had seen the plane which was why he said, "Two Three Foxtrot has the traffic." Imagine a clock, and with Jim facing the twelve o'clock position, he looked a little left to where the eleven o'clock position would be, and up, to catch a glimpse of a twin-engine plane that's going to pass over him at an altitude 3000 feet above Jim's.

Philip Gagnon

There was plenty of separation between them, and Jim had seen the plane without the help of ATC, but flight following was the way to go. While the planes that had filed flight plans would always have the right of way, ATC does their best to help you also. Sometimes though, they would vector you way out and away from their airspace. There was no way to know in advance how busy they'd be.

Jim was thinking back to last week when he was on his way home from East Grand Lake and called ahead to Bangor ATC for flight following. The controller at Bangor initiated flight following and gave Jim a code to set on his transponder. Everything was normal until about five miles from the Bangor Jetport. That's when the ATC guy called Jim on the radio.

"Floatplane Two Four Two Three Foxtrot, Bangor Tower."

"Two Four Two Three Foxtrot," Jim said.

"Two Four Two Three Foxtrot, turn left to a heading of One Four Five and descend to and maintain 3000 feet."

"Two Four Two Three Foxtrot, turn left to One Four Five, descend to and maintain 3000."

That was it, and you couldn't argue. They had a job to do, and that came first. The big jets got the right of way, and with the new heading and altitude change, he was putting Jim out to pasture. Instead of being perpendicular to his original heading, Jim was going a little backwards. He did as he was told and maintained the new heading and altitude.

After seven minutes on that heading, Jim was fairly well out over the sea. He knew he was way beyond the landing paths of the jets flying into and out of Bangor. He picked up his microphone and keyed it.

"Bangor Tower, Floatplane Two Four Two Three Foxtrot."

Ten seconds go by, then twenty, thirty, and no response, so Jim tried again.

"Bangor Tower, Floatplane Two Four Two Three Foxtrot."

Again no answer.

Did the radio quit? Had the electrical system shut down? Any number of things could have happened.

The first thing Jim had to do was correct his heading so he

could get back on a path towards home. He turned to a heading of Two Nine Five degrees and after getting on course hit the "Reset Position" button on his "Loran" to guide him home.

Jim reached over and reset his transponder to the correct 1200, or "One Two Zero Zero," which was the standard VFR setting if you were not under the watchful eye of ATC.

If Jim stayed on his current heading, he would pass the northern side of Navy Brunswick airspace, so to be safe he turned a little right to a new heading of Three Two Zero. That should take him inland enough and well away from Navy Brunswick. Once he was certain he would be clear of them, he corrected his heading for home. He knew the area by heart.

A voice on the radio brought Jim away from reminiscing the past of that messed up flight and back to reality. Portland Tower was calling again.

"Two Three Foxtrot, Portland."

"Two Three Foxtrot."

"Two Three Foxtrot, contact Navy Brunswick at 128.5. Have a nice day."

"Two Three Foxtrot, 128.5. Thanks for your help."

Jim set the radio to frequency 128.5 which was that of Navy Brunswick. He waited before keying the mike to be sure he didn't step all over a conversation already going on. When he was certain the airwaves were not busy, he made the call.

"Navy Brunswick, Floatplane Two Four Two Three Foxtrot."

"Floatplane Two Three Foxtrot, good to have you with us. Pressure is Two Niner Niner Three. No traffic at this time."

"Two Niner Niner Three, Two Three Foxtrot."

Jim reached over to his altimeter and adjusted the thumbscrew to the numbers given him by Navy. Once adjusted to the right pressure number, he was at the correct altitude for the area he was flying in.

Altitude is the height above sea level. An altimeter uses the changes in atmospheric pressure to determine the changes in altitude. There are many complicated gauges used by pilots, but they were easy to understand once you were properly educated.

Navy Brunswick had been contacted by Portland ATC to expect Jim's call. The Navy ATC had the specifics of Jim's flight as they were provided to them by Portland. If they needed anything or were not clear about something, they would call Jim and ask. Other than calls about traffic, a controller would talk to you on the initial contact and then when they release you to another ATC. No other conversation would be necessary. Those people were all pros.

The Town of Brunswick was on the coast in the Gulf of Maine, and the Naval Base with its airport was close to the ocean. Jim was going more inland and he wouldn't be with Navy Brunswick for long. He was on a course towards Bangor, and they would take him soon.

There was a funny thing about the weather around Bangor that Jim had noticed over the years, and it was another reason he checked different weather sources before flights. When you were west of Bangor, the weather could be perfect, but after you passed through Bangor and were east of the city, the weather could turn in an instant.

All pilots had a local number they used to get the current and forecast weather conditions for their area and all along the intended route of travel. Those weather guys were always dead-on, and their briefing sometimes included current reports by pilots who may have experienced weather-related incidents along your route.

But there was something about Jim's trips through Bangor that usually would include having to fly around fast-moving storms. He assumed it must be something to do with the mountain ranges just to the north of Bangor. While it had never been a real problem, Jim always remained cautious.

It seemed like he just talked to Navy Brunswick when the radio came to life again.

"Floatplane Two Three Foxtrot, Navy Brunswick."

"Two Three Foxtrot."

"Two Three Foxtrot, contact Bangor Approach at 125.9. Have a great day."

"Two Three Foxtrot, 125.9. Thanks, you too."

Glassy Water

Jim set the dial to the frequency of 125.9 and waited to be sure the channel was not being used. If it was busy, he would have to wait until there was an opening and then make the call. There was quite a bit of chatter on the channel. Nothing to do but listen to the conversations being played out and patiently await his turn. Bangor ATC knew he was coming because Navy had contacted them.

There was a passenger jet with a customer on board who had become violent. While the reports from the pilots of the jet said the situation was under control, the sound of someone beating on the cockpit door could be heard while they had the radio mike keyed. The cockpit door could not be opened because they had no idea what was happening on the other side. Bangor ATC cleared the flight for a straight-in and expedited approach to the active runway.

According to Jim's calculations, he was still 30 or so miles from the jetport and had plenty of time to call in. As long as Bangor ATC acknowledged his position before he got within 20 miles of the airport, he would be fine. If not, he would have to take a route well clear of the airport while dropping to 2000 feet, and then he could safely pass by at ten or more miles out.

While there were many controllers working the tower at Bangor, that channel was busy with only one and the passenger jet. A situation contained, but another unknown problem. The jet was 25 miles out and on a straight-in approach. The pilots were on edge and rightfully so. The radio chatter was constant.

Jim was around 20 miles out and had already made his decision. Looking off to the right, he could see the big jet floating through the air. There was no chance he would get to use the radio without stepping all over someone else speaking. And that was an emergency situation.

With the jet coming in from his right side, Jim began a descent down to 2000 feet and turned left. The airport was straight ahead and could be seen easily. He reset his transponder to 1200 hoping to send a message to Bangor ATC that he was terminating flight following. They were busy enough and Jim didn't want to be a bother.

Philip Gagnon

Flight tracking was something requested by the pilot in VFR conditions and could help the local ATC with traffic decisions. The controller had contact with you and more times than not, would have you deviate from your altitude or heading so they wouldn't need to re-route the bigger planes. It also allowed you to fly closer to, or directly through the controlled airspace, but only with their permission. You could break it off at any time if you were the proper distance from any controlled airspace and below the required altitudes. That wouldn't apply to large Class B (B for big) terminal airports like Boston where ATC can have control over large swaths of landscape and airways.

Because Jim was close to Bangor, he left the radio frequency alone. He could clearly see the jet and would watch as it continued on to the airport. The chatter on the radio had switched to the pilots of the jet complaining of a person trying to force open an emergency exit door.

A stewardess gained access to the cockpit and told the pilots that three men were taking over the entire passenger section of the plane. It began with one man, and he was subdued. But two others became involved and got him free, so now the three of them were terrorizing the passengers and crew.

Everyone was told by the men to stay in their seats or they'd be beaten. The flight attendant explained the men were given too much to drink, and it all started when she refused to serve them any more. It wasn't terrorism or planned, offered the pilots.

While Jim was scanning the area around him looking for any other traffic, it was hard to take his eyes off the jet. He was hearing first hand the problems they were dealing with and could only feel sympathy for them. Looking at the jet floating towards Bangor, it was impossible to tell there was anything wrong. Until an explosion occurred near the rear of the jet. Jim saw it but couldn't tell what it was. The radio then told him.

"Bangor, Transworld Flight Zero Six Romeo has suffered a cabin breach and catastrophic engine failure. Looks like they got the emergency exit open and it ripped off the plane taking out an engine. Requesting multiple ambulances in response to an anticipated hard landing."

"Roger, Transworld Flight Zero Six Romeo. All requests are being taken care of."

Other than the smoke coming from the engine and a quick shift in the plane's altitude and attitude, the pilots were holding their own keeping it in the air. The aircraft was a trijet, a passenger jet with three engines. It looked to be a couple of miles out and still floating towards the airport. They would be approaching at speeds in excess of 125 miles per hour. But it appeared from his angle to be floating in the air and slowly gaining on the runway. The radio was still buzzing.

"Bangor, Transworld Flight Zero Six Romeo," broadcast the jet. "We have been advised the human threat on board the aircraft is now fully contained. Two of the perps injured themselves badly when the door blew and the other was overwhelmed by passengers. All flight components are still operational, and we expect to make a rough landing."

"Roger that," replied Bangor ATC.

If the pilots got the jet down in one piece it would be a miracle. So much to deal with.

The jet was over the runway threshold now, and other than the smoke and obvious door missing, everything looked normal. It settled on the runway and rolled out normally. At least, that's what it looked like from ten miles away. Up close, it was probably a rough landing, but a job expertly done. Fire trucks, ambulances, and police cars swarmed the jet. The radio had gone silent. Jim changed his frequency to the local 122.8 used by VFR Pilots.

Feeling good for those involved, Jim continued out around Bangor's controlled airspace and stayed at 2000 feet so he was well below any jets taking off from the airport. The weather on the other side of Bangor was overcast with occasional sunny breaks. He could see a few showers out ahead of him. They looked like sheets of gray, and he would fly right through the light ones. As long as his visibility remained decent, he was in good shape.

Another thing about flying in Maine was there were so

many lakes, you could use them as a road map to find your way around because they all had a unique size and shape. Once you were familiar with them, flying using maps became obsolete.

Coming up on East Grand Lake and with the camp in sight, the plane was slowed to the proper speed for deploying the flaps. Then speed was reduced to 70 miles an hour as it descended towards the lake. Jim had slowly pushed the propeller pitch control knob all the way in for maximum pitch and adjusted the horizontal stabilizer trim wheel. There was a little bit of a crosswind, so Jim would do a cross-control landing. That's when you dipped a wing into the wind and applied pressure to the opposite rudder pedal to keep the plane straight.

At around five feet above the water, he flattened the plane out and then felt it sink from underneath him. As he was about to touch down, he gently pulled the yoke back to give the plane a nose-up attitude and applied a little throttle to soften the landing. The plane settled down on the lake's surface. He retracted the flaps and step taxied towards the camp. Once Jim was close, he chopped the power and idled to within twenty-five feet from shore where the engine would be shut down, allowing the plane to glide up to the dock.

The light wind made it easy for him to get out and grab the dock by himself. He tied the plane against huge bumpers that were attached to the dock and then removed the generator. Jim unlocked the shed and unhooked the power cord to the old generator. The new one was installed and hooked up to the power cable. After starting the motor, the gauges were checked for power going to the water pump. One last test of the spigot on the side of the camp and water poured out of it. He shut the generator down and re-locked the shed.

The broken generator was taken to the dock and put in the right seat of the plane. The whole job took fifteen minutes. Now that everything was ready for the return trip home, the ropes were untied from the dock and the plane was pushed away from the bumpers. Jim loved to fly. And having someplace to go made it even better. Hanging close to home and boring holes in the sky could get old quick. Given the chance to go on a trip made flying much more enjoyable.

The plane was away from the dock, the windmill engaged, and after taxiing out from the shoreline, was set for takeoff. Flaps were extended, horizontal stabilizer wheel adjusted properly, water rudders retracted, and power was applied. Without the weight of the 110 pounds of fuel that was used on the way up, the plane was off the water and airborne quickly.

While climbing out, Jim gave thought to whether he should use flight following or just fly around the controlled airspace on the way home. He decided to go the most direct path and maybe see how things were going with the jet from a bird's-eye view. He switched the radio to Bangor Approach at 125.9. When he was about 20 miles from the airport, he made the call.

"Bangor Approach, Floatplane Two Four Two Three Foxtrot," Jim said after keying the mike.

"Floatplane Two Four Two Three Foxtrot, Bangor," the controller responded.

"Two Four Two Three Foxtrot is a Cessna 180 floatplane, 20 miles east your location, level at 4500 feet, destination Sebago Lake, requesting flight following."

"Two Three Foxtrot, squawk Two Six Six Two."

"Two Six Six Two, Two Three Foxtrot."

The controller didn't ask Jim to ident probably because he was the only plane on radar east of Bangor. The numbers 2662 were dialed into the transponder.

"Two Three Foxtrot, radar contact, eighteen miles east of Bangor, continue your current heading, maintain 4500, pressure is Two Niner Niner Five."

"Straight at 4500, Two Niner Niner Five, Two Three Foxtrot."

Five miles out from the airport Bangor called.

"Two Three Foxtrot, Bangor."

"Two Three Foxtrot," Jim replied.

"Two Three Foxtrot, change your heading so you fly directly over the center of the runway."

"Fly over the center of the runway, Bangor, Two Three Foxtrot." That was so he would be at the best location concerning incoming and outgoing aircraft.

Once over the airport, the jet was in view. It was off the main runway but not at the terminal. The emergency equipment was all around it, and the passengers had deplaned on an emergency chute. At least it was all in one piece. The complete story would be in the paper tomorrow. Bangor was calling.

"Two Three Foxtrot, Bangor."

"Two Three Foxtrot," Jim replied.

"Two Three Foxtrot, turn left to Two Six Zero. If you need to adjust from that for a straight line let me know."

"Left to Two Six Zero, Two Three Foxtrot, will do."

Once he corrected it was close enough of a heading to get him where he was going. The radio came back to life.

"Two Three Foxtrot, Bangor."

"Two Three Foxtrot."

"Two Three Foxtrot, traffic at your three o'clock. A pair of F-16 jets will pass below you at 2500."

"Two Three Foxtrot, roger."

The jets were hard to find. Camouflage colored and blending in with the ground made them difficult to spot. At the last minute, Jim saw them as they screamed by. *What a blast that must be.* The Air National Guard had a base at Bangor Airport and the jets were always in the air. What a great job.

"Two Three Foxtrot, Bangor."

"Two Three Foxtrot."

"Two Three Foxtrot, contact Navy Brunswick at 128.5."

"128.5 Two Three Foxtrot, thanks."

The radio was set to the right frequency, and when it was clear, Jim keyed his mike.

"Navy Brunswick, Floatplane Two Four Two Three Foxtrot."

"Floatplane Two Three Foxtrot, pressure is Two Niner Niner Three. We have a pair of P-3 Orion's working radar patterns in close to the Navy base. They will not be near you but wanted to let you know in case you see them."

"Roger that, Two Niner Niner Three, Two Three Foxtrot."

After twelve minutes, they were back on the radio.

"Two Three Foxtrot, Navy Brunswick."

"Two Three Foxtrot."

"Two Three Foxtrot, contact Portland Approach at 124.7. Have a nice day."

"124.7 Two Three Foxtrot, thanks, you too."

After switching the dial on the radio and checking to be sure it was clear, Jim made the call.

"Portland Approach, Floatplane Two Four Two Three Foxtrot."

"Floatplane Two Four Two Three Foxtrot, pressure is Two Niner Niner Six. No traffic at this time."

"Two Niner Niner Six, Two Four Two Three Foxtrot."

The rest of the way would turn out uneventful except for when Jim's cell phone rang. Knowing who it was he pulled it to his ear and said, "Hello, whoever this is I can't believe you called me while I'm flying an airplane. Everyone knows cell phones interfere with a plane's ability to communicate and fly safely. My tail section just snapped off when the phone rang, and I'm dropping out of the sky."

"Very funny, smart guy," Sam deadpanned. "You're breakin' me up."

"Oh, it's you, Sam. How goes it?" Guess the joke was off the mark.

"Great, where you at?"

"Just east of Auburn."

"Any chance we can go out and do some touch and go's?"

"Two Three Foxtrot, Portland."

"Absolutely, hold on, Portland is calling."

"Two Three Foxtrot," Jim said over the radio.

"Two Three Foxtrot, traffic at your one o'clock, heading southeast at 7500, will pass one mile in front of you. And a Lear at 8500 inbound from Bangor will pass a half mile on your north side."

"Two Three Foxtrot, roger."

"Okay, Sam, you want me to pick you up?"

"If it's good for you."

"I'll do it. See you in a bit."

Jim closed the phone. Sam had a place on Little Sebago Lake that was tricky for floatplanes. It was a long narrow lake with its share of rock piles and more than its share of boats. Fall was not a bad time of year for boat traffic, but the rock piles never moved. There were other seaplanes on the lake but of the smaller variety. Little Sebago had many homes and camps around it so noise was always a concern.

After canceling the flight following, Sam's lake was dead ahead. The plane would glide in with no power, and most people would never know it was on the water. But taking off was something that couldn't be concealed very well. There had been complaints recently that had filtered down to Sam, but they were sporadic. Jim would take off on cruise power to keep the noise down, but on a narrow heavily populated lake it was difficult to keep everyone happy.

Jim did a power-off full stall landing just before he got to Sam's house and then idled towards shore. He killed the power and coasted to the dock. Sam took hold of the plane and in one smooth motion, he pushed it away and stepped on the passenger side float. He opened the cabin door and pulled himself up in the passenger's seat. The motor was fired up, and they were idling back towards the middle of the lake.

"You forgot to yell, 'Clear!'" Sam said. "Who taught you how to fly?"

"You did. Sorry, I forgot."

Sam never hesitated to remind his friend to be sure no unsuspecting soul was near the aircraft when he was going to fire it up. You needed to visually scan the area around your plane and with a window or door open yell, "Clear!" prior to starting the engine. It was a good safety procedure to remember.

"I got a call from the farmer who owns the land around the lake up in Naples," Sam said. "He wants to speak with us."

"How did he get your number?" Jim asked.

"Somehow he found out we like going to Richard's, and

he called the restaurant. I don't know why, but whoever took the call gave him my number."

"We haven't done anything wrong, have we?"

"I can't see how. Even landing in the middle of the night wasn't against the law. He didn't want to explain himself over the phone. I asked a few questions, but he was adamant we meet in person."

"When?"

"That's why I called you," Sam said. "If we have the time today, he was going to be down by the lake on horseback, so he could check on a beaver dam that's causing a brook to overflow. He would be able to meet with us at the shoreline if we wanted. Or he said we could drive up later today and meet him at his house."

"It has to be today?" Jim asked.

"Kinda set in his ways, and it didn't seem he wanted me to suggest any other day than today. He totally controlled the conversation. A sort of, 'do this, do that, and don't talk back.' I couldn't get a word in edgewise."

"You talked to him. What should we do?"

"I think it boils down to are we comfortable going up and meeting him at the lake or driving over later and going to his house."

"I just have this uncomfortable feeling about flying over and meeting him. It doesn't set right with me. I'd rather drive up later."

"Good, I'll call and tell him what, four this afternoon?" Sam asked.

"That's good. I'll idle around while you talk."

Sam pulled the cell from his pocket and made the call. It rang and rang, but there was no answer and no machine. That didn't surprise Sam. The guy was probably old fashioned and didn't believe in cell phones or answering machines.

"I'll try him again later. There was no machine. Let's head over to Big Sebago."

"Do you want the left seat now or after we're over there?" Jim asked.

"It would be more comfortable for me if you took us over, and we switch on a stop. I haven't been up with you for a while and would feel better with a little more room to work with."

With that said, Jim set everything for takeoff and eased the throttle in to the cruise power setting. He rolled the prop knob back to match it, and they were off.

Sebago Lake wasn't far so Jim kept the speed at 80 and flew over slowly. They landed on the big lake and allowed the plane to stop. Then they switched seats. Sam did a number of touch and go's and with the courage of a seasoned pilot flew back to Little Sebago and landed near his home. He idled the plane to twenty-five feet from the shore. Then he killed the power. Jim got out on the float and grabbed the dock. After helping to secure the plane, Sam tried the farmer again. He answered on the second ring.

"Hi, this is Sam Arends. We spoke earlier about meeting today?"

"I was expectin' you to show up by now," the farmer said.

"Sorry, sir, I tried calling you a while back, but I didn't get an answer. I was going to tell you we'd be driving up."

"That's too bad. I wanted a ride in your plane."

"You should have told me that."

"I ain't much for words. Figured you'd show up, and we'd go."

"We can head your way now by car and be there in thirty minutes."

"See you then," the farmer said.

Sam hung up and told Jim, "I can't tell you anything new. I don't understand where he's coming from."

"Are we going in the Chevelle?" Jim certainly hoped so.

"No, I need to do an oil change before I use it again. You know how fussy I am about that."

Boy, did Jim ever know. Sam was a stickler when it came time to do any maintenance on things he owned. One time, they were invited to play a tennis match for fun with Jim's brother and a friend of his. A friendly doubles match with a case of beer to the winner. They left Sam's house in the Chevelle with Jim driving, and Sam made him turn around and take the car back to his garage because he forgot to change the oil. They ended up being an hour late for the tennis match and got smoked anyway. They just didn't play enough together to be any good.

The trip would be made using Sam's regular car. Actually, a pickup truck with a standard cab. Jim asked him why he didn't get a double cab with a seat in the rear, and Sam simply said, "Because no one ever rides with me." He had no kids so why the extra room? He figured it for a waste of money.

They made their way up Route 302, which was also called Roosevelt Trail, through Raymond and then eventually into Naples. After the causeway, they turned left on Route 114 and continued up two and a half miles to a farmhouse that was on the left side of the road. Sam pulled into the driveway and parked the truck. There were no other vehicles in the dooryard. They got out, walked up the small set of steps, and onto a wrap-around porch. The entry door to the house was just beyond the steps and was opened before they got to it.

"Come in," the farmer said.

They did, and the farmer told them to sit at the kitchen table.

"Coffee?"

Both men nodded yes, and nothing more was said until the farmer put down cups of coffee in front of everyone.

"You look like nice fellas though these days you can't tell a good egg from a rotten one. I don't mean nothin' by that, except only time will tell if you really are nice or not. My name is Rupert. I own 5,180 acres of land between here and the other side of the lake. The lake is named after my great grandfather and is called Lake Paul. It's landlocked by land I completely control, and I have miles of acreage all around that wet spot.

"The only way to get near it with a vehicle is on the loggin' roads we built over the years. Most of them have grown over, and only four-wheel-drive vehicles can use them now. I don't have any loggin' goin' on at the time bein' and haven't for six years. Some parts of the woods are due to be logged again beginnin' next year. You with me so far?"

Both men nodded yes and said, "Yes, sir."

The farmer liked that. He was not used to getting any respect. He might decide to be nicer to them.

"Anyway, I know you have been in and out of the lake with that airplane of yours. I can't believe the racket that thin' makes."

Jim turned a few shades of red while Sam was gnawing his fingernails.

Rupert continued, "Over the years, there have been many planes that have come by on floats and gone in like you do and then come back out again. I checked with the wardens, and they told me it was part of the trainin' you had to do. They had a fancy name for it that I don't remember, but all those other planes, none of them ever made the racket that one of yours does.

"So I figure you must have one of them fancy ones with lots of power and such. Them other ones seem to flutter through the air like butterflies with no place to go. But that thin' of yours blasts out of there with authority. And when you circle around to come back in, well, it's fast. I like that.

"I want you to do me a favor, and then I won't complain about the noise you make. You still with me?" Rupert asked.

"Yes, sir."

"I got kids and such that used to help me out, but they have other thin's to do and are not interested in the land. My daughter has a small plane, and she used to fly over the land lookin' for illegal tree cuttin' and trespassers. Now she tells me she's sellin' the plane and won't be able to do it anymore. I don't have no vehicle, just my horse to get around on, and I can't keep an eye on all that land. Heck, you fellas are in and out of there every week, and it wouldn't be that hard to do.

"I need somebody that don't mind lettin' me know if there's anybody in a boat on the lake, or if they see someone cuttin' my trees or burnin' my wood. And that's where my problem starts. I can smell the wood burnin' down by the lake at night. I can't see the smoke because it's dark out, but I've been smellin' it the last few nights. Someone's down there, and I know it. And they're burnin' my wood and trespassin' on my land. You still with me?"

"Yes, sir." The men knew Rupert would tell them when they could speak.

"I ain't askin' you to be the police or nothin' like that. Just to give me a call when you see somethin' and let me know. I'll take care of it from there. What do you think?"

Sam spoke first. "Sir, we are new to float flying and have been using the lake to practice touch and go landings for a few months now, and I'm sure we would like to help. But can I ask you a few questions first?"

"Don't know why not."

Sam was afraid what he was about to mention might be taken the wrong way, but he had to ask.

"No disrespect, and if you think I have said something disrespectful, it's not intended to be that way. But isn't the lake and the ground below it the property of the state?"

"What does that matter? Nobody can get near it unless they trespass across my land. And my land is posted. There is no public access to the lake. Unless you fly in, and then you couldn't come on my land without permission."

"But, sir, we haven't seen any no trespassing signs anywhere around the lake. If you weren't telling us right now, how would we have known we couldn't stop and go on the land?"

"I didn't ask you here to argue with me about my land, or who has rights to it. It's always been like that and will continue to be like that. I asked you a question. You interested or not?"

Sam swallowed his tongue and then regrouped.

"Yes, sir, we'll call you if we see anything out of the ordinary. But we're only on floats for another month."

"Just promise me if you're on wheels or floats, you'll pass by my land and keep a watchful eye out for me. I'm not askin' for a steady schedule."

Both men nodded their approval and said, "Yes, sir."

"Good. Now when can I get my plane ride?"

"How about Saturday?" Jim asked.

"That's good," Rupert said. "I was goin' to ask you to take me up today and give me a look-see around my property, but now that I think of it, I'd have to leave my horse tied to a tree and that wouldn't have worked at all. I'm glad you drove up."

"How will you get over to the lake Saturday?" Sam asked.

"My neighbor has a four-wheeler. I hate the thin'. But other than my horse or walkin' it'll do."

"Then why don't we meet up at ten o'clock on the north shore of the lake? If you have any fluorescent tape or even a white rag, tie it to a bush or tree you want us to pull up to. And one more thing. When I called earlier today, there was no way to leave a message. Can you get an answering machine or cell phone, so if we need to talk about something on your property, we can get a hold of you?"

"I ain't buyin' none of that stuff. When you call, I'll be here."

There you have it. Sam and Jim got up and said their goodbyes. *How do you argue with perfection?* They jumped into Sam's pickup and headed back to Windham.

Jim was the first to speak. "That went better than I thought it would. Anything is better than getting yelled at for the noise the plane makes."

"I was surprised at the way the meeting went, too. You heard for yourself it's a one-way conversation."

"That's okay. I'll look forward to buzzing around his woodpile looking for trespassers. It'll give me something to do."

"It would have been nice to be able to talk and warn him about our friends. At the very least to tell him they drive a newer black car with chrome wheels so he could watch for it. I just couldn't put the words together."

"I had the same feeling. I really think it's them staying in the woods by the lake. But if we mentioned it today and were wrong, well, I didn't think we wanted to be on Rupert's bad list. It was probably better left unsaid for now."

Sam pulled into the Naples Shopping Center so they could grab a couple of sodas and a snack at Tony's Foodland, the best store in the world according to Jim who knew the owners. His name was Tony Accuosti, and he ran the place along with his wife, Merrie. Tony built that store and others to be the best food stores around.

The place was packed with more interesting stuff than the stores the Chinese people ran in Aruba. Tony was a master and knew his business. His grocery store was the best around, and he and Merrie could go head to head any day of the week with the best of them. It was only a matter of time before a biggy came and bought them out. That would be a huge loss, but they worked their fingers to the bone for years and could use an extended vacation.

Getting back in the truck, they left the parking lot and pulled out on Route 302. When they entered Raymond, Jim figured it would be a good idea to stop at Richard's and wet their whistles.

"You're not back on duty for a few days are you?" Jim asked.

"No, what are you thinking?"

"Stop at Richard's for a couple and give the people on your lake a break from the noise for today. I'll leave the plane at your place tonight and grab it tomorrow. Maybe we can get you more left seat time late in the morning."

"I like the sound of that. Maybe I'll have the guts to fly out from my lake. Let's make it a plan."

Sam turned into Richard's and stopped short of the building. There was a car parked out front that looked familiar to him, but he wasn't sure. It was black.

"Doesn't that car look like the one those dudes had?" Sam said. "The two guys and the girl? The ones that had sunglasses on? Our new friends?"

"How many newer cars do you see like that with those chrome wheels on them? My guess is not many. That has got to be theirs."

"Maybe we should pass on stopping this time."

"I think you're right," Jim said. "We don't need any trouble. Pull over out of the way, and I'll call Richard and see what's going on."

Sam brought the truck to the end of the parking lot and pulled into a space. Then he shut the engine off.

"Hi, Richard, it's Jim. Have you got a minute to talk?"

"Hi, Jim, sure. What's up?"

Jim hated that expression but let it slide.

"Are there two guys and a girl together in the bar or restaurant?"

"Not that I know of. We're a little busy tonight, but I've been in and out of the kitchen and always eyeball the crowd. I don't remember a group like that, but I can take another look if you like."

"If you don't mind. Sam and I are out in the parking lot, and a car in front of your building looks a lot like the one those three drove when we had the little incident outside that involved the cops."

"Okay, give me a few minutes, and I'll call you back."

"Thanks."

After seven minutes passed, Jim's cell rang.

"Hello?"

"Hi, Jim, I don't see a threesome, but there is a guy and girl with dark glasses on sitting out front by the window. I talked to Rene, who's serving them, and she told me they were asking questions about you. And of course you know Rene, she likes to talk."

"That's not good," Jim said. "They asked questions only about me?"

"When things calm down, I'll ask her for more details, but she said they were just curious if you lived in town and stuff like that."

"Thanks, Richard, please call me when you know more."

"I will, bye."

"That didn't sound good," Sam said.

"I can't figure it out. Why are they asking questions about me?"

"All three of them are in there?"

"No, Richard said only the girl and one guy. He didn't

seem to recognize them."

"What do we do now?" Sam asked.

"I'm going to call the police. Tell them they're here."

"But we don't know if the authorities already found them and dealt with it. And even if they didn't, I'll bet you get the cold shoulder. It seems the cops only move for the big-ticket problems. Something tells me they'll blow you away."

"I'm going to call anyway. At least to report they're here."

The guy and girl came out of the restaurant just then and looked over in their direction. Then they got in the black car with the shiny wheels.

Sam had an idea and said, "I think we should follow them and see where they end up."

Jim didn't like it. "They looked right at us. Richard said they were sitting in the front next to a window. They probably saw us come in and park over here. I'm afraid they may know more about us than we can imagine."

"Did Richard say if they wanted to know anything about me?"

"Nothing about you, just me. But he only spoke to Rene briefly. He'll call back after he has time to talk to her more."

"What did they want to know?"

"If I lived in town and stuff like that," Jim said. "Of all the waitresses they could have had, they got my old flame, Rene. She has all the goods on me. And we know she has no problem letting them be known."

"That's terrible. Let's hope he has good news when he calls back." Sam thought any news would turn out to be bad.

They watched as the black car backed out of its parking space and then turned in their direction. Both Sam and Jim kind of slid down in the seat of the truck but quickly realized that was stupid. The girl and guy were looking right at them.

The black car came right towards the pickup truck and turned away at the last second. It sped towards the main road and after a quick stop, entered the westbound traffic. They were gone but left both men sitting in the seat with their mouths open.

"Think we should follow them?" Sam asked.

"If they didn't see us in the truck, I'd say yes," Jim said. "I'd love to know where they wind up. But we can't very well hide if they've made us. Let's go in and see Rene."

After parking the truck in front of the restaurant, they went in. Rene was behind the bar mixing drinks for customers.

"Hi, guys. Good to see you. A couple was just here asking about you, Jim. They seemed real nice."

"What did they want to know about me?"

"I gotta take these drinks out and then I'll be back. Can I get you a beer before I leave?"

"Yes, please."

Jim thought being nice would get him the most accurate information. He and Rene dated for a while and then moved in together. They didn't last long as a couple, fighting constantly and at times throwing things that occasionally found their mark. After two terrible months, she moved out and that was eighteen years ago. But that being history, they now had a friendly relationship. At least Jim hoped so.

Rene returned and went behind the bar to mix more drinks. Jim was extremely anxious for some information but knew better than to pry Rene. She would tell him when she was ready. Never the kind to do more than one thing at a time, Rene was very slow, but she was steady. Without so much as a word, she finished up and left with the drinks in hand.

Jim was ready to explode. He knew she wasn't doing it on purpose but felt as if his blood pressure had doubled. He fought against the urge to yell something out and instead turned to Sam for some conversation.

"I need to get some information on these guys," Jim said. "How am I going to do that?"

"I know it doesn't look good right now, but we need to pay attention, and we need some time. We should have told Richard to let us know if he saw them."

"That's just it. Richard didn't even know it was them. They didn't draw any suspicion because there were only two of them. Even if all three came in at once he probably wouldn't have realized it was them. He wasn't outside when they were flipping out."

Rene was back with a large tray of empty glasses.

"I have another drink order to fill. Have you got the time to wait?"

"Sure, Rene, whatever is best for you. But did they want anything personal about me?"

"They seemed very sweet and sincere. They asked if you lived around here, and where you worked. I was busy, but I think that's it."

"And what did you tell them?"

"Just what everybody in town already knows. That you did live here and worked at McAllister's. They asked where you lived, but I got called away before I could tell them."

"Then you didn't get the chance to tell them where my house is?" Jim asked.

"No, I didn't get the chance. Two of the other girls called in sick tonight, and we're busy. I left their bill on the table before I was called away, and they left before I had a chance to get back over to them. I gotta make these drinks now."

"Please don't talk to those people about me, Rene. I don't know why they need to know stuff, and I would rather they didn't get any more. Please?"

"Whatever, Jim. I'll be sure to keep my mouth shut."

"Thanks, Rene. I appreciate it."

"No problem. I gotta get busy."

Jim would leave her a good tip before he left.

Richard came behind the bar with his chef's apron on, pulled two cold beers out of the cooler, and placed them in front of Sam and Jim. "On me," he said.

"Thanks, Richard," Jim said. "I've already talked with Rene about what you and I talked about earlier. So I'm all set."

"Good. Is everything okay?"

"It is, but I got to figure out what these people want. I have no idea what they would need from me. Other than when they showed up here, I've never seen them before."

"Well, if they come by again, I'll call and let you know. I saw what they looked like, so next time I'll recognize them."

"Thanks. Busy night tonight?" Jim asked.

"Best night in a long time. People from the local motels up looking at leaves. I don't understand it. They come from all over to watch leaves. Maybe that's why I need to stay in the food business. I don't know about anything else."

"You're the smartest guy we know," Sam said, "and the hardest working."

"That will get you another beer on the house. I've got to get back to work. Catch up with you two later."

"See ya, Richard. Thanks for the beers."

Rene was shaking her head. "You two are the worst brown-nosers I ever met. You'll do anything for a free beer."

"You know Richard's a great guy," Sam said. "He just needs to hear it occasionally. Sometimes it happens when he's near the beer cooler, and we're thirsty."

"Nice idea. I'll try that on him just before he writes my paycheck."

Rene was called out to the dining area, so Sam and Jim had the bar to themselves.

"Let's go over what we know about this trio," Sam said. "The three of them showed up here, I guess because of the girls they picked up. They drive a newer black car with chrome wheels, and one of them has no problem waving a gun around while speaking a foreign language you understand."

"I just don't get it," Jim said. "Why are they asking things about me?"

"They must know you somehow. Why else would they have the questions?"

"I'm not sure, but I have to find out. What else do we know about them?"

"Just that you think they're living in the woods. That's all of it. We don't have much."

"If we can find out where they're staying, we'll be one up on them."

"Are we still planning on some flying time tomorrow?" Sam said. "We could get lucky and see smoke by the lake. You never know, maybe we'll see their car from the air."

"Right, just like in the movies."

It was time to leave, and they left money on the bar for the tab. Jim passed Rene on the way out and put a ten-dollar bill in her hand. Her eyes opened wide, and the smile on her face was genuine. She loved money. She also looked good tonight.

Sam and Jim left the restaurant, finishing their conversation.

"I have this thing about taking off too early from either of our lakes," Jim said. "Why don't we plan on leaving at nine?"

"That's fine. You can drop me at home, and we'll meet tomorrow morning around then."

They drove to Sam's house unaware of the tail that was following them.

The black car with the two cousins in it stayed a safe distance back. It was getting dark out, and they blended in well with the other vehicles. Tonight they would get a two-fer. Finding the homes of those two may eventually lead them to the home of their target. They were convinced Jim Kamae was friends with those men.

Jim pulled into Sam's driveway and came to a stop by the front door. They said their good nights, and then Jim left. He was thinking of maybe stopping back at Richard's for one more before he went home. He had to pass right by the place and it was still early. *Why not?*

The cousins were still there but stayed far back. They followed the pickup as it headed back towards Raymond from Windham on Route 302. The traffic was light, but then again to the cousins, it was Hicksville. There were not that many people who lived around here. It was mostly woods with more trees than anything else. They watched as he made a right turn at the bar. It was probably going to be a long night. The Impala continued on to the far end of the lot and the lights were shut off. The pair would wait for him there.

Jim entered the bar and went straight to the men's room. When he finished there, he went back to the bar and grabbed a stool. It was one of those nights where you needed a few drinks to forget about your problems. Richard came out and grabbed a beer for his friend.

"Can I get a vodka shooter?" Jim asked.

"Anything you want," Richard stated.

"Thanks."

Jim downed that shot and figured one more would be enough. He swallowed the second and would have a few more beers. It took a few minutes for the vodka to work its magic. We all lived like we did when we were younger. At least Jim did. He used to have four vodkas, drink beers for hours, and still act relatively straight.

But as the body increased in age, it didn't process the liquor quite as well. It usually took some kind of shock to the system to get you to wake up and realize you were not as young as you used to be. Like getting pulled over for drunken driving and finding out the cop wasn't believing your story about only having two or three beers.

Richard didn't want to deny his friend the drinks he wanted and made sure they kept coming. But he wasn't fool enough to let anybody get behind the wheel of a vehicle when they drank too much. Those people were sent home in a cab, and that way Richard could sleep at night. But Jim was a friend, and he knew where his house was, so he would personally drive him home.

Jim stayed another forty-five minutes and then decided to leave. That's when Richard asked to let him do the driving.

"I don't want to see you get in trouble," Richard said.

Jim understood. "Thanks, but I'll be fine."

"If you by chance get pulled over and arrested for DWI, you will lose your pilot's license also. What are you going to do if you can't fly? And your insurance. How could you afford it?"

Well, that hit home like lightning striking a tree. Jim would become one of those plane owners who could only wax the equipment. That didn't sit well with him.

"Maybe you're right. You want to take me home in Sam's truck?"

"My car is right out back. Give me fifteen minutes, and we'll go. Can I get you another beer while you wait?"

"That and my bill," Jim said. "I'll pay Rene when she shows up."

Twenty minutes later, Richard came back to the bar and asked Jim if he was ready to go. Together they went out through the back of the building and got in Richard's car. After a few minutes to warm it up, they made their way out to the main road. Richard eased the car out into traffic and drove towards Jim's house. He would be between the warm sheets of his bed with his lovely wife in short order.

It would turn out to be a long night for the cousins.

Chapter 14

The following morning, Rupert and his trusty horse, Camelot, were headed over to the lake from the farm. Rupert could smell the smoke during the night and was hoping to see some in the morning. So far nothing, but he felt it was worth a trip down to the north side of the lake to have a look-see. Strapped to the side of the saddle was his Remington six-shot semiautomatic shotgun.

Sometimes he liked to shoot from the saddle and pretend he was a cowboy. Even at his age, why shouldn't he be able to have a little fun? When he first started shooting a few years back, Camelot would rear up just like the horses did on TV. He must have been spooked by the noise of the gun. It must have spooked Rupert, too, because when he got home, his underwear was covered with brown stains. *What a thrill*, he remembered thinking at the time.

Today the gun would only be used to scare trespassers away. That's if he could find any. He had a date tomorrow with those two young fellas to go up in the plane and thought if it was going to be possible to see any trespassers, that would be his best chance. But how could he shoot at them? *That ain't gonna work.* Maybe if he saw them he could figure out where they were camping and then go out later with that awful four-wheeler of the neighbor's. He should be able to shoot from the seat of that. He would have to practice some before he went out.

Calls to the police in the past about trespassers never got any results. The cops were not interested in nature walks through the woods. They only want to draw their guns and shoot at bank robbers.

Glassy Water

Rupert didn't feel his age was an issue. At 86, he still felt feisty. Standing 5 foot 5 and weighing 138 pounds, he looked like an eagle that could easily catch his prey. 138 pounds of pure muscle and a small amount of fat. *Well, a little extra fat under the arm muscles and on the back of the legs, but hey, them youn' kids today had the same thin'.* He believed he could beat the crap out of most men past the age of 60. Age was nothing but a number. Always think positive and good things would come of it. His daddy told him that.

His daddy also told him they should share the land they owned by letting the public use it for recreational purposes. That statement by his daddy never made any sense to Rupert. It was his land, and he would do whatever he wanted to do with it. He paid the taxes and was responsible for managing it. He ain't never seen a time when the general public used something and didn't leave their trash all over the place. *No siree, them people will never be allowed on my land while I'm still suckin' air.*

He don't even like the fact them darn airplanes come in and use his lake. If he'd known a way to keep them out, he would have done it. *Shootin' at them didn't work.* He shot at them planes in the past, but they were too far away. Ammunition wasn't cheap, so he gave up on that. He couldn't believe he would be going up in one, but what choice did he have? It was the only way to cover some ground quick, and even though he lived on the land his entire life, he ain't been on very much of it. There was just too much territory to cover. But Rupert had always been of the frame of mind that too much wasn't always enough. If he could, he'd own the whole state and kick everybody out.

It was a beautiful fall day, and Camelot led the way over to the lake. The logging roads were perfect for horseback riding, and Rupert was even approached once by a club that wanted to use his trails for giving horseback rides to members of their club only. Rupert refused, telling the club if he let them use the trails, everybody would think they could, and he would never be able to have control again.

It was because Rupert was like that his own kids didn't want to be near him. And Rupert couldn't care less. He had never

Philip Gagnon

married, and all those smart-alecky kids were pushed on him by a local church. If he could care for them temporarily while they find them a permanent home, the church would be forever in his debt. It was the one truly weak moment he had in his life. The church could never find anyone who wanted the little scalawags, and Rupert found himself having to bring them up.

When Rupert was young, he ran away from home a bunch of times, but always came back when he ran out of money. He tried to force his own kids in to running away at a young age and offered them money to do so. But these kids nowadays like all the comforts of home and wouldn't think twice of leaving before they were darn well and ready. Rupert had sunk so low at one time, he thought suicide was the only answer. But he talked himself out of it when he realized the little brats would inherit everything he had. *Wait until they see the will. They get nothin'. A slap in the face would be too good for them.*

At about an eighth of a mile from the lake, Rupert heard the sound of a plane, the unmistakable sound of the Cessna workhorse. If that's a seaplane, he knew who it would be. It used to give him anxiety because he felt powerless to stop the planes from using his lake. But now he felt differently, especially after meeting them young fellas yesterday. They had something he needed.

It was the first time he was down by the water with his gun when a seaplane was close by. If that opportunity had presented itself a while back, he'd have put a few holes in the bird. But times they do bring change, and even Rupert knew he had to adjust. He didn't like it, but in the end, he would still win out. *"One for all"* and *"All for me."*

The seaplane had slowed, and he could tell they were going to make a splash and then leave again. Maybe a bunch of times. Rupert got down from Camelot and tied him to a tree. There was a small clearing in the brush where he could get to the water and see down the length of the lake. Rupert stood there and imagined he was on board the big bird as it floated through the air with ease.

He wondered if they would let him take the controls and

fly the rig. He'd never before had those thoughts about flying. The idea of going up with them tomorrow was now front and center in his brain. The excitement filled his chest as he anticipated watching the plane touch the water then accelerate and take back off.

It was not to be though, as the plane landed and the power was cut off. They were at least half a mile down the lake, and Rupert's eyes weren't what they used to be. It didn't bother him to see his two new friends loitering on his lake, but at the same time, he had never seen it happen before.

One of Rupert's new buddies got out and was fiddling with something up by the front of the plane. Then he saw his other friend come out of the same door and work in the same area. They were too far for him to do anything, so he just watched. He would find out tomorrow what they were up to.

Chapter 15

The cousins were driving up a logging road when the plane could be heard overhead. There were new areas that needed to be scouted for camping and they did not want to stay in one spot too long. After finding a place to hide the car, the trio made their way down to the water. The plane had landed and was now sitting still on the lake.

Jose found a rock he could climb onto at the shoreline and pulled out the binoculars he swiped yesterday from Bradlee's, a local sporting goods store. It was the best pair they had on display and were very expensive. The new camouflage gear the three of them were wearing was paid for. They were on a budget and needed to manage their costs.

"That is the same plane that landed and took off from the lake the other night," Juan said, "and the same one that was here making noise the morning after we arrived. Maybe they own the lake?"

"I have read that lakes this size belong to the state they are in," Jose replied. "This one is different because one person must own all the land around the lake, and it is private. If the state owned the land, they would have to give the public access to it."

He was speaking as the adjustments were being made to his fancy binoculars.

"Well, well," Jose mused. "So we meet again."

"What are you talking about?" Juan asked.

"Our friends out there with the airplane are the same ones we met when we drove the hitchhiking girls to the bar. They are the same two guys we ran into, and Anncherry beat up."

"Oh, then it is a small world," Anncherry said. "Me and

Juan followed them around last night. These guys hang out at the same bar as our target, and we wanted to see if they would have met up with him last night. One of them went home, and the other must have spent the night in the restaurant because we never saw him leave, and we stayed there until two in the morning. We were going to get around to telling you about it."

"Things are definitely bringing us closer if these two are his friends," Jose said. "Too bad Uncle Paul could never get us a picture of what our target looked like. The job would have been done long ago, and then the time would have come to leave this dive."

"It is too bad we could not have arranged for a picture some other way," Anncherry said. "Now the only way he can be identified is to have someone point him out."

"It was known to us this job would not be easy, and we promised Uncle Paul it would be taken care of," Jose said. "It does not matter how long it takes, the job will get done. Hopefully, we do it quickly before it gets much colder."

"I hate it already," Anncherry said. "Me and Juan are not awake yet from our late night out. Maybe we can go and stay in a nice motel room with heat and hot water. I will stay all winter if you do that for me."

"Our money is much too tight," Jose said. "I do not want to come up short when it is time to go back home. But I guess if the funds get too low, we can always stay at our new home in Massachusetts."

Juan was shaking his head no. "We would still have to pay to heat it and have enough money to eat. No one will give us jobs. When our visa slips were made out we said our trip here would only last for ten days. I do not know if they will be looking for us when the time is up, or if we will be given an extension."

"I forgot all about that," Jose said. "They will not mess around when it comes to us overstaying our visas. Especially if we do not contact them beforehand."

"I think the focus should be on getting our work done first and then worry about the other things after," Anncherry said. "If we went to a hot spot in Windham, do you think it is possible to come up with a photo of our guy on the internet?"

"That is why we bring you along," Jose said. "If our target has one of those internet pages, we would be all set. I have never accessed them before, but I have read they have much personal information on them. Maybe even pictures. Let us head that way now and see if we get lucky."

The cousins retreated to the car in hopes of finding a quick solution to their problem.

Chapter 16

Rupert continued to watch the plane with interest. He was yawning now and knew he would soon have to head home for a nap. It just didn't make sense to him. He felt he was in better shape now than he'd been for years, but was finding it harder to stay awake.

A light wind had come up and was pushing the plane farther away from him. Not that he cared, but he was curious if they had broken down or suffered from some other problem. Rupert was aware the wind direction played a big part of landing and taking off in an airplane. If the wind picked up much more, they would probably need to take off coming right at him. He could stand at the shoreline and wave to his new friends. If they ever got the plane going before he fell asleep right there in the woods.

Chapter 17

Jim and Sam were both mechanically inclined and liked to perform most all of the maintenance on their vehicles. That also included working on the airplane. Most pilots wanted a licensed airplane mechanic to perform the work on their planes and then have the mechanic either take a flight with them after the work had been completed or take the bird up themselves if they were licensed pilots and qualified to do so. Why crash and burn when your wrench-pusher was having a bad day and forgot a few bolts here and there? Let the mechanic sweat it out.

The voltage regulator on Jim's plane had an adjustable level that would either increase or decrease the alternator's output. On takeoff from Little Sebago earlier that morning, Sam had noticed the output was over 16 volts, and if left alone could cause damage to the electronics that were being used during that time.

After Jim became aware of the problem, he shut down the master electrical switch that in turn eliminated power to all of the electrical equipment. The plane could still be flown and the engine would still work, but they would be without anti-collision lights, radio, transponder, and anything else that needed electrical current in the cockpit.

It was no big deal as a lot of the smaller planes that were flown away from airports for recreational use didn't have those big-ticket items on board anyway. They would make a stop on Lake Paul and fix it. All they needed was a screwdriver.

Their only problem was there's no way of measuring the adjustment, and therefore, after a takeoff and seeing what the output was, another stop might be required for a second adjustment. Their goal would be 13.5 to 14 volts.

The voltage regulator was in a very accessible spot right on the firewall behind the oil dipstick access panel. After sixteen minutes, they were back on their way.

The wind had picked up some but not enough that it would affect the 180 on takeoff. You could land going with the wind also but needed to be careful with the airspeed and nose attitude. To be safe, and if possible, takeoff and land into the wind. The beauty of float flying was if the lake you were on was big enough, you always had that option.

At airports, you would be staying straight on the runway, and might have the wind blowing at you from an angle. Flying in the wind was a challenge most pilots cherish. Then there were those who would show up at the airport and spend more time waxing the plane than flying it because they didn't like the wind. And there was nothing wrong with that. They preferred not to pound their equipment on a windy day. It was the same as the person who wouldn't take their sports car out in the snow. Each to his own.

The two of them crawled back up into the plane with Sam in the left seat. He got the windmill going and prepared for takeoff. Jim thought of giving his friend a little ribbing about yelling to "Clear!" the area around the plane before starting it out in the middle of the lake, but decided against it knowing Sam was already very nervous. Jim knew that feeling from first-hand experience.

Jim had been taught to fly in an old Cessna 150. If you could imagine two grown men squished into an area where you were actually rubbing shoulders, it would give you a feel for the size of the cockpit. If you or your instructor had bad breath or any body odors, it was known of immediately. The act of passing gas in the cockpit would be a cause for death threats. It was difficult to explain how anyone would feel at 3000 feet above the ground, stuck in such a tight space with someone you would come to hate.

Some CFIs or "Certified Flight Instructors," go out of their way to make you feel comfortable. Then there were some who go out of their way to make it anything but comfortable for you. If you were lucky enough to get the instructor who had a good-paying job and a nice life at home, chances were you would breeze through the flying lessons with ease and confidence. Should you be one of the unlucky ones who got the unemployed instructor who was going through a nasty divorce at the time, you would probably only survive the first lesson and swear you'd never fly again.

The first thing the instructor did on the first day was put you in the left seat, have you taxi out onto the runway and then fly the plane. If he was successful making you think you already know more than you really knew, then he'd have you locked in as a student. And he was right. There were not many things you'd do in your life that would equal the thrill of that first flight.

One thing that was better would be when the instructor cut you loose for your first flight by yourself, or your solo-flight. That would equal any thrill you could imagine. Not like winning the lottery but a definite contender for second place.

After your first lesson, if you chose to return and could afford to come back, you would be taught things like how to preflight your plane, how to properly check and fill the oil level, and what things to look for around the engine compartment like bird's nests. Birds see those big things with wings and think they are their mothers. There was a great spot inside the cowling for a nest. Sometimes right in the air breather.

Filling the gas tank was very important. You needed a stepladder to do that because the tanks were in the wings and filled from the top. After the tanks were filled, you were taught to take a special tool to a valve under the wing that was plumbed into the gas tank so you could see if there was water in your tank. Sometimes you might see a small amount from condensation, but it was always best to check that after every fill-up.

Then there was ground school. There, you would learn everything you needed to know about flying concerning rules, regulations, how to properly use maps and plan flights, how hot and cold affected flying, how winds impacted flying, how a plane's gauges worked, and hundreds of other things. By the time you were done with ground school and actual flight training,

Glassy Water

you'd have a complete basic knowledge of flying.

You would have accumulated and paid for around 40 hours of flying time and 40 hours of ground school. After you passed all the required tests to get your license, the plane you learned to fly in became available to you as a rental. Or maybe the airport would have other rental planes. But you were only qualified in the Cessna 150. If you wanted to fly anything else, you needed to prove you were capable or would be required to have more training.

Jim made a big splash when he bought the 180. The differences between the 150 and the 180 were like pussycats and tigers. For one thing, the 150 had a tricycle style landing gear and the 180 was a tail-dragger. The 150 was a small two-seater with a small cargo area behind the seats. The 180 was a spacious four-seater with a large cargo area behind the seats. The fuel supply in the 150 would last a little more than 2½ hours at 110 miles an hour. The 180 would last more than twice that long at 155 miles an hour. Bigger fuel tanks being part of the reason.

When Jim climbed in the left seat of the 180, the difference he felt was like going from driving a Volkswagen to driving a Mack Truck. He didn't have the confidence to fly the thing. He'd bought the plane and could fly it if he wanted but was afraid to do so.

He couldn't even get insurance for the plane because he had no time in that model. Insurance could be obtained when he had 100 hours of time, but it wouldn't be cheap. Regular insurance rates were not available until you had hundreds of hours in that type aircraft.

Another huge difference were the engines. The C150 had a 100 horsepower engine while the C180 had a 230 horsepower engine. All pilots were required to have a special certification for flying an aircraft with an engine rated at more than 200 horsepower. The torque delivered by the muscle provided from the 230 horses could, and would, take the aircraft sideways off the runway if you didn't have enough opposite rudder applied when applying full power under certain load conditions.

Another pilot Jim knew was kind enough to help him learn

how to fly the 180 while on floats. Learning to fly the 180 on wheels would come later. It would be months before Jim finally found the confidence to take her up on his own. His knees shook so bad they bounced off the side of the cockpit. But after getting her up and spending some time flying around was quickly put at ease. His first water landing by himself was very exciting. He knew well how nervous Sam was today.

With the throttle pushed all the way in, the plane was coaxed up on the step of the floats, and it moved across the water with ease. Sam pulled back on the yoke, and the winged wonder lifted off the lake. Once he was about 50 feet above the water, he threaded the throttle control back from full power and then rolled the prop control back also.

Full power was not needed once you were well clear of the water, and if you climbed out at a reasonable speed of around 80 miles per hour, it helped with cooling the engine. The plane gained altitude to about 500 feet above the ground, and the plan was to go around for a touch and go. The alternator was steady at 14 volts.

Sam took the plane out over the woods and kept going southwest until he was far enough away that he would be able to turn back and land the plane into the wind that's now coming out of the north. After making his turn back towards the lake, he lined up for a straight-in approach.

He set the plane up properly for the landing and glided in for a smooth touchdown. Then he pushed the throttle all the way in and immediately lifted back off the water and began his climb into the sky. Enough fun for now, he wanted to head back home and try his luck on the narrow lake. Sam's confidence was building and that's good. It would be the second time he'd landed on Little Sebago Lake.

The plane was brought up to 1000 feet and pointed for home. He took the speed to 125 miles per hour and had the lake in sight within minutes. He'd be landing with a small crosswind, but it should be no problem. The plane was gently banked so it could be lined up with his water runway and was prepared for landing.

Keeping the plane straight, he gently pulled back on the

yoke and began to flare out his landing just above the water. Sam gave it a little throttle to cushion the landing and settled onto the lake's surface, where he'd chop the power and idle home. He allowed himself a smile knowing that any landing you walked away from was a good landing. *But it really was a good landing!*

Jim's wife had dropped him off at Richard's that morning so he could get Sam's truck. It was noontime now and they decided to drive into town for lunch. Sam had a few more days off, and Jim was on workers' compensation because of a sore back.

He'd been idle for a month now and was dying to get back to work, but his doctor wouldn't clear him. Jim said he felt 100 percent, but x-rays showed some swelling in his lower back. If he didn't get back to work soon, he might go nuts. Being able to fly was the only thing that kept him sane.

The Windham Burger King was always busy. Nothing like a booming cash business when the economy had gone down the tubes. Sam and Jim went inside so they could grab a table and relax while they ate. The lines at the order counter were long but moving quickly.

As they were standing in line to place their food order, Jim was looking around. His eyes settled on a black car with chrome wheels and three occupants parked among the vehicles on the other side of the building. He couldn't see what they were doing, but it appeared they were just sitting there. He called it to Sam's attention.

"We're just seeing too much of those three lately," Sam said. "I'm leaving if they're coming in."

"Let's keep an eye on them and see what they do," Jim said. "If they get out of the car, we leave. Order for me will you? I'm calling the cops."

Sam nodded, and Jim moved off to the side where he could have some privacy. He'd put the sheriff's office non-emergency line on his cell phone a couple days before and now was calling it.

"Sheriff's Office, Deputy Winslow."

"Hi, I made a report a few days ago in Raymond about an

assault at Richard's Restaurant and I was…"

"What's your name?"

"Jim Kamae."

"Spell it please?"

"Jim 'J i m' Kamae 'K a m a e.'"

"What's your street address?"

"Burger King in North Windham."

"No, sir, your home address."

"What's that got to do with this? I'm try…"

"I need the information for the report."

"57 Johnson Lane, Raymond."

"Raymond, Maine?"

"Yes."

"And your Date of Birth?"

Sam was pointing out the window. The black car was backing out and turning to leave.

"July 8, 1967"

"And the number you can be reached at?"

"732-3479"

"I'll have the deputy on duty call you. Thank you. Bye."

Jim slammed the phone shut and wanted to shout some four-letter words but thought better of it. Sam was over sitting in a booth and Jim joined him.

"They wanted all my personal information and then said a deputy would call back. How does that make sense?"

"It doesn't and it's not supposed to," Sam said. "There's nothing you can do about it. Enjoy your lunch."

Jim was about to take a bite of his Big King when his cell rang.

"Something tells me I shouldn't answer it." But he did.

"Hello?"

"Jim Kamae?"

"Yes."

"This is Deputy Tim Swick with the sheriff's department. How can I help you?"

"I reported an assault at Richard's Restaurant in Raymond a few days ago, and I just spotted the car they were driving. They were here at Burger King."

"The sheriff's office has questioned the suspects regarding that report, and the ones who matched your description had an alibi for the time the assault occurred. That alibi checked out, and we're still investigating the incident."

"How could they have an alibi when they were busy beating us up?"

"I can't discuss the details of an ongoing investigation. Is there anything else I can help you with today?"

Jim could think of a number of things, but none of them could be explained without a bunch of four-letter swear words.

"No thanks."

"Okay, bye."

"I think I'm going to be sick," Jim said, "and I don't think I have any faith in the law getting the job done. I'm going to buy a gun."

"That's the way it is today," Sam said. "So much liability that no one wants to accept responsibility. If there's no blood, they're not going to go out of their way. And why should they? It's your word against theirs."

"I get it. I was just hoping for some help. You want to go look at some guns after lunch?"

"I keep one of those cans of wasp killer next to my bed. You know, the ones that shoot 20-foot sprays. I keep it fresh by buying a new can every year. Take the old one and put it on the other side of the bed. Cheaper and less mess than a gun."

"Maybe you're right. If I shoot somebody in my house, they'll still throw me in jail. I'll get two cans of spray. I'm sure that would make Sharon feel better. She doesn't like guns either."

"What are your plans for this afternoon?" Sam asked.

"I'm going to change the oil in the plane."

"Can I drive over and help you, and then we can take our own cars to Richard's for a couple?"

"Sounds good," Jim said. "Only this time, let's drive by and make sure our friends aren't there, and if not, we park out back. I think that while I'm there I'll drink at a table in the bar where I can see out the window. That way I'll see them coming."

"Maybe we should start carrying cans of wasp spray in a holster."

"You think that's funny, but it's not such a bad idea. I'm going to see what's also available for mace. I'm sure they have some of those James Bond type gadgets you can hide on yourself."

"Let me know what you find. I'd be interested in some of that too."

When lunch was finished, they drove back to Sam's where Jim got in the plane and flew it home. By the time Sam arrived, the engine should be cool enough to work on. In the meantime, Jim would use a spray wax on the windshield to clean it. The wax was also excellent for helping with visibility when flying in the rain. The rainwater would bead up and fly off the windscreen. There were no windshield wipers on these babies.

Chapter 18

The cousins had no luck with the internet trying to find their target on Facebook. Some people used it, some did not. Jose did find one of those "Pop-Up" ads explaining that excessive red eyes could be cured without surgery, even if you were born with them. The ad gave a doctor's address in Augusta, Maine, and he was accepting new clients.

"That would help us clear up a life-long ailment and make us look normal," Jose said.

"It would make the whole trip worth it," Anncherry added. "I think we should check it out."

"I agree," Juan chimed in. "We have lived with this problem our entire lives and it would be nice to look like everybody else."

"What about our job?" Jose said. "Should we pack up to make the trip and deal with it later?"

"It is worth a call to see what is involved," Anncherry said. "We would need more money if we are going to stay longer and pay for a doctor."

"I could call Mom and have her wire us more money," Jose said. "That should not be hard for her to do. Let us find a phone and see what the doctor says."

The cousins drove out to the causeway that was all but empty. Finding a phone booth next to a restaurant, Jose went into it and called the number from the ad he had written down. The woman who answered was very helpful and explained the procedure. It was a newly developed saline type of eye additive taken by the patient the same way you would have used any other eye drop. There were different levels of treatment. The price she quoted was reasonable.

Jose explained the doctor they used back home described it as a type of "ocular bleeding redness," and the three siblings had it their entire life. The only benefit it had for them was they could see very well in the dark, even with sunglasses on.

The woman told him the doctor would have to see them before anything definitive could be decided as far as their ailment. That being said, the doctor could see them that afternoon. They scheduled the appointment and received directions from the woman on how to get there.

Not wanting to leave any loose ends, the cousins went back to their campsite and packed everything away in the trunk of the car so they could take it with them. They just moved to another new spot and had gotten set up but preferred being safe more than being sorry. Anncherry hit a tree that wrecked the Mustang and it had been hidden out of sight in the woods. The trio began to depart the area so they could make their way to the doctor's office.

Chapter 19

Rupert and Camelot were out for an early afternoon ride and were a little farther from the farm than they would usually travel, but he wasn't tired and was following a hunch. That would be the highlight of Rupert's day, thinking he had a great idea that might just turn out right. He wasn't going to sit and watch TV all day long like other people his age. He was a doer, and he was doing something.

A shiny metallic object caught his eye in the distance, and it looked to be coming his way. Someone was on his land, and they would pay for trespassing here. He gently released the strap holding the Remington shotgun in its holster and brought the gun up across his chest. A black car was coming in his direction and on property that belonged to him.

At about a hundred feet away, the car came around a corner and Rupert was in its path, sitting on his horse. Rupert brought the gun up and aimed it in their direction. He didn't intend on putting a slug through the windshield but wanted them to think he wasn't kidding. They made no effort to slow, so Rupert let go of a round aiming just above the car.

Rupert's aim was bad. The slug tore the passenger side mirror right off the Impala. Brakes were slammed on and the car came to a stop thirty feet in front of them.

Camelot was doubly spooked by the gun and the car so he reared violently. Rupert was thrown from the saddle with the gun flying off to his side and in the woods. Camelot was doing a strange two-legged dance that made the animal look like he was crazed. The horse went ten feet towards the car then reversed direction and trampled his owner. Camelot was out of sight in seconds. It looked obvious the old man had not survived the weight of the horse. His mid-section was ripped in two and his head crushed.

The cousins decided to turn around and find another way out of the woods.

It would end up taking weeks to find any remains belonging to Rupert as the animals would be constantly fighting and tearing apart what was left of him, dragging the pieces off in the woods for further chewing. Rupert's bones ended up scattered about the forest, cleaned of any meat and then covered by the leaves that were falling from the trees.

Camelot ran crazily for five miles until he ended up at another farm that would welcome him as one of their own. The horse was unknown to those people and unless someone came looking or asking about him, the new owners would say nothing of their new prize. *After all, the price was right.*

Chapter 20

Sam arrived at Jim's and the two men dove into the chore of changing the oil. A metal plug at the base of the oil pan had a nipple that a rubber hose could be slid over to keep the oil from spilling into the lake. The hose would be put into a container large enough to hold all the oil that was coming out of the engine.

While Sam was draining the oil, Jim was pulling the oil screen which was located on the other side of the motor. This type of engine didn't have an oil filter like a car but a screen you would periodically remove to inspect for debris. It would be cleaned and reinstalled. Jim wanted to change his oil every 25 hours of engine use. Some pilots would go 30, or even 50 hours before an oil change, but some of Sam's perfectionism had rubbed off on him.

When Jim came around from the screen side of the engine to Sam's side, he could see his friend looking down under the plane as if he lost something. Sam was holding a quart of oil in one hand.

"Miss the hole a little?" Jim asked. He already figured Sam had spilled some oil.

"I should have gone and grabbed a funnel," Sam said. "I had some miss the hole and run down the side of the engine."

"I'll go get some more rags and a plastic bag to clean it up."

After a half hour of carefully cleaning the spilled oil, the job at hand was done. Leaving the plane tied to the dock, and after making sure the area around the plane was clear, Jim started the engine and let it idle at the dock while making sure there were no oil leaks. Satisfied, he shut the engine down, got out of the plane and locked the door.

They arrived at Richard's and surveyed the parking lot. With the coast clear, they drove around to the back of the building and parked.

"I don't like having to hide like this," Sam said. "Those people must realize we would have talked to our friends here and been told they were asking about you."

"I think you're right," Jim said. "Why would they keep coming back to ask the same questions? Hopefully, we've seen the last of them."

Entering through the front door they were greeted by their friend.

"Hi, guys, how are things?" Richard asked.

"Good, thanks. How is everything with you?"

"Very well. Time for a beer?"

"Yes, please."

"Step right this way then." And into the bar they went. Jim grabbed his beer from the bar and left to sit by the window. Sam and Richard joined him.

"So what's new?" Richard asked between sips on a bottled water.

"We were doing some work to the plane and figured now was a good time for a beer," Jim said. "I didn't tell you guys this before, but I may have to go to Aruba for a closing on my second house." His friends knew he'd already sold the house by the airport in Wayaca Residence.

"When did all this happen?" Sam asked.

"We've had a contract for two months now but thought it was going to fall apart because of financing. Sharon called while I was on the way here, and told me she received an e-mail saying all the documents have been finalized and a closing date is set for next week. We figured we'd go down and make sure everything went smooth."

"Good," Sam said. "That should be the last chapter in that book."

"I certainly hope so. But we'll lose our shirt on the sale."

"Why is that?" Richard asked.

"When you buy property there, the government takes 6% of the gross sales price as a transfer tax. It used to be 3% but they changed it in recent years. Periodic real estate taxes themselves are not unreasonable, and this tax is one of the reasons why. It's not uncommon for buyers to make offers considerably less than the asking price because of that tax. In our case, the offer was more than 20% below the current actual appraisal. It's kind of a buyer's market.

"Real estate sales have slowed tremendously since we bought, and the broker told us many people on the island were in must sell situations which put pressure on prices. We just wanted to move on so we agreed to sell. We could do the whole deal by signing and sending documents FedEx, but Sharon and I would feel more comfortable being at the closing."

"Will you stay at the house until you close?" Richard asked.

"I don't know. I'll leave that up to Sharon. I'm not sure if I want to see my Dutch neighbors."

"I can understand why," Richard said. "The last time we talked it sounded as if they'd set you up."

"That's the feeling I have," Jim said. "We could stay at the Costa Linda. Our neighbors live inland from the tourist hotels, and we'd never see them."

"What's the Costa Linda?" Richard asked.

"It's a large time-share hotel that's on the ocean. The beachfront is beautiful and the grounds are immaculate. It was our second time on the island and we stayed there with my sister and a friend of hers back in 1996. When we arrived, the hotel made an error with the room we were assigned. They made good on the problem by putting us up on the top floor in a front unit that was on the water. It had a massive open front deck with a private hot tub overlooking the ocean. We were immediately spoiled.

"Needless to say, it was because of that experience that we decided to buy property on the island. Aruba did have its share of problems back then. Most of the sewage from downtown was dumped in a river that flowed to the ocean just below the high-rise hotels. When the wind was blowing the right way, the ocean water in front of the hotels would have pieces of toilet paper and other waste in it. The waste was broken down but at times you could tell what it was. Sometimes you could even smell it.

"Over the years they corrected that and now it's nonexistent. Did I tell you how the septic systems work on the island?"

"I don't remember anything about that," Sam said.

"All they have is holding tanks. There are no leach fields used. At least not at individual homes. The homeowners, yours truly included, have electric septic pumps that are hooked to garden hoses, and then the septic juice was used to irrigate their plants. Palm trees in particular loved the juice. Sometimes it's hard to keep any liquids in the tanks."

"Wouldn't that ruin the groundwater?" Sam asked.

"There is no groundwater on the island that's used. The island is actually a desert. Some of the fancy hotels and subdivisions like the Divi Divi and Tierra De Sol have man-made ponds on their golf courses making it look like fresh water is abundant. But all of the island's drinking water comes from 'W.E.B.' the company that operates a desalination plant on the coast. The water lines in most cases are just under the ground's surface, and will heat up as the day wears on. Most individual homes don't have water heaters, and the people shower in the afternoon. The cold water is quite warm at that time."

"What do they do when the septic tanks are full of solids?" Sam asked.

"Just like here, there are many septic companies that will come and pump the tank. Then it's taken to an area below the dump and discharged."

"Not in the ocean I hope," Sam said.

"Not directly. It's only a matter of time before they'll be forced into building a septic treatment plant. It's the same with the dump. When we left, they had just started recycling and garbage control. Up until then, they dumped everything in a pile that's at the ocean's edge on the south side of the airport. They would burn and bulldoze the waste. It's a huge pile. I would guess the length of three football fields and the width of five and then four stories high."

"There is definitely some history there," Sam said. "I mean with four stories of trash. Is there anything else about the island that's interesting?"

"Yeah, there is. New Year's Eve. I've never seen anything like it in my life and hope I never witness it again."

"Witness what?" Richard asked.

"Let me begin with the week leading up to New Year's. The inhabitants of the island are big on celebrations. Every holiday we celebrate here and a lot of their own. They have holidays for different things we never heard of, and the next day is also a day off from work holiday so everybody can sober up. We were invited to attend a bunch. We never went, but we saw the aftermath.

"Folding chairs of all types lining the main streets for miles and shacks set up all along the route that sold beer and liquor. Most of the shacks had beer and liquor logos on them. Empty cans and bottles littered the sidewalks and gutters. They would clean everything up but only in good time, or island time. There's no hurry for anything."

"Just like in all the songs," Sam said.

"Yeah, but New Year's Eve was something I'll never forget. The government allows vendors around the island to set up trailers and sell fireworks. They're only allowed for a number of days before the holiday, and I think it's either five or seven days, but I don't remember. All the trailers we saw were owned and operated by Chinese vendors.

"They would cut a hole in the side of a 35-foot container and hinge the cutout portion so it could swing down like a door, exposing the inside of the trailer. The cutouts were very large because they wanted you to be able to see all the fireworks available for sale. The vendors had a counter that ran the full length of the opening so you had a place to pile up your purchases. And pile them up they did.

"They had fireworks unlike anything I'd ever seen before. And the people who were buying had no problem lighting the fireworks off right after they bought them, and then they'd go back and buy more. You'd see a mother standing there with her kid who would have a pile of fireworks in front of them on the counter. She paid and then the kid would take the bag and start lighting them off."

"Sure, let's see what can be destroyed with this stuff," Sam said. "Kids with explosives are never a good mix."

"I know what you mean. There were some kind of firecracker mats that are bought in a roll, and they came in different sizes. I saw some that stretched for more than fifty feet. They were loaded with firecrackers that were all fused together. The mat was rolled out and then lit at one end. It went on, and on, and on, with the firecrackers exploding until the last one was gone. The mats were a foot wide and wider, so you can imagine how many firecrackers were in a mat.

"The paper waste from the exploded fireworks was everywhere and looked like small brown leaves. I never saw any of it cleaned up. And they lit these things right in the roadways. People would line up beside the mat to watch it continuously explode. The bigger the mat the longer it would take. The larger ones could go on for ten minutes or more.

"We'd see these things as we were heading out to the store. When we drove back by on our way home, you'd see the same mothers and their kids standing at the trailers buying more fireworks. Money didn't seem to matter, fun did."

"Mind boggling how people can burn through their money," Sam said.

"But New Year's Eve was unbelievable. Our house was on a hill that overlooked the most populated areas on the island. We had a clear view of the cruise ship terminal and all of the low-rise and high-rise hotels. Some of the fireworks that were set off by the locals sounded like explosions you would only hear in a war zone. I can't explain how really loud they were. But louder than anything I'd ever heard before.

"We were out on our lanai at about 11:00, and I swear there was not one square inch of landscape on the island that didn't have some sort of aerial fireworks display blasting from it. The loud explosions were continuous, and the rockets were everywhere. The fireworks intensified minute by minute, and it maxed out and stayed that way from 11:30 until 12:15. All of the sky was lit up in every direction we had a view of."

"Way too much fun, but there must have been collateral damage, right?" Sam said.

"Of course. In the days following, leftover firework's trash from the fun was everywhere, along with empty cans and bottles of beer. There was no organized effort to clean it up.

"Then there's the animal problems that arose because of the war zone like activities. Posters were placed about lost and found animals in every store. Pets that were allowed to run loose ran constantly to try and find shelter. Most would end up lost.

"While there are people on the island that take good care of their pets, there are more people that don't. Every female dog you saw, without exception, showed the signs of recently giving birth to a litter of pups. And these mothers are allowed to run wild while they should be home with their babies if they were still alive. That's the saddest part of living there. Dogs had missing eyes, ears, legs, tails, and other obvious injuries. There are a few organizations that are working for animal rights, but it'll be a long uphill battle."

"Let me know when I almost have you asleep," Jim said.

"No way," Richard said. "I was from another country, but I've spent most of my adult life here. I also know firsthand the differences you can encounter between different cultures. This is interesting to me."

"Me too," Sam agreed. "I always envied you for traveling there, but I think I've heard enough now to satisfy my wandering needs."

"I could go on for hours," Jim said. "One other thing about the fireworks. About a week after New Year's, some people were still setting them off, but one early evening when it was just getting dark, we were out on the lanai when down at the base of the hill we lived on, somebody touched off a bomb. I say bomb because it was like battlefield loud. Hundreds of birds took flight to escape the noise and flew right by our house. We were sure most didn't come back that night because birds don't fly well in the dark."

"Now you know why I'm against fireworks," Jim continued. "There's nothing wrong with a little fun, but it should never be at the expense of others or animals. Down there they couldn't care less. That was the thing I hated most, animals suffering."

"We have the same problems here," Sam said. "They may seem extreme down there because it's a small place with no restrictions. But we have animal abuse that equals that of anybody, anywhere. People are the problem. Anyone can get a pet, but not everyone can properly care for it. I think people should have to pass some type of animal care course and be held somehow accountable for their pets' well-being. I don't care if it's fish in an aquarium. If you don't change the water or feed them correctly and cause them harm, there should be a law that holds you accountable."

"You're right," Jim agreed. "But it would be impossible to police that kind of activity. Most animal abuse is covered up in some cases by simply disposing of the pet in the trash. Who's going to tell anybody? And then they sometime later decide they want another one and the cycle starts over."

"But that's just it," Sam said. "The most common denominator in the equation is people. They are the problem. As people, we're responsible for breeding and domesticating these animals. They're our responsibility. We need to be held to a higher standard. There's no need for animal abuse. People who breed dogs just to make a quick buck should be put in jail. I know there are always lawbreakers, but we need to try and get this right."

"I read an article that said we euthanize between four and six million cats and dogs in one year," Jim explained. "And that's just here in the U.S. If that's not disgusting, nothing is."

"Unlike our prison system, when we run out of room for inmates we build more space to house them, the animals have no voice and no rights," Sam said. "In most people's eyes, the only way to control the animal population is to euthanize them. And that's completely backwards. Euthanasia is only meant for overly sick or seriously injured animals. But now it's used on perfectly healthy animals as a means of controlling the population.

"People cause the problem and should somehow be forced to deal with it ahead of time through education and punishment. Start by neutering your animal. And there's another sad fact concerning animals. Money. People don't want to spend their money on them. Once the animal is broken or in need of repair, they don't want anything to do with it anymore."

"That is a heartbreaking fact," Jim said. "People parting with their money. If it doesn't put a smile on their face, or provide comfort of some type, they're not going to part with it."

"It all boils down to responsibility. On every level. People need to be made to see and understand this."

"Ready for another beer?" Richard asked.

Both Sam and Jim nodded their heads yes.

"Be right back."

"You remember Shadow and Pebbles?" Jim asked.

"How could I forget them," Sam chuckled. "You treated those two dogs better than most treat their own kids."

"That we did but don't tell anyone that. Some people just don't get how anyone could care so much about animals. But we did love those dogs more than anything in the world. We got them as puppies and had them fixed when they were old enough.

"Sharon and I planned on having our animals neutered, but the real reason was because we both knew that deep down in our hearts if one of our dogs had a litter, we'd never have been able to give any of the puppies up. We'd have kept them for better or for worse, and would have been one happy family. The hardest thing for me to understand about people is how they can push their animals into having litters of babies and then sell them just to make a buck."

"As you said earlier, it's disgusting," Sam said.

"My mother, Winifred, has donated monthly to the Humane Society for decades. In Shadow and Pebbles memory, we donate every month to the Maine Friends of Animals, the Humane Society, and the World Society for the Protection of Animals. It really makes the heart feel good when you know you're helping a little. Even a few dollars is a big help."

Richard returned with their beers and a shot of vodka for each. "Hope you don't mind, but I wanted to buy my good friends a round of beer and a shot of vodka."

"How do you say no to that?" Jim said.

Sam was not much on the shots but didn't want to insult his friend.

"Thank you, but only this one please," Sam said. "You know how much of a lightweight I am with the vodka."

Boy, do they. A few years back when Jim's brother had a bachelor party, they held the shindig in the back of Richard's restaurant where there was a huge open dance hall with a bar that was built along one of the walls. Even Richard had too many that night, but it was Sam who stole the show.

Vodka shooters were the main theme towards the end, and the ones who couldn't handle their booze were the first to show it. Sam was the first when he got up to sing with the band. The band players were drinking also and didn't mind a little fun. They gave Sam the lead mike and got him going on "Take Me Home Country Roads," by John Denver. The band-mates were singing along in perfect harmony and making it sound good when all of a sudden they stopped singing and playing their instruments. Sam kept right on singing by himself, and it must have taken fifteen seconds to finally realize something was different.

Everyone in the place watched him with big grins on their faces. He couldn't hold a tune for nothing. Sam sang so bad it gave new meaning to the word "Stank!" Everyone laughed at his expense, and he sucked it right up and laughed with them. Good thing he only drank beer the rest of the night. Those were good memories.

It was dark out now and because there were no lights in the parking lot they couldn't see anything, so the men moved over to the bar. Business was slow tonight and Rene was off. Richard's wife and another girl they hadn't met waited on the tables.

Glassy Water

The door coming in from the parking lot opened, and Jim turned so he could see who it was. It wasn't anybody he knew or had seen before, but it was a woman, and she was dressed in a sheriff's uniform. Watching her walk in Jim could see she didn't have a gun at her side. There was an L section in the bar three seats away from where Jim and Sam sat, and she took the first seat in the L so she was looking directly towards them. Richard went over to see what she wanted.

"How can I help you?"

"I'll have a Budlight and a glass, please."

Richard just stood there with his mouth open.

"It's okay," the lady sheriff said. "I'm off duty and don't have any weapons on me. I can be a civilian in my uniform, but I have to follow the law like anyone else. It's not against the rules if you serve me."

"Coming right up," said a stumbling Richard. This was a first for him.

He delivered the beer and then tried to engage her in conversation by introducing Jim and Sam.

"My name is Richard, and these gentlemen here are my friends, Jim and Sam."

"Pleased to meet you all. My name is Jill Berry. I guess it's obvious what I do for work."

"Yes, ma'am," Richard said. "My wife and I own this place."

"My name is Jim Kamae. I work at McAllister's in Windham as a machinist."

"Yes, the bicycle manufacturer," Jill said.

"Hi, I'm Sam Arends, and I work at the Portland Jetport in the tower."

"You mean as an air traffic controller?"

"That's right."

"Someday I'd like to learn how to fly," Jill said. "It's always held my interest."

"These two are pilots," Richard said, "and Jim has his own plane."

"That must be fun. Do you fly a lot?"

"Every chance we get," Jim replied. "It's nice to have a place to go that's some distance away. If you had to stay local and poke holes in the sky every time you went up, it would get boring fast."

Jill liked these guys. They seemed genuine, and it was nice to talk about something other than police work.

"When you say a place to go, do you have one?" Jill asked.

"My Aunt Barbara has a camp on the other side of the state," Jim said, "and it's one hour and ten minutes of flight time. More than four hours by car. That might not sound like a long time flying, but after you've been sitting still in the same seat for an hour, you're ready to get up and stretch. But what's really nice is you can either fly up there on your own or with the help of guys like Sam here who will watch you all the way."

"I don't understand."

"To fly to my aunt's camp in a straight line involves flying into controlled airspace that you need permission to enter. If I decide to fly around and avoid entering the controlled airspace, that would take me an extra fifteen minutes to make the trip. My plane uses 13 gallons of fuel an hour, so from a cost standpoint, you can figure that out. And the extra time in the seat feels more like an hour. So I ask for flight following once I'm up in the air, and they take me up there a lot quicker. Plus they alert me to other traffic that may be of concern."

"Sam watches you all the way up?" Jill asked.

"If I were to begin on this end for a trip, flight following would start with Portland, and then they would hand me over to the next ATC at the airport controlling the airspace I would soon be entering, and then as I'm leaving their area they hook me up with the next airport in line and their ATC. When I reach my destination, I radio the ATC I'm currently with and ask to cancel the flight following."

"That sounds real interesting. Maybe someday when you go up I could catch a ride and see what it's like."

Usually at that part of the conversation, Jim would change the subject because he didn't like giving plane rides to just anyone who happened to come along. They'd agreed to take Rupert up only because the old man made them feel like they had to, or he'd complain about the noise they were making. But Jim hadn't been doing real well lately with the law. Maybe having someone he could eventually confide in or ask for information would help his cause. The idea of some insider law help definitely made him feel better. *Why not be friends with her to see if she could help him?*

"Do you live local?" Jim asked.

"I got a place about twenty-five minutes from here up in Naples," Jill replied.

"Sam and I are going up tomorrow if you're interested. We have a friend who owns a great deal of land, and he wants us to fly him over it. There will be three of us in the plane, so there's plenty of room."

"I'm off tomorrow, so that would be great. Where do I meet you and when?"

"The plane is at my house just up the road from here on Panther Pond. You can meet us there if it's good for you, and we told our friend we'd pick him up at ten o'clock, so we'll want to be airborne five minutes before. I'm sorry, I'm getting ahead of myself. The plane needs to go through a preflight first, and then there is taxi-time out on the water and stuff like that. Show up at my place around twenty minutes of ten, and we'll be fine."

"I'll look forward to it."

Jim drew her a map showing the directions to his house.

"I can find that easy enough," Jill said, and she ordered a second beer. Jim and Sam decided on another one also.

"Two is my limit. I have to watch my figure."

If she had a figure, you couldn't tell anything about it with the uniform she was wearing. She was pretty though, with blonde hair hanging down over her shoulders and those deep blue eyes. She stood about 5 foot 2 inches and couldn't have weighed more than 105 pounds. *What made her want to be a cop?*

Richard came over and joined the conversation.

"You should ask which one of them will be flying the plane tomorrow," Richard said.

"Why is that?" Jill asked.

"They each have a different set of skills. And both have good days and bad days."

"What kind of skills?"

"One of them is good at flying, and the other is not so good at flying. Both of them have lots of bad flying days."

Of course, Jim and Sam are doing everything possible to keep a straight face.

Surveying the two of them kept Jill clueless.

"They don't want to offer anything on the subject."

"That's because they don't know which one is which," Richard said. "They both think they're the absolute best, but it's only a personal observation of mine."

"What kind of personal observation?" Jill asked.

"Nothing I can share in their presence. It would only serve to fatten the head and stroke the ego of the one who hasn't made all the mistakes. And then he would start messing up more."

"Maybe I should reschedule."

The three men started laughing, but Jill still didn't get it.

"Richard is being facetious," Jim said. "He hasn't got a clue what he's talking about. I don't think he would know the difference between the front and the rear of a plane."

"That's why we leave him to the cooking and drink delivery," Sam added. "That way we know he's safe."

"It's good to see you guys have a sense of humor," Jill said.

"All I can say is you want to bring that sense of humor with you tomorrow if you go up with them," Richard said. "Consider yourself fairly warned."

They all had a good laugh, although Jill's appeared to be forced.

"I can see Richard has succeeded in rattling you," Jim said. "He's really only joking. We're good pilots."

"Okay, I'm game," Jill said. "I guess we'll find out tomorrow."

"You won't regret it," Jim said not slurring any words but trying real hard not to show the effects of the drinks.

Glassy Water

Beers were finished and goodbyes said. Jill left first, and fifteen minutes later, Jim and Sam left. Time to go home for a good meal and then a good night's rest. Both men would sleep well tonight while dreaming of flying.

Jill went to bed hoping she wouldn't regret her decision.

Chapter 21

At nine o'clock the next morning, Jim was at work checking out his baby. The condensation that built up on the windshield had to be cleaned; any excess water in the floats had to be pumped out; the oil was checked; the engine compartment was looked over for bird nesting materials, and a general preflight inspection was performed. He always checked for water in the fuel even if he didn't put new gas in. With four people on board and not having to travel far, he figured the two hours of usable fuel would be enough. The plane would be lighter without full tanks.

It was a breezy day with the wind coming out of the northwest at 10 to 20 knots. The whitecaps were building, and you could see the wind-streaks blowing across the surface of the water. A lot of seaplane pilots didn't like to pound their floats when the water was angry with whitecaps. It also delivered a pounding to the aircraft.

On Jim's lake, there were numerous coves and shorelines that offered shelter from the blowing winds. There were miles of undeveloped shoreline that belonged to families who had owned the land since the lakes were made. A lot of the lakes were not actually formed until dams were built to hold the water back. The dam at Panther Pond was completed in 1925.

Those families built modest camps where the best beaches were but kept the balance of their land undeveloped. The camps would be rented to vacationers during the summer months and were still operational today. The property would pass on to future generations with the guarantee no further development or splitting of land would take place. The family who was in control of the land could not sell it.

One huge tract of land was given to the Boy Scouts of America in the late 1920s and was called Camp William Hinds. It was donated by the father of William Hinds who died in a tragic accident. It was a gift that was meant to keep giving forever in memory of his son.

There were three other large parcels of land that had been kept intact and were used as private recreational retreats. All of those large land areas combined made up a good chunk of frontage that was not developed on the lake. Because of those large undeveloped tracts of land, Panther Pond was one of only a few lakes that were not overly developed. That left many stretches of frontage without camps or houses, and those areas offered shelter from the wind so Jim could take off from calm water on windy days.

Today the plane would taxi over to Betty's Neck where there was half a mile of waterfront with no development. That shoreline was sheltered from the winds coming out of the northwest. The water they take off from would be as smooth as it would have been with very light wind, and there would be no pounding of the equipment. It just took a little extra time to taxi over to it.

Jim was out by his garage having coffee when Sam pulled in with Jill right behind him. The road to Jim's house from the main road was dirt and more than a mile long. Jill got out of her car and started in on Sam.

"I should arrest you for driving so fast on a dirt road!" she snapped. "The amount of dust you left for me to eat was pathetic! If I had wanted my nose powdered today, I would have done it before I left the house instead of riding behind you and eating your rubbish!"

Sam looked like a ten-year-old getting chewed out. "I'm sorry, Jill. I didn't mean it. I didn't realize it was that bad."

"What, you can't take a joke? I was only pulling your chain."

Everyone had a laugh, and the day of fun began.

Jim gave her a quick tour of his waterfront land and said

they'd all have coffee when they got back, and he would show her the house then. Sharon came out on the deck and introduced herself.

"Hi, I'm Jim's wife, Sharon."

"I'm Jill. Pleased to meet you."

"There aren't many people who want to ride in that machine with this crew," Sharon said. "In fact, you're one of the few that dare to."

"That's what Richard told me last night. Why didn't he want to come along?"

"He gets more than his share of time in the air," Jim said, "but Saturdays are a big lunch and dinner day for him so he's already cooking."

"The phone in the house is ringing so I have to go," Sharon said. "It was a pleasure meeting you, Jill, and I'll see you when you get back."

"Bye, Hon," Jim said. "Sam, why don't you take the left seat today? Flying with a little weight in the plane will sharpen your skills up."

"I'm not big on crowds when I'm learning something," Sam said. "You know how nervous I get."

"You wouldn't know it to look at him, but he can get nervous," Jim said while looking at Jill.

"He looks like the type who'd feel right at home on a football field," Jill said.

"I just get embarrassed when I make mistakes. The less people around to witness them the better."

"I promise not to make fun of you unless we crash and burn," Jill said.

"That's not on the schedule for today's flight, so it can't happen," Jim said. "You'll have to call ahead and make a special request for those flights. Sam is always the pilot on those days."

"At least we can agree on something I'm good at. My confidence was shaken there for a minute."

"All joking aside, we do take this seriously and try our best to be as proficient as possible," Jim said. "I give you my word you're in good hands. That's when I'm flying. Sam will have to speak for himself."

More laughs and it seemed to calm Sam. He decided to go ahead and fly the plane.

"You had mentioned the left seat," Jill said. "Is that important?"

"This particular plane can be flown from either front seat," Jim explained. "The same controls are available from both sides. Sometimes it might come down to something as simple as being right or left-handed, and what you're used to. The same levers and pedals needed to fly the plane are easily available from each seat, but the gauges required for flying are not.

"While being taught to fly you're trained in the left seat. When you're learning, there are some exercises that are taught while relying completely on the gauges. Like hood-time, which is when you cover your eyes with a visor that comes down over your forehead and acts as blinders so you can't easily see out of the cockpit without the instructor noticing.

"Then the instructor has you stare down at the floor while he banks the plane sharply in different directions, including up and down, in order to disorient you. When he's done, the plane won't be level or straight. Then while you're dizzy, and depending on what kind of an instructor you had, your head comes up and you must correct the plane to level and straight flight by using the gauges on the dashboard.

"The main gauge for this lesson would be the artificial horizon. This instrument identifies the position of the plane in relation to the earth's horizon as it would be seen by looking out of the cockpit. When we're flying VFR flight, or 'Visual Flight Rules,' we rely on the earth's horizon as a reference for flying level. If you're flying IFR flight, or 'Instrument Flight Rules,' which requires a lot of additional schooling and flight time, you're relying solely on your gauges to maintain your plane in flight.

"The point I'm trying to make is the important flight gauges are directly in front of the left seat, which is why the pilot in command uses the left seat in training. There are more technical reasons for flying the left seat such as prop rotation and torque, but we won't get into them right now. I've only heard of a few VFR pilots who are left-handed and prefer the right seat."

"So this plane can fly IFR because you have the gauges to do it?" Jill asked.

"No," Jim said. "First off, the pilot needs to be IFR Certified, and I'm not. It's very expensive and takes a long time for that certification. Secondly, the plane must be IFR Certified, and this plane is not. That requires special radios and instruments. It's more complicated than I could explain. Until we win the lottery, we'll fly VFR."

At the plane, the door was opened. Jill climbed aboard and got in the back seat. Because of her weight, Jim would have her sit on his side of the plane in order to balance the load. Sam was 225 pounds on one side and Jill and Jim together were 270 pounds. Rupert weighed a little more than Jill, so they'll switch sides when he climbs aboard.

Jim was slender and could enter the plane from either side and then crawl across the front seat without damaging anything in the cockpit. Not so for Sam. The passenger side of the plane was tied to the dock and for him to get in the left seat, he had to walk a tightrope that stretched from the right float to the left float. It was a 3/16 inch steel cable attached to the front of the floats, and you must hang onto the propeller for leverage while crossing from side to side. Jim wanted to yell, "Clear!" when Sam was holding the propeller but decided against it. Too much fun at his friend's expense may come back to haunt him.

After Sam boarded the plane, had his seat adjusted, and seat belt on, Jim told him to have everything ready to go before he untied and pushed the plane away. If he pushed off and for some reason the motor didn't start, the wind would have them on the rocks in a matter of seconds. Just thinking about it would make Jim tear up.

Jim watched his friend turn on the gas valve to the proper "Both Tanks" position, prime the engine with the fuel primer, and turn on the master electrical switch. He looked to be sure the water rudders were down and then untied the rear rope securing the plane's float to the dock. Because of the wind, he had tied an

Glassy Water

extra rope from the dock to the step above the float that's used to climb up in the cockpit. That rope would hold the plane in place while he removed the front rope that was securing the float to the dock.

After checking with Sam and making sure all was a go, he untied the last rope from the dock and yelled, "Clear!" Sam fired up the motor and allowed it to idle. Jim was still on the dock holding the rope he attached to the step while the wind was keeping the plane in place at idle. Jim wanted the engine to warm up a little before pushing the plane away and jumping on the float.

When it felt right, he told Sam he was pushing off, and as soon as Jim was on the float, Sam increased the throttle enough to move the plane forward in the wind. Jim climbed aboard and closed his door. He looked back at Jill to make sure her seat belt was fastened.

"There's just enough wind to make docking this thing with only one person a nightmare," Jim said. "I've done it before but don't like doing it often. It's one of those things you need to know how to do because you could leave by yourself in the morning with a light wind and come home to a big blow. There are a few different ways to handle it, but in every one of them, you have to be quick and sure-handed. It's also handy to have an alternate place to put the plane until the winds die off. I'm lucky because I have a neighbor deep in the cove who lets me dock there when the winds pick up."

"So it's something you have to stay up with, the wind I mean," Jill said.

"If the plane is at my dock, I check the forecast every few hours. And I check different sources. I don't want to end up with my equipment on the bottom of the lake or on the rocks. Some storms can develop quickly and are severe."

"Have you ever had a time when you came home and found it windier than you thought it would be?"

"More often than not. I don't mind leaving the plane at the dock if the winds don't exceed 15 knots. But a few times, they would forecast for 5 to 15 knots, and I'd come home and see 15 to 25 knots. And you can't do anything about it. You could cause more damage to the plane trying to move it than you would riding it out. As long as the dock stays in one piece, the plane should be fine. But nobody likes to watch their equipment beat against a dock like that. Now, if I'm the least bit nervous, I move it the day before."

"When is it too windy?" Jill asked.

"For some pilots who just fly wheels, anything over 15 is too much. At 10 knots, the water begins to create whitecaps. Today's wind is gusting to about 20 knots and this is nothing. When it comes to float flying, it's not so much when is it enough wind to keep you from flying, but when is it enough to ruin your equipment by pounding it over the waves."

Jim continued, "I've flown wheels when the wind has gusted to 30 knots, and it can be a challenge, but it's not a problem."

"Sam, taxi over to that far shoreline and from this position let's go to our ten o'clock, and we'll begin our takeoff run from there," Jim said. Checking the clock on the dash it showed 9:55. They would be a few minutes late meeting Rupert, but he would hear them coming.

"What about the wind where we're going?" Jill asked.

Jim turned and stared at her. "You ask a lot of questions for an adult. Sorry, just kidding. We're going up to Lake Paul in Naples. It's a narrow lake that's oriented in a north and south direction. We'll be able to land almost directly into the wind, and the gentleman we're picking up will be on the north end. There will be very little wind at the shoreline where we're meeting him because of all the trees."

After idling across the lake, the plane was 200 feet from the shoreline and there was only a small chop on the water. Looking out beyond the end of land where the lake opened up, they could see the big waves rolling by. The trees where they were now offered protection from the wind, but the pilot had to be ready when he passed by the last of the trees that would shield them because then the wind would hit the plane and push it sideways while also trying to flip it over.

Glassy Water

Sam had the plane ready for takeoff and pushed the throttle to its maximum. Because of the wind, he'd take no chances with a lower throttle setting to reduce the noise of the prop and engine. He brought the plane up on step and glided across the water like a boat until he reached takeoff speed, and then he eased the yoke back to lift the plane off the lake.

They flew past the point of land that's providing the protection from the wind and felt it blowing against them as the plane was pushed sideways, and the wind got under the left wing and tried to roll it over. Sam corrected to keep on a straight and gradual climb, then at 100 feet above the water, he wound the throttle knob back until he had 25 inches on the manifold pressure gauge. He then rolled the propeller pitch control knob back to 2500 RPM. Now the plane was climbing out at 25 square, or 25/25, and the noise from the propeller and engine had been greatly reduced. Cruise was 23/23.

The plane was climbing out and around the WGAN transmitting tower that was the tallest architectural structure in the world when it was built in 1959. It lost that designation a year later to another transmission tower built in Missouri. The tower in Raymond had support cables that stretched out for thousands of feet from the tower. While the tower itself was well-lit at night, the cables had no illumination. During the daytime, the cables could be easily seen.

Leveling off at 1000 feet, the plane was aimed towards Naples. A few minutes later, Lake Paul was in view and Sam steered so he could enter the landing pattern on a left-hand base and then turn final, which would take him into the wind. An experienced pilot would come down to about 25 feet above the lake and keep the plane level with power until he was close to the spot where he wanted to land, which wouldn't be far from where he needed to stop the plane. An inexperienced pilot like Sam lacked the confidence to land so close to the shore. He would land farther out in the lake so as to have plenty of room to lift back off should he misjudge something with the landing.

A big part of having confidence was being the owner of the aircraft. It could be very nerve-racking when you had to worry about making mistakes in somebody else's plane, and more so when they were seated right next to you. Even if it was a best friend it could be a challenge.

Sam came in and flared the plane 6 feet or so above the water. He felt the plane sink from under him and cut the throttle for a power-off landing. The more it sank, the more he pulled back on the yoke, and the more speed the plane lost. The plane settled onto the lake, and Sam let it bounce over a few waves until it slowed enough for him to add a small amount of power to propel it through the water to their destination.

The water was calm at the shoreline where they would be meeting Rupert, so getting him aboard should be easy. On the way in, Jim was looking for a white flag or some fluorescent tape that would help locate their friend. Sam's knees were still shaking from a case of the nerves and the high of still being in one piece, so he wouldn't be much help. Jim told him to run parallel to the north shore until they could find the old boy.

It took fifteen minutes to idle over to one side and then back to the other, with no sign of Rupert. Jim had seen a place where they could stop the plane and get out on the land. Sam headed there, killed the power 20 feet from the shoreline, and coasted into the spot. Jim went out on the float so he could catch a tree branch and rotate the plane 180 degrees then move it backwards into a small clearing.

With everyone out of the plane, they decided Sam would stay with it while Jim and Jill searched for Rupert.

"I didn't want to bother you guys while the two of you were busy, but I live just up the road from here," Jill said. "Is the guy you're looking for the owner of this land?"

"Yes, an old guy named Rupert," Jim said.

"Rupert's my neighbor. I have only lived here for three months, and I've met him a couple times. Not the friendliest neighbor, and he keeps to himself. Our homes are a quarter mile apart so we can't see each other's house, but I stopped in to introduce myself, and he told me to get off his property."

"That sounds like our Rupert."

"Then he sees I'm out on my four-wheeler and waves me

over. Nice as pie and asking me about my ride, but that's all he cared about. No, 'How are you?' 'What's your name?' or anything. Just, 'Will that thing hold me and my gun if I wanted to do some hunting?' Long story short, he asked to try it out, and what could I say, so I let him. It's an automatic so anyone can drive it. He takes it in a big circle and then comes back and thanks me. Then the old-timer walks away, but at ten paces, he turned and said, 'It was nice to meet you. My name's Rupert.' Strangest guy I ever met."

"Did he know what you did for work?"

"I don't know how. The only conversation we ever had, I just told you about. It was another neighbor who told me about all the land he owns. But I didn't know the name of the lake. It can't be seen from my house so it didn't come to mind."

Jim and Jill continued their conversation while moving through the brush.

"Sam and I just met him the other day. He contacted us and wanted a meeting. We were worried it was about the noise the plane made, but it turned out he needed our help for a mutual problem we have. We're going to fly over his land today so we can look for some trespassers he thinks are camping on his property. He seems to get upset if anyone steps foot on his land."

"Amen to that," Jill said. "Must be impossible for him to sleep at night if he's worried about a few campers. I mean the guy owns thousands of acres. How can he be sure they're even on his land?"

"I think he believes all the territory for as far as he can see belongs to him. He can smell smoke at night and even though you and I both know it could be coming from a neighbor's house, Rupert's convinced it's his wood being burned. We agreed to fly him over the land so he could see for himself. It would be impossible to cover all his land even with the plane, but we were hoping to see signs of smoke. The tree cover is so thick it's difficult to see anything else."

"You mentioned a mutual problem. What did you mean by that?"

"Did you hear anything about an assault that took place at

Richard's earlier in the week?" Jim asked.

"One of the other officers told me about it. That's why you saw me there last night. I wanted to see if it was for real or not. Chinese food is one of my favorite meals, and someone said it was good there. I was curious about the type of crowd that hung out there, and now that I know, I'll never go back."

"Me neither, now that I know the cops hang out there. Who wants to drink with the fuzz around?"

"I know what you mean," Jill said. "Makes me uneasy too."

"As far as the problem goes, we made the complaint after a fight with three people, and then later, I saw them up here on the lake while I was flying. I believe they're staying in the woods."

"So you think the same people who assaulted you are camping in the woods by the lake?"

"I believe they were. I don't know about now."

Jim scanned the woods and then said, "Have you been through here on your four-wheeler?"

"No. I didn't know him well enough to ask his permission."

"Rupert said logging roads were the only access into the lake, and most of them had been grown over. Four-wheel drive would be about the only way around. Let's see if we can find one of those roads."

Making their way through the thick brush, they came to a logging road that had been built 150 feet away from the lake. It was grown over but in otherwise good shape. Jim wouldn't be surprised if a regular vehicle could use it.

"Must be a couple miles from here up to his house," Jill said.

"At least that far," Jim said. "I never really paid a lot of attention to how far it is." He took his belt off and hung it from the branch of a tree. "You go that way for about five minutes, and I'll do the same this way. Let's meet back here in ten minutes. It won't be exact, so whoever gets here first waits for the other."

"I'll just call you on the cell phone."

"Check yours for service. Ours don't have any out here

Glassy Water

until we're up in the air."

"Nope, I don't have any either."

"Okay, see you in ten minutes."

Fourteen minutes later, they were both back at the starting point.

"I didn't see anything," Jill said.

"Me neither. We landed five minutes late to begin with, but he would have heard us well before then. While cruising the shoreline took fifteen minutes, and just spending another fifteen out here, never mind the time it took us getting to the road from the shore, he's over forty-five minutes late. He probably just forgot about it."

"He's earned the right to forget a few things at his age," Jill said.

"Let's head back to the plane. Maybe Sam and Rupert are enjoying each other's company while trading jokes."

When they were back at the lake, there was no sign of Sam and the plane had been tied to a branch. Thankfully the wind didn't shift around from the south, or the plane would be on the rocks. Jim shouted for Sam and got a reply.

"I'll be right there!" Sam yelled back.

After thirty seconds, he appeared from out of the thick brush.

"Sorry, I had to check the soil over there for drainage," Sam said. *A polite way of saying he had to pee.*

"No signs of Rupert?" Jim asked.

"Not a soul to be seen," Sam said.

"There's nothing for us to do here, so let's fly around a little and then head home."

After they were all aboard, Sam got the windmill going and idled down the lake far enough so when he turned the plane, there would be plenty of room to take off. While they were waiting for Sam to get to his spot, Jill wanted to know more.

"I don't want to be a pain, but can I ask a question?" Jill was looking at Jim.

"I was only trying to be funny earlier about your asking too many questions. Please ask all you want."

Philip Gagnon

"When you say the plane is up on the step, what are you talking about?"

"When Sam applies the power so we can begin our takeoff run, you'll notice the nose of the plane will begin to go upward. Sam will pull the yoke all the way back making the nose go up even more. As the plane picks up speed, he will push the yoke forward so the plane ends up skimming across the water like a boat. That's called being on the step because there is a step section on the float that is wider and bigger than any other part and performs just like the bottom of a boat.

"But basically, it's the difference between plowing through the water as compared to riding on the surface. You're on the step when the floats are riding on top of the water. And Sam will control getting the plane on step. If he pushed the yoke forward, the front of the floats would go under, and he could end up with the propeller striking the water which would cause all kinds of problems."

Jim went on, "I remember a time when four guys I knew overloaded a 180 floatplane with gear for a fishing trip. Not only did they pack the plane as full as they could, but a canoe was also tied to one of the floats. The fuel tanks were filled to capacity. I witnessed this from down on my dock because they were departing from the cove in front of my house. The plane was taxiing out, and the back of both floats were underwater.

"The pilot gave it the pickle, which is slang for full power, and they plowed through the water for what seemed like forever before coming up on the step. The lake's surface was smooth meaning there was no wind. The plane went a long distance but couldn't lift off the water. Two things worked against them. Being overloaded and having no wind.

"The problem with a situation like that one is the engine will overheat and could cause internal damage. The engine in this type of plane is air-cooled and relies on air movement to cool it. By working the engine so hard and with little or no result in forward movement, it translates into high cylinder head temperature, which left unchecked could be disastrous for the engine.

"Realizing the plane wouldn't get off the lake and seeing he had high cylinder head temperatures, the pilot chopped the power and returned to the dock, where they unloaded some of the goodies on board. That was at 7:30 in the morning.

"They didn't unload much because the back of the floats were still underwater when they came back out at 10:00. But by then the wind had picked up to about seven knots, and that would make a big difference. The plane went a long way to get up on the step, which told me they were still grossly overweight, and after it was on the step, the plane traveled a long distance before lifting off. The pilot knew if he was able to lift off now, the fuel used to get them to their destination, which was in Canada, would cut the plane's gross weight down considerably and bring them more into balance."

Jim continued, "I would never abuse my equipment like that."

"I'm not even a pilot, and I wouldn't have wanted to be aboard that flight," Jill said.

Sam reached his destination for the takeoff run, and Jim couldn't help but notice he was a lot farther than he needed to be. But everyone's comfort zone was different and better safe than sorry. If there were houses near the shoreline, Jim would have gone most of the way down the lake so he would have some altitude when going over them to help keep the noise down.

With the plane turned into the wind and all levers, elevator trim wheel, and other components set for takeoff, Sam pushed the throttle in and off they went.

With the new knowledge Jill had gained today, she now watched Sam's every movement and what it did to the plane. Before, she was happy looking out the window. When Sam made things happen to the plane, and she understood for what purpose it was being done, it gave her a thrill. Maybe she would learn to fly after all.

Sam wanted to fly over Rupert's house and see if the old boot would be out in the yard, but Jim thought better of it. Maybe he was taking a nap or something. "No," Jim said. "Let's go up to 1000 feet and look around his empire." Twelve minutes of that gave them an aerial view of all the trees they wanted to see. And that's it. Even the logging roads couldn't be seen from the air.

"We may as well head home," Jim said. "We're good on fuel, but I don't want to stretch it." The gas gauge needles were bouncing off the empty mark, but Jim usually went by time spent flying. He always kept close tabs on that number.

Back at the dock, the winds had calmed some, and Jim tied the plane securely. Sam and Jill got out and they went to Jim's house. Once inside, Sharon had coffee ready, and they all had a cup. Jill was impressed with the setup, so Jim gave her some history of how they came to own the house.

"Ever since I was a toddler, my parents would rent a cabin at Plummerville, which is a group of seasonal cottages on a beach across the lake from where we are now," Jim began. "In 1961, my parents bought this lot from Carl and Larry Murch, father and son landowners who were then, and still are now, highly respected in town. My dad, Henry, built a wooden platform so we could pitch a tent on it and also built an outhouse nearby. As the years went by, Mom and Dad saved their money and in 1966, they began to build this house. It was originally built as a seasonal camp and later converted to a year-round home.

"My parents relocated to Florida and sold us the place in 1992. We added the tennis court in 1997 and had the house completely rehabbed a few years later. We love it here."

"Are you any good at tennis?" Jill asked.

"He's so bad at it that even his own wife won't get on the court with him," Sam joked.

"You're one to talk," Jim said. "You don't even know which end of the racket to hold and which end to hit the ball with."

"I admit I have my issues, but you're stretching it a little aren't you?"

"I stand by my statement. I think we should go out and hit a few. That is if you can keep the balls from going into that big fat mouth of yours."

"You're on, Skinflint. Let's make it interesting and put a wager on it."

"No problem there, Pork-round. Put your money where your mouth is. To answer your question Jill, which I couldn't do before because I was so rudely interrupted, you can come out back and judge for yourself."

"Can I get some strokes with the winner?" Jill asked.

Wow, Jim thought. *That was spoken like she knew what she was talking about.*

"Okay, but you must know we don't play easy ball when a girl comes on the court," Jim said. "We don't want to hurt you, so you'll have to sign a medical release first."

"I can take care of myself."

On his way to get the rackets, Jim had an uneasy feeling they may have been set up. *How would that be possible? She can't be much more than 5 feet tall and 105 pounds soaking wet.* He knew he'd find out soon enough.

Out on the tennis court, which was built in the woods behind Jim's house, Jill was awed. "I've never seen anything like this. It's so beautiful."

"Thanks," Jim said. "Sharon and I coordinated the whole thing. Right now, I'm ready for some butt-kicking. What do you say we all meet at Richard's tonight for dinner so you can try his Chinese food, and then I'll go into the details of how we built it?"

"I like the sound of that," Jill said. "It's a deal."

Sam was already on the court running his mouth like he was Pete Sampras or something.

"Don't hurt yourself warming up, Twinkle-toes," Jim teased. "Jill is already drooling so she can play me because you're stinking up the court."

"You better worry about yourself, Slim-Jim," Sam yelled. "I'm gonna take it to you, and you're gonna wish you never got out of bed today."

"Bring it on, Slowtrain. Let's see what you got other than a big mouth that is."

"You're gonna get more than you want, Toothpick, but first I need to warm up."

"Warm up? C'mon, Bullwinkle! What's the problem? You need someone to hold a match to your rear-end to start your engine? We don't want to have no forest fire here!"

"HaHaHa smart guy. You just wait until you have to eat my first few serves. After that, I'm gonna drive the ball down your throat."

"Do they really play or is this the show?" Jill asked.

"They're just getting warmed up," Sharon said. "It takes them a while to hate each other, then they warm up for tennis. And this is nothing. You should hear them when they drink beer while they play. You have to cover your ears."

"You got two balls in your pocket and one you've been bouncing around for ten minutes," Jim said. "Send it over to me so I can show you how the game is played."

"Okay, here it comes, but I warned you. If you end up with bruise marks all over your body, don't blame me."

The ball was sent over the net, and Jim sent it back like you should when you were warming up. Nice and easy. They kept a rally going until Sam totally fanned one, and the ball sailed by into the fence.

"That's why we put up them ten-foot high fences," Jim chuckled. "For people like you who need glasses but don't think you look good wearing them."

"Go ahead. Run your mouth. Gives me something to aim for. I'll take a few serves and then be ready to play."

"Really! You already look all worn out to me! And don't get any blood on my court! Take your serves and let's go!"

"Don't you want a couple of serves?"

"That's a typical ploy to stall. You want Jill to come in for you now?"

Sam fired a couple of serves that were in. Jill was impressed. Jim wasn't.

"That all you got, Fatboy? This is gonna be a short match."

"I'm all set. Say your prayers, Beanpole."

"Up or down," Jim said as he rolled the racket in his hands. He had a P on the base of the handle that stood for the make of his Prince racket. P was up and d was down. Anything in between and Jim would call it any way he wanted because he owned the court.

"Up! And don't you cheat me!"

Jim stopped spinning the racket and held it so they both could see the P was up. All the balls were given to Sam so he could begin the match.

The first set ended with Sam on top at 7 games to 5. Both men were quite good and the more they competed, the better they were, which was typical for part-time players. Jill was a seasoned pro who won a pair of state titles with her college tennis team. Her size and speed made her an excellent singles player. Looking at these two guys, she figured they were solid 3.5 level players. And from what she could see, they would easily be 4.0 level if they worked more often on their game.

The second set began with Sam firing an ace down the middle. After some name calling and body gestures, the games continued. With Jim serving at 5 games to 4, Jill could see that Pork-round was beginning to show fits of fatigue. He was charging the net hoping to end points early, only to have Beanpole consistently pass or lob him. With no go-juice left in his tank and the score 40 to 15, Toothpick let go of a sweet slice serve that made Fatboy look like his feet were in five-gallon buckets of cement. He never moved, and the ball caught the line. One set apiece.

After a lengthy break and more name calling, the deciding set began. Sam started with a double fault, and the bickering would be non-stop from there on out.

"What's the matter, Alice?" Jim yelled. "Confused about what part of the ball you're supposed to hit?"

"I'm just checking to see if you're awake! Now pay attention!"

He did, and Sam double faulted again.

"Gee, Poop-for-Brains, can I have a couple more of those?"

"Go ahead and taunt me. Don't forget we have witnesses to your unethical behavior. I'm surprised they're not booing you."

"Ya, ya, ya. You're just killing time. Let's see if you can

still toss the ball above your head without passing out."

Sam went on to hold serve and take that game but fell flat as the set moved on. The rest of the way wasn't pretty. Sam was fading fast and didn't have the energy to charge the net anymore. Of course, Jim was just getting warmed up and was serving again at 5 games to 2 and 40 love. He smacked an ace down the centerline and then began his corny victory dance.

"Game, set, and match, Chunk-a-lot!" Jim yelled, who had his racket turned around and was strumming the strings like it was a guitar while his left hand was changing cords. His feet did a funky shuffle that even Sharon was embarrassed to watch. Jill had seen enough.

"You got anything left for another match?" Jill asked.

"I can play all day long," Jim said. "Unlike my chubby buddy over there, I got the wherewithal to go the distance."

"I'm just having a bad day," Sam said, "and I didn't want to embarrass you on your own court in front of an audience. Next time will be different."

"Oh, I can't wait to see how you'll play the next time," Jim said. "Maybe if you wear your wig that makes you look like a girl, you'll feel better knowing you play like a girl."

Jill was on the court and ready to hit a few so she could get warmed up, but the guys were still going at it on the sideline. She couldn't believe what they'd given her to use as a racket. It could have doubled as a sandbox shovel.

"You need an hour or two for a break?" Jill chided. "Or maybe to take a nap? Let's go!"

"Hold your horses. I'm coming. Woman thinks she's the boss or something."

Jim took his place on the court and hit the ball to Jill. She swung at it and totally whiffed the shot. She continued to look rusty, and Jim's ego swelled with confidence. After five minutes, he began hitting strokes that passed Jill on either side.

"You're wasting all your good shots during practice," Jill said, who would save her good stuff for the game. "I'll take a few serves, and we can begin. Because it's your court, I'll even let you serve first."

She let loose a couple of so-so serves and then a couple of second serves. She had pretty good spin on her second serves, and all of her practice serves were in.

Jim began and won the first game on his points off serve. Jill would need a few games to get used to his style. And the crappy racket. It turned out she would only need two games before she was serving for the set at 5 games to 2. She had an accurate, hard serve that always fell in. Not able to match the speedy serves of her opponent, she would get the job done with placement. Jim would have to adjust his game if he was going to beat her. She finished the set after a 40 to 30 lead with a crisp backhand shot that passed Jim while he dove for it.

"Not bad for a beginner," Sam offered. "I can't wait to see how you'd play with your own gear."

"I've played a little," Jill said. "I can hold my own."

"I had to go easy on you," Jim said. "You know how it is. Being a gentleman and all."

"I appreciate the special treatment. Are you good for another set now, or should we wait until after you take your nap?"

"I can't believe what my ears are hearing! I'm trying to be nice, and in return you're insulting me for my kindness!"

"Save it for someone who wants to hear it. You got three?"

Jim did have all three balls in his pocket, but he wasn't going to tell her.

"Only two," Jim said. "I think one went out in the woods behind you. Why don't you go and find it?"

"I'm not falling for that trick. If you don't have three, then let's play with two."

"I'm getting a little sick and tired of your attitude! I guess I'm gonna have to show you some manners! Ready?"

"Bring it on, String-bean!"

Jim began strong and played well throughout the set. But this Jill character was just too accurate for him. Instead of speed, she was taking it to him with finesse. Jim was returning everything she sent him, but he was consistently sailing the ball long while trying to keep her back on the baseline.

At 5 games to 2, Jill was serving for the match at 40 to 15.

After a long rally, Jim wanted to really show his power and tried to pass her fast with topspin on her backhand side. Not enough topspin made his shot wide and long. Crushed and beyond words, he stumbled to his chair and collapsed into it.

"What's the matter big man?" Sam chided. "Girls a little tough on you today?"

"You saw how she played," Jim said. "She was sandbagging me. I had to take her on so you wouldn't slit your wrists when you lost to her. I'm the only one who can be man enough to say I let her win. Next time she won't be so lucky."

"Next time, I'll have my own racket, and you'll be lucky to get a game off me," Jill said.

"Okay, you beat me fair and square, but I'll need a rematch. When will you be able to play again?"

"I don't have anything planned other than work, which can sometimes be a floating schedule. Let me check on that and get back to you."

"You do that, Missy, and hold your breath until then because I'm not going to be so kind next time."

"All talk no action. We'll see."

"It's after three o'clock now," Jim said. "Shall we all meet at Richard's around five?"

Jill and Sam nodded yes and said they'd see them then. Once they were gone, Sharon told Jim about the phone call she'd taken when they were getting ready to leave in the airplane earlier in the day.

"I took a call from our broker in Aruba. He said they want to move the closing on the house to the middle of next week."

"That's good," Jim said. "At least we know it's going to happen."

"I already called my boss, and he said to go and take care of our business. We don't have to go. They can send us the originals FedEx, and then we can overnight them back."

"I know, but I'd like to have a little more time in the house we built. After putting everything we had into it, you know we're going to miss being there. I'll leave that up to you. Either we go, or we do everything FedEx. What do you think?"

Glassy Water

"Even if we were to book our flights now, the price would be the same as it would be tomorrow. And that's if there are seats available. I say let's enjoy the rest of today and make a decision later."

"As always, well thought out. Let me get showered and cleaned up. Then let's go to Richard's and have a drink."

One hour later, they arrived at the restaurant well ahead of Jill and Sam. They ordered drinks and began to relax. It was a slack time before the dinner rush, so Richard sat with them. They had a laugh when Jim filled him in on the tennis matches that were played. Their new friend was quite the player. Richard had tried tennis a few times with the guys but would need lessons before he could give them any kind of a game. Because of that, he understood the difference in the level of play. He thought Jim was really good.

"You're joking me," Richard said. "How could she beat you?"

"Don't let the size of the package fool you," Sharon said. "She told me she played before, and I'll bet from what I saw it was on some kind of competitive level. She didn't make many mistakes."

"Easy for you to say while you were all comfy and cozy sitting in your chair watching us," Jim said. "She was as tough an opponent as I've ever had. She didn't make any mistakes."

"She was definitely in control," Sharon added. "I had goosebumps because she did things easy that most men seem to struggle with."

The front door of the restaurant opened and in came Sam. He looked ready for a drink. Richard flew out of his seat and ran behind the bar so his friend wouldn't have to wait long for it.

"Not to be rude but gimme that," Sam said. "I'll have another in about two minutes. I'm so dry it's pitiful. This is going to be the best part of the day for me."

"I can see why after the shellacking you took out there today," Jim said. "Richard admits he needs lessons and maybe it's time you were truthful with yourself."

"Not one of my best performances, I'll admit. It's hard to

be perfect when your host lends you a tennis racket that has a picture of Mickey Mouse along with his signature on it."

"Your racket was as good as Jill's."

"Right. And hers had Minnie Mouse on it. You stacked the deck on us, and in the end, it came back and bit you. She's good at tennis."

"Sharon was just saying she thought Jill might have played competitively."

The front door opened and in walked the subject of the conversation. Jill took a seat next to Sharon. Richard couldn't believe it was the same person he saw yesterday in a policewoman's uniform. She was stunning. Richard had a good memory and was behind the bar getting her a beverage before she asked for one.

"It's good to see some people still dress to impress," Jim said. "I'll admit, you do look good."

"Well, shucks there, Beanpole, you sure do know how to sweet-talk a girl."

"Okay, let's get right to it," Jim demanded. "Where did you learn to play tennis like that?"

"Same place you did. On the tennis court."

"I can see that being charming with you is not the way you like it. Seriously, you killed me today. Sharon thinks you played competitively."

"I did in college. Our team went to, and took, the state championships two years in a row. I played both singles and doubles and didn't lose many games. I never dropped a set."

"I knew it! You could've at least told us a few tidbits so we would have an idea of what we were up against."

"Sorry to disappoint you, but that's not my style. Especially when competing against 2.0 level players. I like to keep them guessing."

"You seem to forget something, Sweetie," Jim said. "The cook here is a good friend of ours and a strong 2.0 player. He doesn't take kindly when being made fun of, and he'll remember that when he prepares your dinner. Last I knew, he had some tasty extras he could add to the meal of a smart-aleck. Extras that will make your mouth burn."

"I've known Richard half as long as I've known you, and I can already tell he's twice the gentleman. I'll take my chances."

Richard liked the girl. "Ready for menus?"

"Yes, sir," Jim replied.

The menus came and the food was ordered. Jim and Sam always had the "Three Delights," and Richard made sure to load it with lobster meat. They convinced the girls to try the same. Jim also ordered a large serving of the house fried rice. He could have made a meal out of that alone, and Richard always gave them plenty.

"So how was it you were able to build the tennis court in the middle of the woods like that?" Jill said. "I've played on a lot of courts but never one as beautiful and well designed."

Jim's head swelled with pride. "Are you serious or joking? I don't know you well enough to tell."

"One hundred percent serious. I'll start joking later and begin with the Minnie Mouse autographed racket you gave me to play with. I think if the racket had been in the original packaging, it would have said it was suitable for kids aged 4 to 6 years."

"He does that on purpose," Sam said. "He wants you to think there won't be any tennis that day so you don't bring your gear. Next thing you know, he has an itch to play and out come the toy rackets. You'd think I'd know better, but I still get taken on occasion. I'm going to start leaving a bag of gear in my car."

"You tried that once," Jim said, "and I'm sure you remember it didn't turn out well. The dirty laundry was never taken out of the bag and cleaned. Next time we played, I had to find a shirt and shorts so you wouldn't have to play in your jeans. And then you broke a string on your racket and threw it in the trunk. It stayed there for a month before you took it to get restrung. I think you like using my rackets. I know you like Mickey."

"Think what you like but wait until our next match when I bring my game and my own gear," Sam said. "I saw what Jill did to you today, and it looked easy to me. I'm going to wear a pair of hot pants and a halter top and flash you. I saw it work."

Philip Gagnon

"I think Jill was asking about the tennis court and doesn't care about you having diarrhea of the mouth," Jim said while eyeballing Jill. "My parents bought the back lot the tennis court is built on a few years after they bought the waterfront lot. The Murch family offered the back lots to every waterfront landowner, but only my parents and the next-door neighbor bought the lots directly behind their camps.

"To this day, the rest of the land is still held by Larry, who has said he'll take it all to his grave with him. The neighbor who bought the other back lot never did anything with theirs, so everything around the tennis court is heavily treed and untouched, which really adds to the beauty of the setting.

"Our lot size was 15000 square feet, and the outside dimensions of the tennis court took up a total of 7200 square feet. Sharon and I cut every tree and shred every branch to clear the lot. We hired a guy with heavy equipment to pull all the stumps and haul them away. Then we had forty truckloads of fill brought in and made a base that was twelve inches thick. The base was graded and compacted with the pitch required and then left alone over the winter so it could settle.

"It was paved eight months later. Then the green vinyl coated perimeter fence was installed, and the tennis court was painted and lined. We chose the dark green court and the lighter green out of bounds area because of the setting in the woods. Not including the price of the land, the whole thing cost $35,000. We were real happy with the way it turned out."

"I'd be honored to be invited back so I can play on it again," Jill said. "I've never seen a court in such a beautiful setting. I was impressed."

"I'll bet you were," Jim agreed. "Maybe we'll let you come back once more. I have a racket with broken strings that I'll let you use next time, and I won't take no for an answer."

The food arrived and another round of drinks was ordered. The talking completely ceased while Richard's exquisite meal was devoured by all. The only sound heard during the meal was, "Please pass the fried rice." Richard sat at the next table with a wide grin on his face knowing they were pleased.

"I've got to bring my mother here," Jill said. "She'll fall in love with this place."

"Everyone loves Richard's food," Sam said. "The first night he opened for business, he expected a handful of people. It was him in the kitchen and his wife waiting the tables. They got mobbed. The restaurant was almost packed. Somehow they survived that night, but now there are at least two waitresses on weeknights and four on weekends. And that depends on the time of year. In the summer, he needs even more people on staff. That's a lot of business."

"Sharon and I recommend it to everyone we know," Jim said. "Richard doesn't disappoint."

Looking at Jill, Sam had a question.

"Did you see Rupert when you drove by his house?"

"Ever since I met the man two months ago, I've looked in his dooryard as I drive by. Not once have I seen him out in the yard. Today was the same."

"I'm done with my meal, and if everyone will excuse me, you can find this tennis pro at the bar drinking a beer," Sam said. "I'm going to take a minute and call Rupert. I doubt if now would be nap time for the old bugger."

Sam went to the bar and was joined by the others in less than five minutes.

"How is our friend?" Jim asked.

"There was no answer," Sam said. "It just rang and rang. I'm not nervous or anything, but we might want to look in on him tomorrow if we can't get through on the phone."

"I can stop over in the morning if you want me to," Jill offered. "It'll give me an excuse to go on my four-wheeler."

"I'll give you a call early and report what I find out," Sam said. "I'll try and raise him around nine."

The gang made tentative plans for the next day and said they would call each other. With their bellies full and drink quotas reached, they said goodnight to each other and Richard, then left to make their way home. *Pleasant dreams for all.*

Chapter 22

The cousins returned in the early afternoon not looking at all like they had for all of their earlier days alive. The doctor asked them to stay in the area for the night so he could adjust the level of medication the following day. Normally he would not work on Saturday, but after seeing the dramatic results of the first treatment on the redness in their eyes, decided a more reduced level would give the desired results, and he wanted to be the one who made the adjustment. The trio couldn't believe the doctor almost came to tears because he had to come in on a Saturday. Back home in Aruba, a doctor would work any day of the week. For a price. Money bought anything on the island.

The cousins had been told all their lives there was no cure for the condition they were born with, but a new medical breakthrough had delivered results they never would have imagined. It would not come as a surprise to find out that it would take many years for the treatment to reach the shores of their homeland.

Once the doctor adjusted the second treatment and had it applied properly, the cousins were in shock when they looked in the mirror that was held in front of them. One by one they uttered the same phrase, "I cannot believe it."

The medication in the form of eye drops would have to be taken twice weekly for the rest of their lives. And because it was new, it was expensive. They had to purchase all the medication through the doctor and could get six months' worth at a time. The only real problem was they had to pick it up from his office in person. No one of them could pick up for the other. That meant a trip to Augusta, Maine, once every six months for the foreseeable future. They would somehow make it work.

Proud of their new look, the sunglasses they had always worn were now hanging from the "V" cut in their shirts. It was going to take a bright sun before they would want to wear them again. The doctor said reasonable exposure to the sun's rays would help with the recovery. It was like the beginning of a new life for the three of them, and they held their heads high. Maybe it was time for a change of lifestyle at the same time. Jose had pocketed a beard trimmer and razor at the Alive'n Well store next to Tony's Foodland. He had a plan in the works.

"You think we should start going to church on Sundays like all the good people do?" Juan said. "I mean, just look at our eyes. It has to be some kind of miracle we were able to find out about the treatment and then have it work for us."

"If it was a miracle and God had a hand in it, then he would have delivered the results without any financial attachment and would have ended the transaction with, 'You are welcome,' " Jose said. "Instead, we paid dearly and was well worth it, but my point is it was not an act of God, we did say thank you, and their response was come back soon. As in after you refill your wallet. It is all about money. Nothing happens in this world unless it is driven by the money."

"Do not go soft on us Juan," Anncherry added. "We already know our souls are so black that nothing will clean them up. Why change things now?"

"It is just that I feel really different today. Do you think we should reconsider why we are even here? Uncle Paul never did get his leg broke, and I have an idea that if we continue on, a jail cell will become our new home. It gives me a bad feeling."

"This has already been covered before," Jose said. "The three of us made a promise to Uncle Paul before he died, and we will keep it. If you want to go home, then go right ahead. But you need to decide if you are with us or not."

"I am with you. But do you not have a new outlook on things? We have spent our entire lives hiding our eyes, and now it is like we are free of the burden. A new life has presented itself for us. I am completely with you. It is only that I do not want to spend my new life in jail."

"That is easy to avoid," Anncherry said. "We make sure we do not get caught. And you are right about a new life for us. I do not think anyone has ever seen us without our glasses on, so we have a new identity. The one without the glasses. And we will not be ashamed to go without them anymore."

"Anncherry is right," Jose said. "We need to be careful and finish our work here. Uncle Paul is planning on us to do him justice."

"I am only saying the guy did not get the job done," Juan explained. "Maybe Uncle Paul is asking for too much."

"Nonsense," Jose said. "A deal was made, and his money taken. We may be thieves, but we do not steal from family."

At least not yet, Juan thought.

The Impala was back on familiar ground. The logging roads were just as beautiful as when the trio had left them. Out of curiosity, the cousins made their way back to where they encountered the old man on the horse. When the Impala arrived on the scene, the car was stopped and all three got out. The marks made by their car and the horse were still visible along with some animal tracks.

But that was it. No one else had arrived at the scene. It had been cleaned up, but then again it had not. There was a small amount of blood in the dirt, and it looked like something had tried to clean it up, or scuff at it, with a paw. After knocking heads, the thought was that concealing the evidence would be best for their situation.

Off the side of the road, branches were found that the trio used to smooth the ground out while also hiding the marks and blood. When done, you could not tell anything happened at all. While looking around and surveying the area for any other clues as to what happened to the old man's body, his shotgun was found. Just what the cousins needed; another weapon. And they liked the gun because it came with their favorite cost to them. Nothing.

Juan was again beginning to have second thoughts. Were they here to break a few bones or start blowing people away. He was sure Jose and Anncherry would have no problem shooting someone. And Juan did not have a problem either, except he was afraid of jail time. He would go to any extreme to avoid jail.

Satisfied the area was returned to normal, they set out for the new campsite when Anncherry thought of something.

"I think it is obvious all this land belongs to one person, and what if that old man on the horse was the owner? He is gone, and it looked to me like no one came into the woods looking for him. We would have seen signs of some sort that people had come and removed his body. There was nothing but animal tracks."

"That is right," Jose agreed. "What are you saying?"

"If nobody came looking for him, then nobody has missed him. He must live alone. I say we see if we can follow the horseshoe marks in the ground to where they came from. Maybe we will inherit another home."

"I like your thinking. It is worth checking out."

The trio found a place to hide the Impala and began walking the logging road. The tracks were like painted graffiti on a wall. Easy to see. It was more than an hour later when they saw an old farmhouse that sat by itself near the edge of the woods. After a quick discussion, it was decided Anncherry would go and knock on the door to see if anyone was home. The hoof-prints led directly to a barn that was by the house.

After repeatedly knocking and receiving no response, she tried the doorknob but found it was locked. There was no deadbolt, so she went and got a credit card from Jose. The card was inserted past the door jam and against the latch that silently slid aside and the door pushed open. She motioned for her brothers to join her, and they entered the home. The door opened to a combination kitchen and dining area that had recently been used with unwashed dishes in the sink and a half-empty bottle of water that was on the table next to a book.

Jose read many books, and the cover on that one looked familiar. "I have read this book named 'Glassy Water' and it has sections in it that speak of the homeland."

"Really," Anncherry said. "Is it any good?"

"I thought it was poorly written and not a very good storyline. It was very confusing to me."

"Well, I will not waste my time reading trash like that."

Deciding to split up, the trio quickly searched the house but found no signs of human life. Once the home was completely gone over, they met again in the kitchen.

"There is one bedroom downstairs that looks to have the belongings of one male person," Anncherry said.

"Upstairs, there are two bedrooms with furnishings but that is it," Juan said. "No clothes or shoes and the dresser drawers are empty."

"I found mail in the front room, all showing the name of Rupert Shoemaker," Jose added. "This has to be the old man's pad. Want to spend the night?"

"We should camp in the woods one more time," Anncherry said. "The house can be checked in the morning. If no one comes or goes by noon tomorrow, we lay claim to it."

"Let us go and set things up," Jose said. "We need to see if we can get the down-low on our target tonight."

By the time the cousins returned to the Impala, it was getting dark. Finding a spot near where the car was parked, they began setting up camp. The brothers were beginning to gather wood for a fire when Anncherry again had an idea.

"We have not had a good night of beer drinking for days. We should pack everything back in the car and head up to the farmhouse to spend the night. After sleeping in a hotel bed last night, I do not want to sleep on the ground again. If anyone should show up at the house while we are there, we know how to handle them."

"Let us do that," Jose said. "I want to go back to the restaurant and see if we can get some more information. I have an idea that will get us in, and they would not be the wiser to who we are."

"Are all three of us going?" Juan asked.

"No, just me and you. And we will be sporting a new look."

"What kind of look?" Anncherry asked.

"Me and Juan are going to cut our hair to the scalp. We have only been there with glasses on, so without our glasses, and with our white eyes and a new hairdo, it will be like a new identity. With our target's name, we only need to know where he lives. Once that information is in hand, I can see an end to our mission. I am dying to go home and show off our new looks."

"What about the house in Massachusetts?" Juan asked.

"I think we should try to sell it," Jose said. "What can be done to us if they somehow were to figure out it is a false will? These Americans are so stupid. They think hiring lawyers and giving them all their money is the right way to live. If it becomes an issue, a lawyer will get hold of it and tie the problem up in court for a year so he can drive his fees up. It is the 'American National Pastime.'"

"I think it is worth the risk," Juan said. "We call a real estate broker and list it with her. A lot of real estate closings are done over the internet or by mail. If things go right, they will deposit a fat check in our account at Aruba Bank. And if we are smart, maybe we can do the same with the house we found today. Two old men with nobody who cares about them. What could be easier?"

"I like your warped minds," Anncherry said. "Let us go to the house and get you ready for a night in town. You should keep all our gear in the car in case we need to make a fast escape. Leave me a gun and some beer, that is all I need. Should you come back and not find me at the house for some reason, I will be in the woods out behind the barn where we followed the trail left by the horse."

Quickly packing everything back in the car, the cousins then drove out of the woods and headed to the farmhouse. After making a few wrong turns with all three of them voicing opinions on how to drive, the Impala found its way into the driveway. Jose nosed the car up to the barn, and Juan got out so he could open the door. The car was put inside and the door shut.

Anncherry used her special key to pass by the lock again, and they were back in the house. It felt chilly inside.

"I know they use a furnace of some type to heat the homes

in the winter, but how do we turn it on?" Anncherry asked.

"There should be a switch mounted on a wall somewhere in the main living area," Jose said.

He found the thermostat and studied it for a moment before understanding how it worked. Rotating the dial brought the needle upwards and should be set at the desired temperature. The bottom needle pointed to the current house temperature. Good thing he found it himself. Juan and Anncherry would have spent an hour wondering why the bottom needle did not move when they rotated the dial. He heard the furnace fire up and knew the heat would not be far behind.

Both boys went to the bathroom and cut their hair close to the scalp, then shaved their faces for a clean look. Gazing in the mirror was like seeing people they did not recognize. Each was impressed with the results and stood admiring themselves for many minutes. Nothing but a couple of pretty Arubans.

Making their way into the kitchen area, they sat at the table to have a beer before leaving. The first beer was so smooth and went down so fast, another was in order. After a half hour passed by and with the beers flowing, the brothers grabbed a couple for the road and left. Back home in Aruba, you always had a beer between your legs while you drove. The Americans who came to the island taught them to do that. They also taught the Arubans how to drink in mass quantities.

Out at the barn, Juan opened the door so Jose could bring the car out. Juan shut the barn door and got in the car. They drove out the road towards the causeway and went right on Route 302. Eighteen minutes later, they arrived in Raymond. When they got to the parking lot of the restaurant, all the spaces in front were taken, and they had to park away from the building. The new-look brothers got to the front door and held it open for a departing party of two couples. They stared at the men. Jose and Juan had seen them before.

The people leaving paid them no mind and continued on to their cars. The brothers entered the restaurant and took a table by the window. Looking out, it was too dark to see anything of importance.

"Those two are the same guys me and Anncherry followed the other night," Juan said, "and the same ones you saw yesterday morning on the water."

"And do not forget the same two Anncherry fought with also," Jose said. "Our new look has passed the test. They did not even notice us."

"I was nice and smiled at them. I hope you did the same."

"No, I spit in their faces and stuck my tongue out at them. Of course I was at my best."

"It looks like we will have the same girl waiting on our table," Juan said. "Do you know what you will ask her?"

"Pay attention to the master. Let us order a few beers and dinner first. Maybe the crowd will thin a little because it is getting late, and she can have time to talk with us."

Rene came to the table, took their drink orders, and said she would return for the dinner order. There were more waitresses on duty tonight from what Juan could tell. She should not be as busy as the last time they were here and asked her questions.

Rene returned with the beers and prepared to take their dinner orders.

"Is this your first time in?" Rene asked.

"Yes," Jose said. "We are in town to see a friend of ours. Perhaps you know him. Jim Kamae?"

"Oh wow, you just missed him," Rene said. "He and his wife just left with another couple. You must have seen them in the parking lot."

"We did see some people on our way in, but it was too dark for us to see them clearly. I cannot believe it was Jim, and I did not recognize him. Is he still the big guy he always was?"

"Not really sure what you mean by big guy, but Jim is the same lean-mean guy I've always known him to be. You know, not too skinny for his height."

"I am sorry," Jose said. "I meant like the big guy on campus. The one everybody likes."

"That's him. Everybody likes Jim. He's got his airplane, and he built a tennis court at his house. Everybody respects Jim. He's a fun guy. I dated him for a year, and we had fun."

Someone was calling for Rene, and she said, "One minute while I take this order. Sorry, guys. What will it be tonight?"

"We will have two PuPu Platters and another drink when you get a chance."

"Coming right up."

Rene left, and the new-look cousins conversed.

"Now we know what he looks like," Jose said. "One guy was big and meaty, and our target is the skinny one. Did you get a good look at him?"

"I did," Juan said. "I remember the faces of both those guys."

"The plane that landed on the lake was his then. Both of those guys were on it. We just need to know where his house is. Do you want to bet if I can drag it out of her tonight?"

"No way. You are too slick for her."

Jose took a twenty-dollar bill out of his pocket and set it on the edge of the table.

"That is just a little primer," he said.

The brothers sat in silence and enjoyed their drinks while waiting for the dinner to arrive. Eight minutes later, Rene brought the two platters of food and set the dishes down in front of them. It was time to feed the machine. They had been working on lubing the components for more than an hour. The brothers said thank you, and Rene was off again.

They had Chinese food back home, so it was nothing new to them, but the fried rice was spectacular. Whoever made it must have developed their own recipe because they never had any rice like that before. It was loaded with pieces of meats, veggies, and scrambled eggs. *Yummy.*

Rene had spotted the twenty and hoped it was for her. She had her share of cheapskates who didn't like to tip. She'll pay a little extra attention to those two.

She approached the table and asked how their meal was.

"Outstanding," Jose said. "Everything is great, and the fried rice is out of this world."

"Well, I helped the owner develop the recipe for the rice," Rene postulated. "We're really proud of it."

"You should be. It is excellent. Do you eat here often?"
"As much as I can. I love Chinese food."
"Does Jim eat here a lot?"
"If he's not at the bar drinking, he's at a table eating. He loves the place. It's his second home."
"I still cannot believe I missed him tonight," Jose said. "I would drive to his house and see him, but I do not remember his address."
"Oh, it's easy," Rene said. "57 Johnson Lane. Go up Route 85, which is the road at the street light, follow it six miles to Johnson Lane, then in to number 57. You can't miss it. He has the only tennis court in his backyard."
"I think I remember him giving me that address over the phone the last time we talked. I need to start writing those things down."
"The older we are the more we forget. I started writing stuff down years ago. I was forgetting everything."
"If we could have one more beer before we leave, along with the check, we will be good," Jose said.
"Coming right up."
Rene couldn't suppress the smile on her face as she went behind the bar. She would earn that big fat tip and felt good she was able to help two such nice guys out. The one she talked to the most was cute. Maybe she would drop a hint that she was available.
She delivered the beers and check but was again called away.
"I'll be back in a jiffy."
The cousins gulped down their dessert and left enough money on the check to cover it. Jose thought about pocketing the $20 bill but decided not to. She had delivered the goods and earned it. They got up and left the restaurant.
Back in the car, they wanted to drive over to Johnson Lane and check things out. Who knows, maybe the target would be lying in his driveway passed out, and they could just break his leg and go home tomorrow. People in Aruba passed out in their driveways all the time. Once the inebriated individual got home

Philip Gagnon

from a heavy night of drinking, the driveway offered a sense of comfort. They were at home and could be comfortable sleeping anywhere. Why not the driveway? Lie down and turn your head sideways and let the vomit fly. No need to get out of bed to find a sink or toilet. Now that was real comfort.

The six miles driving on Route 85 went by fast, and Johnson Lane was coming right up. It was a dirt road barely wide enough for two cars to pass by one another. They came to a "T" in the road, and the brothers did not remember being told which way to go. Jose knew he should have pocketed the $20 for incomplete instructions. Going right at the "T" took them past dozens of camps lined up at the water's edge. There were no homes on the other side of the road, and no tennis court.

Turning around, the brothers made their way back to the "T" and went straight through. They drove past many more camps lined up at the water's edge. There were no cars or lights at any of the camps because they must have been summertime use only. Jose could tell all of the buildings were on posts, and he could see under them. Everything back home was built on solid concrete pads.

As they continued along, lights could be seen up ahead of them, so the car was stopped. Jose switched off the headlights and backed in the driveway of a camp. It was all woods on the back side of the road, but he could see something was built on a back lot up in front of them. There was a mercury vapor light that lit the entire area up like daylight, so it would be difficult to make an approach without being seen.

The brothers quietly got out of the car and walked down beside the vacant camp to get a view of the lake. Once at the shoreline, they could look into the cove where a plane was sitting tied to a dock. That was definitely the right spot. All the pieces were fitting together, so now they needed to figure out how to get access to the target without anyone else around.

Heading to the car, they made the decision to go back to where Anncherry was holed up and discuss their strategy with her. She was always smart when it came time to be sneaky. Jose drove out the way they came and turned onto the paved road.

They continued for six miles to the light, then turned in the direction of Naples. Twenty-two minutes later, Juan was opening the barn door for Jose to drive in and hide the car.

All the lights were off in the house. That did not bother the brothers because they knew Anncherry would want to be able to see out and not have anybody know she was there. Up on the porch, the door was unlocked and they went in. Anncherry had seen them when they pulled into the driveway.

The cousins grabbed new drinks and sat at the table.

"We found him," Juan said. "It is the slim guy we ran into outside the restaurant when you got tangled up with those girls."

"I do not believe it," Anncherry said. "We had him in our grasp from the beginning and did not know it?"

"And get this," Jose proposed. "He owns a plane. The same plane we have seen on three occasions at the lake."

"We could have been home days ago if we had known this," Anncherry said.

"Do not forget though if fate had not taken us the way it did, we never would have found out about the eye treatment," Jose said. "I think we will all have a different life going forward. Part of me now thinks Juan is right. We have the target to thank for allowing us to have our eyes changed."

"Do not tell me you have spent a few hours out with Juan, and he convinced you to turn soft. Am I the only one who cares anymore?"

"It is not like that. We both care also, but we are trying to see the complete picture. It would be like cutting your losses and going home."

"What losses are you referring to?" Anncherry asked.

"The ones that would land us in jail," Jose replied. "Who knows what mistakes could fall upon us. Do not forget we are in America. Back home, we could sweet-talk our way out of anything we did. That would not be the same here. They lock you up and throw away the key if you are a foreigner bent on attacking their people."

"I do not believe my ears. Are the two of you backing away from our job? You would let this toad order Uncle Paul's leg broke and get away with it? The two of you have definitely turned soft."

"For all we know, Uncle Paul stole money from this guy," Juan said. "He was no saint. We all know of problems he has caused for his own family."

"Uncle Paul was the worst thief we knew," Anncherry said, "and do not forget he was the only one who cared about us, and was never selfish with anyone in our family. I can only remember good times with him."

"He had his hand in everyone's pocket," Juan said, "and he never stopped grabbing money as long as his hand stayed there. You say he never did anything to go against our wishes, but you do not truly know that. He was very slippery."

The cousins all finished their beers and Anncherry brought another round. They may argue, but they were still best friends.

"I am not going home without finishing what we came to do," Anncherry said. "If I have to do it myself, I will get the job done."

"We have no intention of walking away from this and forcing it all on you," Jose said. "We only thought it would be worth a little further discussion. We had the talk and respect your position. We will finish the job. Right, Juan?"

"I am with the both of you, and you know it. I am also appreciative of the things that happened while we were here. To me, we are riding a high, and I would be proud to go home with that feeling. It gives me a nervous twitch that something might happen and ruin things for us. As of right now, there is no blood on our hands. No one can tie us to anything that has happened. I am in hopes it remains that way."

"We will be careful," Anncherry said. "Let us enjoy some more beers. How about we take a few with us, and go out for a walk on our new land?"

The brothers agreed, and they set off for a night-time stroll. They were going to sleep well tonight while dreaming of being home soon.

Chapter 23

Jim saw the car lights shining through the woods. It was still early October and not unusual for an owner to come by his camp for the weekend. Sometimes people were just nosy and would drive in the road to see if there were any camps on the water with "For Sale" signs on them. Or it could be kids looking for a place to park.

Then again, it could also be the people who were looking for him. But he doubted that. He lived out in the woods with no mailing address. Because it was a private dirt road, he was forced to keep a post office box in town. The postal service didn't travel on private roads. Only roads properly maintained by the state or town.

The people who owned the camps on Jim's road didn't get any town or state benefits like those who lived on town maintained roads. If the road needed to be plowed, you had to plow it. If it was a sheet of ice, you had to get it sanded. If you called in a fire or needed an ambulance in the winter, they wanted a fresh layer of sand put down before they would come in. Not good if you suffered a heart attack or had a burning home.

Even in the summer months when the camps were used more often, there was very little traffic. Seeing lights tonight wasn't a cause for alarm but did warrant further investigation. Armed with his newly purchased 20-foot wasp spray weapon, Jim opened the door of the house and told Sharon to keep it locked until he got back.

A mercury vapor light was installed high in a tree so it would give off the maximum amount of exposure over a large area. The lakefront lot had many trees, and the light did a good job with protection. The back lot with the tennis court had no trees and was completely lit up.

The only part of land that was unlit was the dock space where he had the boat and his plane. There was a motion light that lit up the entire area when necessary. Anyone who got near the dock by boat or on foot would trigger the light to come on. Jim never had any problems with theft or vandalism, and he wanted to keep it that way.

The vapor light was high above Jim's two-car garage which offered the only available shaded location facing the direction of the unknown car. He stayed out of sight in the shadows of the garage while he listened for anything happening a few camps away.

The sound of someone quietly closing a car door could be heard, and then a car engine was started. Jim walked out to the well-lit roadway behind the garage and headed towards the car. It pulled out of the driveway three camps down and sped off. It was pitch black and too far away to see what type of vehicle they had. He would have been happy with a plate number.

Jim continued to where the car pulled out so he could make sure no one had broken into a neighbor's camp. After trying the doors and checking the windows, he was sure no one had gotten in. He walked back home and rapped on the door. Sharon didn't answer it. Maybe she couldn't hear him. He rapped again and louder. Still no sign of her.

He knew better than to overreact, but where was she? He went down around to the front and tried that door. Locked. And it should have been. Jim tried looking in through the windows, but she couldn't be seen. Hearing the side door open and her voice calling his name brought relief.

"Jim!"

"Be right up!"

He reached the side door while she was holding it open.

"Sorry," she said. "I had a bathroom moment."

"Well, you definitely had my heart rate up."

Together they entered the house, and Jim closed and locked the door. He told her what he saw and that everything seemed fine.

"What do you say we have a glass of wine and then go to bed?" Jim asked.

"I like that idea."

The glass of wine turned to another, and then they went to bed. A good night's sleep after a day of fun with good company. It didn't get a lot better than that.

Chapter 24

Sleep came fast for both of them and morning just as quick. After breakfast, Sharon turned on the computer so she could check on travel to Aruba. Her first check showed no seats available on flights from the Portland Jetport. Those planes would make a connection in New York and then would have gone on to Aruba. The only other choice was to fly out of Boston, which would be a four and a half hour direct non-stop trip. They'd have to drive to Boston first and that would take close to three hours.

After checking various other airlines, she found many with room, but all were expensive.

"Remember when we used to catch a last-minute flight to Aruba for $200 round trip? It looks like those days are gone. The seats I see available are $800 apiece. And then we can't get two together."

"Is that everything that's available?" Jim asked.

"There are some more here. Give me a few minutes."

After a short while, she was done checking.

"The $800 flights are the best out there. It leaves at 7:15 in the morning, which would be good for us. But once we pay for food and extras, we're looking at a $2500 quick trip. I'm not sure it's worth considering."

"I'm not so sure either," Jim said. "The other thing I hadn't thought of was a money exchange. If we sit in on the closing and ask for a check, it'll be in florins. We'd have to arrange for an exchange, and a sum that size would need to be deposited. A request to forward the funds into our account back here would be created, and we both know the cost of converting the money to dollars, and then having it wired through many

Glassy Water

banks until it finally arrives at ours. Everybody who has anything to do with the transfer takes a cut for themselves. Then there is the fee to the government. It's expensive."

"I wish we could go back in time and do this whole deal over again," Sharon said. "If we'd known how a foreign country taxed our money when we wanted to bring it back here, we wouldn't have made the investments. I would never recommend buying real estate in Aruba."

"Nobody ever told us we had to pay such a large fee to take our money back out. I don't know if other countries are like that, but Aruba is real bad. I would go out of my way to dissuade anyone from investing there. The government charges a sizable tax penalty for taking the money off the island. And that should be a crime itself."

"You've succeeded in ruining my day. I've lost any interest in ever going back there."

"Then I guess that settles it. It would be less stress for both of us if we decide to let the notary transfer the money to the bank, and then have the bank forward the funds here. I'll call the broker at his office tomorrow and give him those instructions. Are we agreed?"

"I think so," Sharon said. "What are you going to do about the truck?"

Jim and Sharon had bought a truck from a nephew of Paul's that was supposed to be in great condition. An 01 Dodge Dakota King Cab with a five-foot bed. Perfect for what they needed it for. The only problem was they trusted Paul and took his word for the truck's condition. The nephew did bring it by the house the night before it was to be paid for. It did look good. In the dark. Supposedly, the entire front end had been rebuilt at a substantial cost. But that's where the misunderstanding began, and they should have known something was up the next day when the nephew insisted on being picked up in their rental car so they could go to the bank and pay him.

The fault was all theirs because they care for and trust their fellow human beings. Although these things occur occasionally over the course of your life, for some reason Jim and

Philip Gagnon

Sharon never gave up on the hope they'd be dealt with fairly. Was it too much to ask for in life that you would like to be treated the same as you would treat others? It was such a shame all men were not created equal.

The truck was paid for and delivered. Everything looked good while sitting in the driveway. When it was started, the engine rapped. A check of the steering showed it needed a whole new front end. *Must have heard him wrong on that one.* Money was spent and the truck fixed. Simple as that. Later, Jim would think having a leg broke on two different people would be worth the money.

Their Dutch neighbor's name was HeRon. He was rich because of his inheritance and smart enough not to trust even his own wife. When he purchased property, the deed would be in his name only because as he put it, "You never know if she might leave me." And like most people Sharon and Jim ever came to know who were wealthy, the main event here was me, me, and more for me. That's also the same guy who came up with the idea of breaking legs. Jim was almost certain now that HeRon set him up for a money grab. But other than Paul, there was no one else on the island they knew.

HeRon also owed them big time. On numerous occasions, he needed help with his equipment and Jim was the guy he'd call. Even though he tried to pay him for his time, Jim would never take anything. Jim was glad to be of help. HeRon soon figured out the good deal and would show up at their house almost every day for help. He could at the very least move the truck.

Wishful thinking.

The people who were buying their house wanted the truck off the property. Who else but HeRon could easily move it for them. His house was 100 yards away.

"I'll call HeRon this morning and see if he can keep it in his yard and then sell it for us," Jim said. "I don't know what else we can do with it."

"We don't have many choices do we?" Sharon said. "We either go and deal with everything on our own or wait and see how our friend will take care of us. Do you think he'll sell it and send us the money?"

"I would plan on him cheating us, and then we won't be quite as disappointed. I'll call him now and be done with it."

Jim looked the number up in a directory he kept on his desk and dialed. HeRon answered on the third ring.

"Hi, HeRon, this is Jim Kamae. How are you?"

"Jim! I am well and yourself?"

There was a slight delay after every word spoken.

"Good, thanks. HeRon, I have new buyers who moved the closing up to the middle of the week, and I can't come down that soon. I need my truck moved off the property. Is there a chance you could move it for me?"

The other end of the line was silent for what seemed like thirty seconds. Jim knew the wheels were turning while burning rubber in the heat.

"I think I can be of help. What shall I do with it?"

The roundabout way of saying, "Will it be mine to keep for free?"

"Can you keep it in your yard and sell it for me?" Jim asked.

An obvious insult. It suggested work of some kind. Everything the guy said was measured.

"I'm not so sure. You know I have much materials in the yard while I build the house."

Or in other words, "I can't believe you ask a favor of me and offer nothing in return. Just give me the truck!"

"If it's going to be a problem for you, I can ask someone else," Jim said.

Like who??

"No, it will not be a problem. I will find a way to make these things work for you."

And you will owe me dearly in return.

"Thanks, HeRon. I knew I could trust you to get the job done."

Really?!

"Yes, I will do this for you. Have you been told of any news from down here?"

"You're the only person I talk to other than the broker."

And thank God for that!

"Ah yes, well, he would not know of any connection, so he would not have told you. Your friend, Paul, is dead. He and his sons were hit by a car out in front of a bar. All three are dead. But the real story, as I am told it, is he sent family over to find you and pay you back."

"That's all crazy," Jim said. "When did this happen?"

It was one of those moments where recent events were flooding through his mind and taking priority over all other thoughts, while at the same time he was really interested in what he was hearing on the phone. Jim moved to a room where he could speak privately.

"I have just learned of it last night. I was going to call you today and let you know."

Uh huh! Right, you were!

"Tell me what you heard."

"Only that your man and his two sons were run over. He had three relatives who were dispatched to repay you for what you ordered done to him."

You mean what you suggested I have done to him, like, "They do it all the time." What a swine!!

"Do you know who sent them?" Jim asked.

"I heard it was your friend, Paul, who sent them, but he was killed in an accident just before they left," HeRon said.

"Do you know their names?"

"I do not. But I can try and find out."

And how much would that cost me?!

"Do you know how the word leaked out that I was the one who paid to have harm done to him?"

"No. I only know it is a small island and loyalty here is very shallow."

Tell me about it!

"Okay, thanks for the information," Jim said, "and thank you for helping with the truck. Can you move it today?"

"I was leaving with my family for a breakfast on the beach and then some quality time with the kids. But I will somehow find a way as it is your wish."

I'm sure you will! Start the truck and move it a couple hundred feet. Such a chore. Oh, I forgot. Open the door to the truck and close the door to the truck. He'll be all worn out. And he hates his kids. I can't imagine what quality time with them would be like.

"Thank you again. Bye." Jim wanted to ask more questions but knew that would get him nowhere while at the same time making HeRon think he was to blame. Somehow, Jim felt deep down that everything pointed to his Dutch neighbor as the instigator.

"I didn't hear much, but I don't have to ask how that went," Sharon said.

"It went just as I expected, and I learned a few things. Paul and his two sons were hit by a car and killed in front of a bar."

"That's terrible! I hope they caught the person who's responsible."

"I don't know about that, but why don't you go on the Diario website and see if you can find anything?" Jim asked.

"Okay."

Jim wanted to tell her more because he loved and trusted his wife, but at the same time, he wanted to protect her from the stupid things he'd done. He would hopefully only have to tell a couple of lies.

"He also said before Paul was killed, he sent some relatives of his over here to find me. HeRon heard it was because I owed him money. I'm not sure what he's talking about, but now things are beginning to come together."

"Why would Paul say that when he had so much of our money?"

"I don't know," Jim said, hoping the subject changed quickly.

"You think those people asking about you at Richard's are his relatives?"

"The same ones we met outside of Richard's that spoke Papiamento, and the same ones we ran into on Lake Paul in the middle of the night. I should have put it together when Sam told me they knew who I was. I wouldn't be surprised if it was them who parked up the road last night."

The phone rang, and Jim answered it.

"Hello?"

"Hey, it's Sam. I just called Rupert's house. I didn't talk to him, but he has company. That's probably why he didn't show up yesterday."

A bomb exploded in Jim's head.

"Who's the company?"

"They didn't say, and I didn't think it was my right to ask. I talked with a guy who told me they were visiting for a few days. He said Rupert was outside doing some chores and would tell him I called."

"Did you call Jill?"

"No, I called you first."

"Well, let me tell you a story."

He filled Sam in on the phone call he had with HeRon in Aruba. Then he gave him his take on what he thought was happening.

"But that doesn't seem possible," Sam said. "It's not that small of a world. How could they have ended up here all the way from Aruba?"

"It is a small world and that's the beauty of the internet. Sometimes it works for you, and sometimes it works against you. Either way, anything you need to know is at your fingertips. And their initial information would have been given to them by my friend before he died."

"Okay, I'll need some time to think about this," Sam said. "So you're assuming they were the ones living in the woods on Rupert's land and are now visiting with him? That doesn't make any sense. Why would the old-timer have anything to do with them?"

"It's only a gut feeling about them being at Rupert's. I could be completely wrong. It could really be his relatives, but he said he had no family he was close to. We haven't known him long enough to guess one way or the other."

"Should I call Jill? She said she could stop over and check

on Rupert."

"Do that," Jim said. "Ask her to get back to you so you know. See if she's busy this afternoon also. If she comes away from Rupert's with the information I think she will, then we need to get together. Let me know."

"You got it."

Jim hung up and filled Sharon in on what he'd been told. She was on the Diario website and found what might be an article about their late friend. But it was in Papiamento. There were papers written in English published on the island, but they wouldn't have any of the gory details associated with a death. They didn't want their visitors from away to think anything like that could happen on their "Piece of Paradise." The Diario would have pictures of a decapitated body on the front page. You know, the stuff that sells papers but only to those who could read Papiamento.

He looked over Sharon's shoulder and translated what he read.

"It says here that Paul and his sons were run down in front of the Talk of the Town Restaurant and Motel. The driver and the car that hit them were not found as of yet and there were no witness accounts clear enough to help with the identification of the car."

Jim and Sharon knew the Talk of the Town well. Back in 1994, which was their first time on the island, Jim's sister, Theresa, had arranged a trip to Aruba with them staying at the Talk of the Town for a week. At that time, the motel was busy and in good condition. The restaurant was open, and they ate there a number of times. The whole experience was another one of the reasons they came back and bought later.

Jim read the entire story, but it was more tailored to how Paul and his sons were well respected on the island and would be sorely missed.

How many times do you read an article that portrays a person as a saint when you had first-hand knowledge they were anything but? Must be a universal issue.

"That's about it," Jim said. "See if you can find an

obituary for him. I'm curious to see who he had for relatives."

While Sharon searched for the information, Jim called his good friend, Richard.

"Morning, it's Jim. How are you today?"

"Good, thanks. What's up?"

Why does he have to say that?!

"After we left last night, did you happen to see those people who were asking for me earlier in the week?"

"No, I didn't. I was stuck in the kitchen after you left."

"Is Rene coming in today to work?" Jim asked.

"She loves the weekend tips," Richard said. "I can't keep her out of here."

"Could you have her call me when she comes in? I may even be down later for a drink, but have her try me anyway."

"Okay, is everything good?"

"Yes, for now, everything is good."

"Okay, see you soon."

"I didn't find an obituary, but here's something else that's interesting," Sharon said while gesturing at the computer screen. "Take a look at this."

"That's our house!" Jim screamed.

"That's what I thought too. What does the article say?"

"That it's to be sold at auction for non-payment of taxes."

"Jim, I've always let you deal with that. We pay all our bills. How is this possible?"

"Because they're a bunch of idiots, that's how. I have spent days sitting in the tax department offices trying to get them to straighten out the taxes on the house. I thought when we left it was all set."

"It's anything but all set! They're trying to tax foreclose our home! You have to do something about it!" Sharon was hysterical now and rightly so.

It would be hard without the proper knowledge to condemn every foreign island in the land but easy to do so with Aruba. If you purchased a government lot with a lease on it, you were guaranteed economic rights to that lot for a 60-year period which started when the lease began and with rights to continue, meaning that unless they decide to put a highway or other road through the land or something else, like, say an airport, you would probably be given another 60-year lease.

The problem is the government doesn't recognize you as an owner of the land even after you were given a deed to the property. Title to the land didn't transfer to you until after you had filed the proper paperwork with the right authority, which authority no one seemed to recognize, and only after a three-year period had expired, and then it was a crapshoot at best.

Before you could file the required paperwork, the home must be completed. Working on Aruban work schedules, that could, and would, take years. Then the proper authority must inspect the home. That was another roll of the dice. You would not be communicated with to know if it would happen or when. Going and beating your gums at the numerous government offices got you nothing in return except a nice thin set of well-exercised lips.

What happened then was the tax bills were sent to the title owner of the land. He, or she, was not going to forward those bills to you, nor would they pay them. He wanted the property to be tax foreclosed so he could bid at the sale. If you didn't step forward and pay the delinquencies, you would lose the house. If there was not a mortgage given by a local bank, there was nothing to stop him. And never would you receive anything by way of postal or via e-mail alerting you to any past due amounts. Even though they had all the information to notify you, it wouldn't happen.

Even after pleading for years to have bills sent so you could stay notified of payments due, you would never see anything in the mail from the tax department. They would not even talk to you after you built a quarter-million dollar home on the property. Because the land was in the name of a different title owner, they could only speak with him or her. Desperate now, you set out to locate the title owner, only to find he relocated from the island months before. But rest assured, he was getting all his mail sent to him. He was Aruban.

The most frustrating thing was that the taxes must be paid,

and Jim's were always paid on time. When the payments you would owe were made, nothing was recorded in your name and were instead applied to any delinquencies the title owner may have on other property he owned. You go in every year with hopes that you'd be given something that would tell you where you were at, but you'd get the same ear full of, "We can't give that information out to anybody but the title owner of the property."

After seeing their house in the paper, the reality of it all began to sink in. And the thought that HeRon and his realtor probably knew about it and didn't tell Jim made him sick. It was all Jim's fault for insisting they go there in the first place. Then trusting people who didn't deserve to be trusted was his second mistake. Hatred was now consuming him, and he made a decision then and there that something was going to change. Jim was going to get a gun, and people would pay. But first, he had to calm Sharon.

"Let's not jump to conclusions here," said Jim, who had already concluded how he would like to deal with this mess. "We've bought and sold a lot of real estate in our day, and why would the notary give a closing date if arrangements hadn't been made to effectuate clear title?"

"I'm totally lost in all of this!" Sharon cried. "How would I know?"

"I'll call the realtor and tell him we can't make the trip on such short notice. All the documents will be sent to us for review. I'll tell him we want an updated closing statement with all the current financial information on it. Let's wait and see what it looks like."

The phone rang, and it was Sam again.

"Jill just got back from Rupert's, but she didn't see him. He was busy somewhere on the property. She met one guy at the door, and another guy was at the kitchen table. I drilled her on their looks, and it appears they're genuine. I asked her three times about red eyes, and she said, 'Definitely not. No glasses on and no red eyes.' It can't be our friends."

"You're right," Jim said. "I just had a hunch. Did Jill say

Glassy Water

anything else?"

"Yes, but it's none of your business," Sam said.

"What's that supposed to mean?"

"Just that the girl thinks I'm neat and wants to see more of me."

"She said that?"

"No, but I could sense it in her voice. And she wants to get together for a beer. Okay, she said you could come too."

"Wow, Romeo, nice job. Maybe I can sleep between the two of you on your honeymoon."

"Don't get ahead of yourself, Swizzle-stick. You may not even get invited to the wedding."

"When does she want to have a drink?" Jim asked.

"Anytime this afternoon. You in?"

"Why don't you call her back and meet her over here? We can cruise around a little in the boat and then go to Richard's for a few."

"I like that. She did mention she would like to see the tennis court again. Maybe have a doubles match."

"Sounds like you had a heart to heart talk with the girl."

"Okay, I told her she needed to see it again. I know she really liked it."

"I like it too. Call me so we can plan."

"I will, bye."

Chapter 25

The cousins heard the four-wheeler enter the driveway, and Jose told Anncherry to disappear. The thought had crossed his mind that someone may show up after the phone call from Sam. He waited until the woman rider got off the machine and came up on the porch. The door opened just as she was going to knock.

"Sorry," Jose said. "I did not mean to startle you. We saw you pull into the driveway. That is after we heard you pull into the driveway."

"I didn't mean to be so noisy. I'm Rupert's neighbor, Jill. I live a little ways up the road from here. I just wanted to come by and check on him. I didn't realize he had company."

"We are relatives who are visiting for a few days. My name is Paul, and that is my brother, Phil. We are pleased to meet you, Jill."

"Pleased to meet the both of you, too. Is Rupert around?"

"He was fifteen minutes ago. He said he wanted to get a few things done out around the barn. Would you like me to go and see if I can find him for you?"

"No, that's all right. He was supposed to show up for a meeting yesterday but never came. He probably didn't come because you showed up."

"We did show up yesterday. I apologize for changing his plans."

"It's not a problem," Jill said. "I was only concerned for him. I'm sorry to have bothered you."

"No bother at all. It was a pleasure to have made your acquaintance. Have a nice day."

"You too, bye."

As she backed her four-wheeler out of the driveway, Jill felt sure those guys were the real thing. She saw nothing that would have made her think otherwise.

"Is she going to be a problem?" Anncherry asked.

"Not in a way I can see," Jose theorized. "Just a curious neighbor who lives out of sight of the house. That is what I really like about these homes. You cannot see any others that are nearby. Even if she was a problem, the solution would be quick and easy."

The cousins were in agreement. It was no problem.

Chapter 26

After Jill returned home, she called Sam. "I just got back from Rupert's after meeting the relatives, but he was busy out on the property, so I never saw him."

"Does everything seem on the level with you?" Sam asked.

"I thought so. Two guys with short hair and clean-cut faces. Spoke intelligently and seemed genuine. Little bit of an accent. And I did notice the one guy I spoke with didn't contract his words."

"Some southerners have some strange twists on the English language. Did they have sunglasses on?"

"No, no sunglasses."

"So you got a good look at their eyes?"

"I did, why?" Jill asked.

"Just curious. They didn't look to be bloodshot or anything?"

"Looked normal to me."

"Only the two guys?" Sam asked.

"That's all I saw. The one I spoke with at the door offered to go and find Rupert for me, but I told him it was fine. That I was checking on him because he missed a meeting yesterday. He told me they arrived yesterday which would explain it."

"Okay, thanks for taking the time to check on him."

"No problem," Jill said. "Are you busy this afternoon?"

"What did you have in mind?"

"Nothing special. Maybe a few drinks at Richard's. Do you think Jim and Sharon would be interested?"

"I can ask them if you like."

"Don't sound so negative."

"Sorry, I thought you were thinking of just the two of us."

"Not at Richard's. Maybe another time, in another place."

"Is that a promise?"

"Can be."

"Can't ask for more than that. Could I?" Sam asked.

"You can certainly try," Jill said.

"Well, how about a doubles match with Jim and Sharon? We show up with our own gear and take it to them."

"I like that plan. Do you want to ask them first?"

"I've got to call him now. Have your gear ready, and I'll get right back to you."

"I'm all packed and ready to go."

"Maybe we could wear matching outfits?" Sam asked.

"What did you have in mind?"

"Hot pants and a halter top. It'll drive Jim batty, and he'll double fault every time."

"Dream on, big fella."

"Okay, I will. Bye."

"Bye, Cutie."

She had to say that...

Chapter 27

Sam and Jill agreed to meet at Jim's. The four of them would go out in Jim's boat, and if there was time when they returned, there would be a tennis match.

Down on the dock, Jim climbed into the boat and started her up. He liked having the engine nice and warm before heading out. The boat was a wooden mahogany 1965 Chris Craft Super Sport that was 20 feet long. The 327 cubic inch displacement 210 horsepower motor was more than adequate for pushing the wooden log through the water. Topping out at 42 miles an hour, the boat would get up and go.

But Jim liked putting around more than anything. Being what was considered a "Utility Boat" because the engine was in the center, she would seat five people comfortably. It was also an inexpensive wooden boat and sharp to look at with its molded fins attached to the side of her, reminiscent of the old cars from the past.

They set out to cruise the shoreline and take in the foliage surrounding the area. Although some of the leaves had blown or dropped off the trees, the coloring still available to be seen was spectacular. The tour included a viewing of the entrance to Tenny River, which connected Panther Pond to Crescent Lake and was navigable by most boats. Camp William Hinds had thousands of feet of frontage on the river as well as the frontage it had on Panther Pond.

Then there was the old music camp that was now a recreational resort known as Kingsley Pines. It butted up to Camp Timanous, which was a private camp for young boys.

There were many small privately-owned camps to pass

before coming to Plummerville, which was where Jim's parents started out. The owners of Plummerville had the most undeveloped frontage on the lake. The camps and land were currently managed by a well-respected family led by Ernest Allen. The rest of the waterfront was made up of camps and homes, and the lake itself encompassed over 1400 acres.

The entire trip was more than an hour and served its purpose by relaxing Jim and Sharon. With the winds calm and the temperatures mild, one could not ask for more.

Back at the dock, everyone got out of the boat and Jim secured it.

"I didn't know life could be so good," Jill said.

"This is definitely a special place for us," Sharon explained. "As we get older, we think we'd like to be in a warmer climate, but this is hard to leave. When our dogs passed away, we buried them here on the lot, and now we cry every time we leave for any length of time. We feel like we're deserting them."

"Sometimes, animals are as good or better than family members," Sam said. "When these two got the little Shih Tzu's, they had to go out and buy a king-size bed because the two little fellas would always lie on the bed sideways. That's what I call puppy love."

"They were our babies," Sharon said. "We'd love two more, but now that we're traveling, it would be too hard on them. We couldn't just leave them behind and go somewhere warm."

"I know the feeling," Jill agreed. "When we were brought up, we were taught to care and love all animals. It stays with you. I have one now that I also have a hard time being away from."

They walked up to the deck, and the four of them sat at the picnic table. Sam was thinking revenge.

"Are we on for a doubles match?"

"It's up to the girls," Jim said. "Personally, I think I'd rather have a few drinks and relax."

"It's too early for that," Sharon said. "Come on. Let's show our stuff and beat these guys."

"You mean kick their butts?" Jim joked.

"Call it what you want, but they won't stand a chance

against us," Sharon said, trying hard to get her mind off their problems.

"Do you want to use our rackets again?" Jim asked.

"Today, we're prepared," Sam said. "We brought our own weapons."

"In that case, there's nothing left to discuss," Jim said. "Let's play ball."

It was a great match and would have been good fun, but both Jim and Sharon had a lot on their minds. They gave it their best but came up on the losing end, 6 games to 4 and 6 games to 3. Sam was running his mouth again as if he was responsible for all the winning points. Jill couldn't make a mistake. She carried him all the way.

"Let's sit on the deck and have a beer," Jim suggested. "Time to relax."

The drinks were brought out and half gone when Sam's phone rang. It was Rupert's relative who he'd spoken with earlier.

"Hello, my name is Paul, the grandson of Rupert. Is this Sam?"

"Yes, Paul, this is Sam."

"I am sorry to bother you, but I do not know who else to call. Rupert went for a ride two hours ago on his horse and has not returned. We are worried that something might have gone wrong."

"It's still early in the day. Maybe he wanted to enjoy some extra time riding."

"He told us he would return in a half hour," Jose perjured. "Now, he is an hour and a half past that. Maybe we are being too cautious, but we did not want to wait until just before dark to let somebody know. We are new to the area and afraid of getting lost ourselves in the woods."

"You did the right thing calling me," Sam said. "I will check on a few things and call you back."

"Thank you, I appreciate it."

Sam explained in detail the call to his friends while the cousins were conniving in Naples.

"We can leave in the plane and be there in ten minutes,"

Jim said.

"I didn't think you'd want to fly because we had a drink."

"One beer shouldn't alter our decision making."

"I'll call and tell him we're on our way by plane."

"Can we go with you?" Jill asked.

"It would be better if you brought a vehicle in case we need it to drive around in," Jim said. "I'm thinking we'll buzz the shoreline a few times. Hopefully, he'll take the time and walk to the shore so he can see what's going on. Maybe we'll get lucky and spot him after we land."

"If we leave now in the car, we should be there in about half an hour," Jill said. "We'll get on the logging trails and see what we can find."

"Take my truck," Sam said, "and if you can't find us, make your way down to the lake and hang fluorescent tape on the tree branches. I have rolls of it under the seat. We'll keep an eye out for the tape if we're on the water. Use the tape on the logging trail to mark where you've been also. If we end up having to hike around looking for him, the markers will let us know you're in the area."

"Grab a roll so we can bring it with us in the plane," Jim said. "We'll mark the locations where we've been too. If we don't hook up before dark, we'll send up some flares, so look for them. We'll hold that position while you come to us."

"Got it," Jill said. "See you there. Let's go, Sharon."

Sam was running to the dock with the tape just as Jim had everything ready to leave. Nothing was being done to preflight the plane because there wasn't time. But Jim wasn't going to jump in and go without making sure of a few things.

He could tell by the way the plane sat on the surface that the floats were not loaded with water. The paint lines on the floats were another indicator of how much water they had in them. He knew how far above the waterline they were supposed to be.

Jim was through the door and Sam pushed off. He climbed aboard, and then Jim had the plane idling across the water in seconds. He waited for the cylinder head temperature to stabilize and then blew out of the cove on full power. The noise of the prop whipping through the air and amplifying the engine's exhaust was probably heard all the way up in Naples.

Less than six minutes later, they were descending down from 1000 feet to buzz the shoreline of Lake Paul. It would be extremely loud for anyone within a few miles of the water but that's the point, isn't it? To get some attention. At least someone's.

Once the shoreline strafing was finished, he landed the plane on the northern part of the lake not far from where they were supposed to meet Rupert yesterday. Jim and Sam decided to shut down the power while still away from the shoreline to see if they got anyone's attention.

"I know you've been concentrating on things, and I didn't want to bother you, but when I called Paul back he told me a neighbor had shown up and offered his help looking for Rupert," Sam said.

"What neighbor?" Jim asked.

"I didn't have time for details. He just said a neighbor had shown up and offered his help."

"How did the neighbor know he was missing?"

"I can't say. Oh, and he said he would try to locate us by hanging a white towel in a tree by the water, so we could compare notes about how to be organized in our search."

"Well, it can't hurt. The more people we have looking the better. At some point, if we can't locate him we'll need to notify the wardens. I think we'd be premature to do that now. The old boy probably wanted a little me time."

"I think you're right," Sam said. "I'm sure his company has already worn him thin. We were nice and did it in ten minutes."

"And we didn't even hang around afterward. I'm fairly positive he's just blowing off steam. Call the girls and see where they are."

"Wishful thinking. We don't have phone service here."

"Oh, I forgot," Jim said. "Okay, let's give this another five minutes, and then tie the plane up at the shoreline and search by foot."

Glassy Water

When it became apparent no one was waving anything anywhere that they could see, Jim started the engine and idled in towards shore.

"Over there," Sam said. "Down the lake a ways. A white flag."

"Okay, I see it. Why is he down there?"

"It doesn't make any sense unless maybe he's seen something."

The plane made its way towards the flag while both men were looking for a place to tie it up and jump ashore.

"About 150 feet to the left of the flag," Sam said. "It's still thick brush, but it's the only spot with a tree limb hanging over the water."

"How did he tie the flag where he did?" Jim said. "You can't see two feet into the woods in that area."

"Hopefully, it'll thin out a little as we get away from the water."

Twenty-five feet from land, Jim cut off the power and let the plane glide to shore. At the last second, he pressed hard left rudder to bring the plane sideways with the tree branch, and the nose of the plane pointed out towards the lake. Sam was out on the float and caught the branch, which broke in his hand.

"It's all rotten," Sam said. "It won't hold the plane."

"I don't want to take the time to look for another place to tie up," Jim said. "Why don't you hold it here while I go and look around? It might be easier for me in the thick brush because I'm so much smaller."

"I'll go if you want me to. I'm not afraid of a few scratches."

"Look at the brush even right here. I'm not so sure I can get through."

"Okay, you go ahead, and I'll see if I can find somewhere safe to tie this down," Sam said.

"If you do come in the woods, bring the flare gun kit with you. Otherwise, I'll come back and if we have to, we'll send the flares from here."

Jim gingerly walked to the back of the float being careful

not to submerge it. When he was as far as he dared to go, he jumped for the shoreline but landed in the water. It was only a foot deep, but it was cold. He glanced back at his friend to see if he was laughing. Sam was pretending to be looking down the shoreline of the lake with a big grin on his face.

He made his way to shore and entered the thick brush. It was almost impossible to penetrate the stuff. Thick wasn't the word for it. It felt like five minutes passed before the brush thinned out some, and even then it was still bad. He tried going sideways towards where the towel was tied to the tree, but that was the worst. It would be easiest to stay straight into the woods and find a logging road.

Jim wished now that he'd remembered to bring his compass. Being in a rush, he hadn't given it a thought. Another seven minutes passed, and he was at a logging road. On the road, he could see tire marks but nothing resembling the hoof-print of a horse. Rupert was not in this section of the woods.

Listening for any sounds that were unnatural and hearing none, he thought it would be best to move the plane to the north end of the lake, which was in the area where Rupert was to meet them yesterday. But he had to find out about the white flag first.

He headed at an angle towards where the flag would be and fought the thicket for a right-of-way. The cracking of branches was constant, but he stopped moving because he heard something. He waited before starting again and heard the noise clearly. It sounded like a male voice shouting for help.

The first thought that came to Jim's mind was that Rupert's neighbor had run into trouble. He waited until he heard the voice again. Then he fixed on the direction it came from and went that way. It took him into heavier brush, so he turned and went back out towards the road.

On the road, Jim jogged in the direction he believed was the right one. He stopped and listened for the voice again. It was coming from his right side in the brush towards the lake. He continued on the road until he was in line with the voice and the water. It appeared to be quite a bit farther from where he'd seen the white flag.

Glassy Water

He entered the brush and pushed forward until coming upon a small opening that had a few bushes in it. *It would be nice going if all of the woods were like this,* he thought. The voice was coming from straight ahead, and he walked that way. His leading foot never touched the ground as he was blindsided and everything went black. He hit the ground with a loud "Whomp!" and didn't move.

Anncherry was standing over him as Jose approached from the rear. He called for Juan to come out from the brush.

"Good work," Jose said. "He is out like a light."

"He never saw what hit him," Anncherry said, "and this space in the woods was such a great find. He will have a hard time finding his way out when he wakes up."

"Let us get this job done," Jose said and grabbed Jim's leg. It took both he and Anncherry twisting and pulling, but it finally went "Snap!" The victim moaned, and his body rumbled like there was an earthquake inside of him.

"How long will he be out for?" Juan asked.

"Not long," Anncherry replied. "I caught him square in the temple."

"Then we best get going," Jose said. "This could not have been more perfect."

The cousins worked their way out of the brush and then walked the logging trail to where the Impala was hidden in the woods. They left the trails and went back to the farmhouse where the beers would flow. Tonight they would celebrate a job well done. "Well-done" like a steak. The trio decided to go to a restaurant for a big juicy steak dinner after a few beers at home.

Chapter 28

Jill and Sharon had been driving along the logging trails at the north end of the lake because that's where Jill assumed Rupert would be riding. They moved down the eastern side and were going slowly with their windows open. With no signs of tape or anything else to let them know anyone was in the area, Jill was thinking the others may be concentrating on the other shoreline.

When the two of them did stop and get out of the truck, they checked the trail for any hoof marks. The ones that could be seen were not fresh. Some tire marks seemed recent but that's it. The trails were so widespread that even Jill wasn't sure where they were.

It became a nasty habit to keep checking their cell phones for service. Jill was also thinking if the guys did launch a flare into the sky, they'd be hard-pressed to see it during daylight hours and only a slight chance if it was dark. The canopy overhead was that thick.

Continuing on for another fifteen minutes, the girls were in agreement they didn't know where they were, so the truck was stopped.

"I didn't think for a second it would have been like a maze," Jill said. "I'm completely lost."

"I was lost when we drove into the woods," Sharon said. "I was hoping you had some idea of where we were."

"I did when we first started out but never could have imagined how complex these road directions were. I'm afraid if we don't try to find the main road now, we may be spending the night out here."

"If I thought we were helping in some way, I'd say let's

stay and look some more, but you're right. We've been at it for quite some time, and from what I've seen, we're not even in the same town as they are."

"The sun sets in the west, and we're on the east side of the lake," Jill said. "If we keep it to our back, we'll eventually hit the main road. Keep your fingers crossed."

There were no immediate roads that went in an eastern direction, so they stayed straight for the time being. Lucky for Jim that they did. The truck came around a corner, and the girls spotted what looked like a body in the road.

"My God, what is that?" Sharon asked. Jill had an idea but wanted to get closer.

"Is that my Jim?" Sharon shrieked. They were both out of the truck before it actually came to a stop.

Jim was in a fetal position with one leg straight out. He was in serious pain and semiconscious. Sharon was hysterical.

"Tell me what's wrong," Jill said to Jim.

"My leg is killing me."

Jill put her hand on his stretched out leg, and he screamed.

"I think it's broken," Jill said. "Sharon, bring the truck over right next to us so we can get him in."

Sharon must have been in shock because she did nothing. Jill stood up and talked straight to her face.

"Sharon, Jim needs your help. You have to get the truck and bring it over here."

The tears were running down her face, and she didn't move. So Jill slapped her. Hard.

"Why'd you do that?" Sharon cried.

"Because you were in shock. Jim needs your help. Can you do it?"

"I'm sorry. What should I do?"

"Bring the truck over here and line the door up so it's beside Jim. I'll tell you when to stop."

Sharon went to the truck and got in. She seemed to be fumbling around with something in the front but then started it up and slowly moved up beside them.

"In a little closer to me," Jill said. "Good, another foot

forward. Stop right there." She did and then was out of the truck and over to help.

"We need to get him up into the seat," Jill said. "Can you use your other leg to help us?"

"I think so," Jim sobbed.

Together they worked him up into the front seat of the truck and got him situated in the middle. He was screaming constantly, and the girls could really feel his pain.

"Let's head to the hospital and get you fixed up," Jill said.

"No, not yet," Jim moaned. "I'm sorry, but I'm real dizzy. Sam had to stay with the plane. We have to tell him to leave."

"How do we find him?" Jill said. "Or do you want me to lay on the horn and hope he comes to us."

After looking around and checking with his mental compass, Jim believed the plane was behind them.

"Can you back up about a quarter mile?" Jim said. "I'm a little disoriented right now, but I came south on the logging road to get here. If going back is north, then that's where he is. I tied some fluorescent tape on a branch where I came out of the woods onto the logging road."

Jill put the truck in reverse and began backing up.

"What about my idea of blowing the horn?" Jill said. "Will he come to us if he hears it?"

"I think he'd try coming to the sound, but the brush is so thick it would take him a half hour to reach us," Jim said. "It would be better if we blow the horn while you make your way towards him and hope to meet about halfway."

Jill stopped the truck when the fluorescent tape was next to the door. It was only a small piece and could easily be missed.

"Straight towards the lake?" she asked.

"As straight as you can go. If you have to go all the way to the plane, it'll take you ten minutes or so. Hopefully, he'll meet you and make it easier. Tell him to call us from the air."

"Got it."

After she disappeared in the brush, Jim held the horn button down. He didn't release it until two minutes passed. If Sam decided against leaving the plane, blowing the horn more wouldn't help.

It was a long wait, but seventeen minutes later they heard the sound of the plane's engine roar to life with full power on takeoff. No sign of Jill yet, so she must have had to go the full distance. Jim heard the familiar sound of the throttle being feathered back from the full power setting. Sam would be back home in a short time. It was so fast he wouldn't have time to call them on the phone. Not that they had service anyway.

Jill crawled out of the woods looking scratched up but in one piece. She climbed behind the wheel and started the motor.

"That was fun," she said. "I can't wait until I can come back and spend a whole day at it."

"Did Sam come to you?" Jim asked.

"He did, but not as far as I would have liked. Out to the edge of the road would have been better for me."

"I'm sorry. This is all my fault."

"Don't say that," Jill said. "We knew what we were getting into. Help me get out of here."

They did very well and were out of the woods in fifteen minutes. Three minutes later, they were on the main road going to Bridgton Hospital. Jim was in extreme pain and had tears staining his cheeks.

"Can you tell us what happened?" Jill asked.

"I honestly don't know," Jim sobbed. "We saw a white flag, and I was heading towards it when I heard a voice in the woods calling for help. I knew it wasn't Rupert because it sounded like a younger male. With the brush being so thick, I couldn't reach him without going back out to the logging road. I entered the woods where I thought he'd be, and the last thing I remember is putting a foot forward, but it didn't touch the ground. I must have stepped in a hole and hurt my leg. I blacked out, and when I woke up, I managed to crawl to the road. I can't even tell you how I knew which direction that was in."

"I think you broke the leg," Jill said. "You were lucky to be in the road. We were trying to find our way out of the woods. We didn't see any signs of Rupert or anything else."

"I wouldn't have made the night. You two saved my life."

"Why wasn't Sam with you? I thought that was the plan."

"It was. After we saw the flag on a branch by the shore of the lake, the closest we could get to it and tie the plane down was a few hundred feet north. When we got to shore, the branch we wanted to use was rotten, so Sam stayed there with it. I didn't think when you went into the woods, if he heard the horn and left the plane, he'd have to figure a way to secure it first. So you probably had to go most of the way through the brush. I wasn't thinking clearly."

"All that matters is you're safe," Jill said. "We'll have you fixed up in no time. Are you doing okay, Sharon?"

"I am now. Sorry about earlier."

"Nothing to be sorry about."

Jim's phone rang.

"Hello?"

"I only got a little of what happened from Jill," Sam said. "Are you okay?"

"Jill thinks I may have broken my leg. I fell in a hole."

"Ouch. That's not good. I know you're in good hands. I'm going to call Paul and tell him we're not involved anymore. Should I have him call the wardens?"

"I would if he doesn't have anything good to say."

"I'll call you right back after I talk to him."

"Wait! I just remembered something. I was following a voice in the woods some distance from where the flag was hanging from the tree. I was on my way to him when I fell. Someone's got to check him out."

"I'm in Jill's car coming your way," Sam said. "I can try to find him if you can tell me where to go."

"Okay, I can," Jim said. "Make the call to Paul. Then get back to me, and I'll tell you where he is."

"I will, bye."

"Is everything okay?" Jill asked.

"I can't believe I forgot about that guy. Here I am telling you the story about me, and I forgot he needed help too."

"We're just as guilty. We didn't give it a thought either."

They drove on in silence until Jim's phone rang again.

"Hello?"

"Paul told me Rupert's home," Sam echoed. "He'd come home not long after he talked to us. He said he tried to call me but there was no answer. I checked my phone for missed calls and there were none."

"Maybe because of where we were?" Jim said. "I've heard of that before. With no service in the woods the signal never went through."

"Okay, I also told him about the voice you heard, and he said the neighbor who offered to help has gone back home. He has no idea of who it could be. Do I still check it out?"

"I heard it, and it was a person," Jim said. "I mean, I think it was a person. I'm not sure what to do. Let me talk to Jill and call back. Where are you?"

"On 85, coming up to 302."

"I'll get right back to you." Jim ended the call.

"Everyone's accounted for except the voice in the woods?" Jill asked.

"Yes, what do you think?"

"Who put the white flag in the tree?"

"We were told it was a neighbor of Rupert's who was going to do it so we could get together with him and coordinate our search."

"Which neighbor?"

"We never asked. We were just happy for the extra eyes."

"And the neighbor is now accounted for?" Jill asked.

"Yes," Jim said. "He went home."

"Someone needs to at least check the location of that voice. Did I hear you say Sam would do it?"

"He offered to. He's in your car headed that way. Your car is an all-wheel-drive, so he could get in there without a problem."

"Tell him to do it. We have a half hour of daylight left. He'd be the best bet."

Jim called Sam back.

"Hi," Sam answered.

"Jill said you should check it out. Do you think you can get on the logging road that's parallel to the shoreline we were on?"

"Yes."

"I tied fluorescent tape to a tree where I came out of the woods when I first left you today. From there, I went south on the logging road about a quarter mile. That's where I heard the voice. It was between the road and the lake. I can only guess it was half the way in. Before you enter the brush, you might try calling out to see if you can get his attention."

"I'll be there in ten minutes. I'll call you when I get back out of the woods."

"Good luck," Jim said, "and be careful to watch for the hole I fell into."

"Got it," Sam said. "Just a reminder for you before using the plane again. The gas tank needles were bouncing off empty. I think I came in on fumes."

"Okay, thanks. I'll be sure to remember that. Bye."

The hospital was coming up on the right, so Jill entered the parking lot and proceeded to the emergency room entrance. A wheelchair was brought out, and Jim was helped into it. He was wheeled inside and taken to an examination room while Sharon and Jill stayed behind. Sharon was given the task of filling out the paperwork.

Nothing to do now but sit and wait.

Chapter 29

The cousins were having a few beers at the kitchen table when the phone rang. Jose took the call.

"Hello?"

"Hi, Paul, this is Sam. Have you heard anything about Rupert?"

"Yes, Sam, hi," Jose said. "I tried to call and tell you that Rupert came home on his own. It was not too long after I spoke with you. He lost track of time while having such a wonderful ride on his horse. I apologize for any inconvenience caused by this."

"As long as he's safe, that's the important thing. And the neighbor who came by to help. Did he return also?"

"He did. He has gone back to his home."

"Good," Sam said. "My friend told me he heard a voice in the woods that sounded like a man in need of help. Any idea who it could have been?"

"No idea. As I said, everyone is back."

"Okay, I'll talk to you later."

"OK." Jose ended the call.

"I think we should have a toast," Juan said. "To a job done well and a steak well-done. To us!"

The trio touched beers and emptied them. After two more rounds, they left for dinner at a restaurant in Windham called the Steakhouse Tavern. They decided to eat there and afterward go and park at Burger King so Jose could check for flights home on the computer.

At the tavern, the trio ordered drinks, appetizers, and then the 22-ounce "Prime Rib Dinner." The idea of the well-done steak disappeared when they saw the menu. They did not like their meat well-done anyway. Meat that was bleeding was more to their liking. All three ordered the dinner with the "Prime Rib" cooked rare. Juicy, bloody, rare. No one ever told them the meat had to be cooked to a minimum temperature to kill off any bacteria. *Oh well, party on cuz.*

They ate constantly for forty-five minutes straight. The waitress could not figure out where they put it all. The meal was washed down with four more beers and two bottles of Merlot wine. A waitress cleared the table when they were done, and after declining dessert in favor of another bottle of wine, the check was delivered. Jose laid his mother's credit card with the check and the waitress left with it. She was back in two minutes.

"Sorry, sir, but the credit card has been declined."

"Please run it through again," Jose said. "There must be a mistake."

"We did try it twice. It was declined both times. Do you have another card to use?"

"No, these credit card companies are such a pain. I will pay you with cash." And he did. But the generous tip given with the card was done away with.

Dragging themselves from the restaurant, the three of them climbed aboard their trusty wheels and set out for the nearest Burger King. Once there, they parked where they would be alone, and Jose turned on his computer. After many minutes of fumbling around with it, he said there was no signal. He could not access the internet.

"Anncherry, go in and see why there is no Wi-Fi," Jose said.

She did and returned with the goods.

"The equipment is offline until tomorrow."

"Why?"

"The girl behind the counter did not know why. She just shrugged her shoulders."

Any other time, that kind of an answer would have had Anncherry over the counter and punching the respondent. But tonight was different. She had a burning sensation inside that was unlike those of past. And the booze had mellowed her attitude.

"We will come back tomorrow then," Jose said.

He started the car and left Burger King for Naples. Halfway home things began to happen. Anncherry's 114-pound frame was the first to lose it. She barfed all over the back seat of the car. She could see all the good tasting food and drink scattered around her. Chewed pieces of meat came out larger than when they went in. The stench was caught by the brothers, and then they, too, became violently ill.

An orchestra could not have played it better. At times, they would all barf together, and then one by one they tried to sing that tune. Needless to say, the car was a stinky mess, and Jose finally made his way into the parking lot of a convenience store. He barely managed to get the car around the back and out of sight before he lost it all over himself. The other two had already done that.

For the next half hour, the cousins barfed and dry heaved until their stomachs were so sore they wanted to cut them out. No one said a word as Jose moved the car back out on the roadway towards Naples. There was still the occasional heave here and there but nothing like the spectacular sing-a-long performance of thirty-five minutes ago.

After pulling in the driveway of the farmhouse, Juan had all he could do to get out of the car and open the barn door. Anncherry had fallen out of her door and was lying lifeless on the ground. *Home sweet home,* she thought. *Just like back in Aruba.* She fought her way to her feet and went to the door where she ended up somehow leaving another round of solids. *God,* she thought to herself, *where was it all coming from?*

With the help of her brothers, and it did take all three of them to turn the doorknob, they fell in through the door onto the floor of the kitchen. One by one, they got up, went to the refrigerator for a beer to wash the mess down, and then went to bed where they would stay for what seemed like the next two days. Could have been food poisoning, but naw, they figured they had the brown bottle flu.

Chapter 30

Sam liked the little rig that Jill had. It was a Subaru Outback station wagon, and was loaded. Heated seats, power everything, and all-time symmetrical four-wheel-drive. The thing was unstoppable. And Sam needed that because he somehow entered the woods from the southern end of the lake, and those logging roads could not be used by anything but a four-wheel-drive vehicle.

There would be some mud on the car before he was done but knew Jill would understand. Thoughts of her crossed his mind as he braved the wilderness roads in the chariot she owned. If only she was with him, they could hold hands or something.

Sam was like Jim when it came to compass headings and directions. Before long, he was on the road that was closest to where he'd been earlier with the plane. He found the fluorescent tape Jim said he tied to a tree. Such a tiny piece he almost missed it. The Subaru was small enough that he could turn it around on the narrow logging road. He did so and reversed his direction. Checking the odometer, he stopped at a quarter mile. After shutting the car off, he got out and listened for any sounds. When nothing was heard, he walked in front of the car checking for marks in the dirt.

There was nothing to see but tire tracks. No scuff marks or footprints anywhere for 200 feet. Turning around, he went behind the car and began searching the dirt again. At 75 feet, he found an area full of shoe and scuff marks. *This must have been where they put Jim in the truck.* Sam listened intently but heard nothing. Calling out to try and get the attention of the lost person did not bring a response. He entered the woods and heavy brush. The sun was on the horizon now, so time wasn't on his side.

Forcing his way through, he eventually came to a small opening in the brush. Looking down, there were leaves kicked aside and marks left in the ground. Continuing on, he entered the brush again and called out to anyone who might hear him. After reaching the shoreline seven minutes later, and then moving 20 feet to the north, the trip back towards the road began. Occasionally, he would stop and listen, then yell again.

When he got back to the car, the sun had set and it was getting dark. Sam wanted to be long gone by the time nightfall hit. After the car was started, he took off in the direction of the main road. The woods gave him goosebumps. It was as if he could feel all the eyes that were watching his every move, waiting for a chance to have a fresh meal. His eyes darted from side to side when he should have been keeping them on the road. Sam could swear he saw sets of eyes in the brush. Later, he would swear the eyes were red. Something was definitely red.

Back on the main road, Sam dug out his phone and called Jim. Sharon answered.

"Hello?"

"Hi, Sharon, it's Sam. How is he?"

"The doctor said he'll be fine. His leg was broken, and they reset it. They're getting a cast on him now. We'll be able to leave as soon as the cast is done. He said it would be about half an hour. That was forty-five minutes ago."

"Okay, I'm at least fifteen minutes away. I'll wait for you at the causeway in Naples. Look for Jill's car in front of Rick's Café."

"We will. Thanks for calling, Sam."

"You're welcome, bye."

Sam drove over to the Alive'n Well Pharmacy and bought a newspaper to read while he waited. They would be at least a half hour. Just as he was backing the car into a space in front of the café, the phone rang, and he dug it out of his pocket.

"Hi."

"It's Jill. Is everything okay?"

"Everything's fine, thanks for asking."

"Don't be sarcastic with me! Out in the woods! What went on in the woods?"

"Oh, and I thought you cared," Sam said. "I found tracks in the road that indicated a scuffle of some kind, or maybe it was where you helped Jim into the truck. I went straight in from that spot towards the shore and came to a small clearing that showed signs of activity."

"What kind of activity?"

"Same as in the road. A scuffle or something being dragged around. Other than that I didn't see or hear anything. I went all the way to the shore and then moved over 20 feet and went back to the road. Nothing anywhere except the footprints and scuff marks."

"Jim said there was a white flag tied to a tree," Jill said. "Did you see it?"

"Only from the water. We couldn't figure out how anyone could have gotten through the brush to tie it there. That brush was the thickest we'd seen."

"Why would someone put a flag where the brush was so thick?"

"Maybe they had some kind of a boat and put it on the branch from the water."

"I guess we don't need to report anything to the wardens," Jill said. "Jim is in a wheelchair now, and on his way to the exit. Sharon said we'll meet you in Naples. See you soon."

"See you in a bit, bye."

"No, wait. You didn't scratch my car any did you?"

"No way. I respect you more than that."

"I bet you do, bye."

"Bye."

Twenty-three minutes later the pickup pulled in next to the Subaru, and Jill rolled the window down.

"Fancy meeting you here," Jim blubbered from the passenger's side of the pickup.

"Don't pay any attention to him," Jill said. "He's on drugs."

"It'll probably be more comfortable for Jim in the pickup

Glassy Water

with the extra legroom," Sam said. "Why don't you come with me, Jill, and we'll follow them home?"

Jill got out of the truck and climbed into the passenger seat of her car while Sharon slid behind the wheel of the truck.

"See you at the house," Sharon called over to them.

Once they were on the road Jill began talking.

"I told Jim about your trip into the woods. He said when you entered the clearing, you should have seen the hole he fell into that broke his leg."

"I didn't see any hole. And I walked right through the clearing."

"Then you must have been in another area."

"Maybe, but the marks and footprints I saw were fresh. Today kind of fresh. How many different sets of fresh marks would you expect to find so close together? And the other marks in the clearing were where Jim said they would be. Directly towards the shoreline from the marks in the road."

"It all comes together except for the hole," Jill said. "That's why it doesn't work. We need a hole to break Jim's leg."

"Did the doctor see any other injuries on Jim?" Sam asked.

"He did have a nasty bruise on the side of his head. The doctor said he may have hit it when he went down."

"Or he was hit with something and didn't see it coming. You crawled through that brush. You could be a few feet away in the right colored clothing and not be seen."

"Sounds far fetched but so doesn't the hole if you didn't find it. And I remember now that Jim said he didn't know what happened to him. He said he must have fallen into a hole."

"I'm getting this funny feeling some people we don't like might have something to do with this."

"What do you mean by that?"

"I'm going to tell you something, and I want a promise you won't get mad," Sam said.

"Why would I get mad? Try me."

"When we first met you at Richard's, Jim was having a problem getting anywhere with the sheriff's department concerning the report we filed on the assault. A few hours before you showed up, a deputy called him and said he couldn't talk about an active investigation. What was frustrating about the whole thing was we had just seen the people who were involved in the assault, and we wanted to try and help the police locate them. The deputy blew Jim away and while he was giving him the riot act, the people drove off. You with me so far?"

"I got it all, so far," Jill said.

"Sorry, that's a Rupert expression. I guess I can't get the old-timer off my mind. Anyway, when you showed up in uniform and all friendly-like, we figured it might help to have a set of ears and eyes close to the front. We wanted to be your new friends."

"You wanted to use me? For information?"

"Now I can tell you're getting worked up over this, and maybe we should wait and finish the conversation at Jim and Sharon's."

"Why? So it can be three on one? I can't believe what I'm hearing! I was beginning to think you and I might have some chemistry together! Boy, did my bubble burst!"

"Please don't think that way," Sam pleaded. "It came out all wrong. And it was Jim's idea, not mine. I think a lot of you."

"Now it's his fault after you started the fiasco! I'm not sure I can trust you anymore! Call and ask them to pull over! I'm going home! Alone!"

Sam did as he was told, and Sharon pulled to the side of the road. Without being told to, Sam got out.

"Please, Jill. It wasn't meant the way it sounded."

"It sounded clear enough to me! Bye!"

She backed up, did a U-turn in the road, and headed for home. Sam came up on the passenger's side of the pickup to get in.

"Why don't you drive and I'll sit in the middle?" Sharon said. "Jim is dozing."

Doing as he was told, Sam came around the front of the truck so he could get in the driver's door when a car pulled up behind them and the blue lights came on. Sam froze in his steps. The deputy stopped and got out of the car while putting his hat on once he was clear of the door.

"Are you folks all right? Do you need assistance?" the deputy asked, trying to begin a conversation to see what he was dealing with.

"No, sir," Sam said. "We were pulled over so we could change drivers."

"Can I see your license and registration please?"

"Yes, sir." Sam opened the door and asked Sharon to retrieve the registration for him. Sam then handed the deputy his documents.

"You can get in the truck while I check these," the deputy said.

Again, Sam did as he was told and waited for the deputy to return. When he came back, he aimed the flashlight in the truck and saw Jim passed out.

"Has he been drinking?"

"No, Officer," Sharon said. "He just had a cast put on a broken leg and is on meds for the pain." Jim had his coat over the cast, so she removed it for the deputy to see.

"Sorry to hear that," the deputy said. "I hope he gets well soon. Here's your paperwork back. Have a nice evening."

"Thank you, we will," Sam said.

Sam put his blinker on and pulled back onto the roadway. He decided to sugar-coat his conversation with Jill for Sharon's sake. He told her she was tired.

"I don't mind telling you she's a nice person," Sharon said. "She was asking a lot of questions about you. I think she wants to get to know the real Sam."

Me and my big mouth, thought Sam. *I think I just saw the last of her.*

"If you get the chance to talk with her, I'd like getting to know her more too," Sam said, hoping Jill would reconsider.

"You can tell her yourself. I'm surprised you didn't already, but she's coming over tomorrow night for dinner. You're going to be her date."

Oh boy...

From there, they drove in silence until they turned on the

Philip Gagnon

dirt road to their home. Sam was thinking.

"Did Jim say anything else about the hole he fell into?" Sam said. "I mean, did he say he 'crawled out' of a hole or something like that?"

"I didn't hear a lot of what he said when we first found him, but on the way to the hospital, he was trying to remember exactly what happened," Sharon said. "He remembered seeing the opening in the woods and hearing the voice just beyond it towards the lake. He was looking in the direction the voice came from and not paying attention to where he was stepping. He thought he must have fallen into a hole and broke his leg."

"I went to that spot and didn't see a hole in the ground. Did he mention anything else that might have happened?"

Like he was ambushed?!

"No, he said he didn't remember. He figured he fell in a hole and passed out when his leg broke."

"Maybe after a good night's sleep he'll remember," Sam said.

"Why? Do you think something else happened?"

"I don't know, but thinking about it leaves a lot of questions. And what happened to the guy who was calling out for help? Where did he go? I crawled all through that area and found no sign of anyone."

"I'll ask him again in the morning."

They arrived at the house and together helped a groggy Jim from the pickup and into the home where they put him in bed. Sharon said she could handle it from there, so Sam left locking the door on his way out.

He climbed into his pickup and went home. Jill was on his mind, but he was alone, and she wasn't coming back.

Chapter 31

Anncherry was the first to wake up and her mouth felt like a herd of buffalo had run through it and left runny deposits on their way out. She had a pounding headache that would not stop. Getting out of bed, she stumbled to the bathroom where she hoped there would be aspirin. Large amounts of aspirin.

There were two thermometers in the medicine cabinet, one in a cup marked "Front" and another in a cup marked "Rear." Wanting to take her temperature, she reached for one of them but buckled over after feeling a sharp pain in her stomach. After a few minutes, she forgot about checking her temperature and spent another five minutes looking through the vanity drawers for anything close to aspirin. Anncherry gave up and went back to bed nearly falling over three times on the way. She had not felt so sick ever before in her life.

Lying in bed, her ears were filled with the sound of someone else bouncing off furniture and ending up in the bathroom where he proceeded to barf or dry heave. You would need solids to come up if you barfed, and she knew none of them had any left. *He must have the dry heaves,* she thought.

Hearing the same drawers opening and shutting, she knew he was looking for aspirin also. She would have called out and told him there was none if only the strength could be found to do so. Instead, she found herself begging God for mercy or death. Give me either, but make it quick and swift.

It was going to be a long day. Better to stay in bed with the pillow over her head and pray for a quick death.

Chapter 32

Jim was up and out of bed feeling better than he looked. Surprisingly, the cast on his leg made the situation very comfortable. He had taken a few pills for the pain during the night, but right now he was feeling good. He used the crutches the hospital gave him and went to the bathroom. When he returned to the bedroom, Sharon was up and putting on her robe.

"You look chipper this morning," she said.

"I feel okay. Other than a few itches I'm dying to scratch inside the cast, I'll be fine. What's for breakfast?"

"Anything you want. I'm staying home today to wait on you."

"You don't have to. I'll be fine."

"No, I want to. Maybe we can find the time to rethink what happened yesterday and deal with the things in Aruba. And don't forget we're having Jill and Sam over tonight."

"I totally forgot about that," Jim said. "Must have been something they gave me at the hospital."

"They definitely took care of you. You were out for most of the trip home. Do you remember anything about last night?"

"I remember going to the hospital but not much after they put me in a room. Must have been the start of happy time for me."

"Well, I'm sure it'll all be talked about tonight at dinner, so I won't bother you with it now," Sharon said.

"Speaking of the Aruba thing, did you get the chance to find Paul's obituary?"

"No, after I saw the picture of the house I never finished up. I'll do it this morning."

"I'll call the realtor and get things rolling with the

paperwork."

Jim grabbed his phone, found the number, and dialed his realtor. He didn't like using realtors to sell his real estate. They made you think they were working for you, but all they cared about was their commission which usually ended up being most of your equity. A realtor was nothing but a salesperson and had nothing to do with the legal end of a real estate closing.

Of course, they made you feel like you would not survive the process without their representation. The title company performed all legalities of the title work and all aspects of the closing transaction. The realtor at that point was a gopher who did what the title company requested, and you didn't need a license to be a gopher. Anyone could hire any title company to do the legal work and prepare the closing.

However, selling a property so far away would have been difficult without help.

His broker answered the phone. "Halo?"

"Esaki ta Jim Kamae en America. Con ta Bai, mi amigo?"

"Do not insult me with your bad knowledge of Papiamento. You speak it like a two-year-old."

"Sorry, Ray. How are you?"

"You already asked me that in your lousy Papiamento."

"Maybe you prefer I speak to you in a language you don't understand?"

"There are not many. Maybe Swahili. You are fluent in that one, yes?"

"I thought that's the same as Papiamento. I must have missed that day in school."

"Good to hear from you. And how are things? How is Sharon?"

"All is well, Sharon is fine," Jim lied. "She sends her best." *Liar.* "Things are good with you also I hope?" *Ahhhh....*

"Could not be better. You are calling about the closing, yes?"

"Yes. We can't make the trip on such short notice. Can you scan and e-mail the closing documents for us to review and FedEx the originals?"

"I can do that," Ray said. "They want to close by the middle of the week, so I will get the paperwork off to you this morning. The notary will prepare a package, and I will take it to FedEx myself."

"Good, thank you," Jim said. "Can you please ask the notary to include an up-to-date closing statement?"

"You do not want much now do you? I will ask, but you will get what they want to give you. I cannot tell you how up-to-date it will be."

"The reason I ask is we saw our house is on the auction block for delinquent taxes owed. You know my battle with them over the years. And you know I paid the taxes when they were due because I insisted you have copies of my receipts showing they were paid."

"I understand your frustration," Ray said. "They have problems here and are aware of them but cannot be interested in fixing them. But you do know that if the notary has said she is ready for the closing, all debts will be paid before a deed is given."

"I understand that all too well. What is missing here are the hard numbers I need to see that tell me what amounts of money are going where and to who. When we closed on Wayaca, they never gave us the statements we asked for ahead of the closing. Isn't there a requirement for the closer to provide a detailed statement at least one business day in advance of a closing so the seller and buyer have time to review the numbers?"

"Yes, there is such a thing in America. But this is Aruba. The same laws do not apply, and you will not come away from the closing completely satisfied. There are no laws here to protect you."

"If you could ask the notary to have the closing documents as up-to-date as possible, that's all I can hope for," Jim said.

"I will do what I can for you."

"Okay, thank you, Ray. Keep me informed if anything comes up. Pasa un bon dia, mi amigo."

"Igualmente."

"Chao." And Jim ended the call.

Sharon had turned the TV on to the local news channel. Jim liked to see the forecast for the winds every morning. There was a breaking news story just coming on.

"The Maine Warden Service and Maine State Police are asking for the public's help in finding anyone of interest in connection with the illegal burial of a man's body in Naples. The body was found in a shallow grave in the woods near the shore of Lake Paul. At this time, no further information is being released because it's an active investigation. More details will be available soon."

"First time I've heard of that," Jim said. "I'd like to know what area of the lake they found the body at."

"Didn't you tell me the ground area around that lake was enormous?" Sharon said. "The body could have been there for years. It may just be a pile of bones from hunters who buried them."

"Maybe you're right. We can ask Jill tonight what she heard about it."

"She should have first-hand knowledge of what's going on."

"I know you're right about that," Jim said. But he had an uneasy feeling about it. And right in Jill's backyard too.

After breakfast was done, Sharon got back on the computer and accessed the Diario website to start searching for obituaries. The edition with the story on Paul didn't have it, so she checked the papers that were written in the following days. It was found in the third edition after the story ran.

"Here it is," Sharon said.

"What's it say?" Jim asked, thinking he was funny.

"I can only read his name. The rest is in Papiamento."

"Let me see what we've got. Right there. Two nephews and a niece. Jose, Juan, and Anncherry Dalmer, children of his sister, Jolanda. HeRon said they came here to return the favor I had bestowed upon Paul."

"I thought you said it was about money. What favor was that?"

Oh boy, Jim let that one slip. He started from the

beginning and filled her in on almost every detail. A few things were left out or embellished to make the story come out the way he wanted it to.

"Why did you hide this from me?" Sharon demanded. "And more importantly, why did you let that idiot, HeRon, convince you it was the right thing to do? I thought you were above such childish behavior!"

"Paul stole from us, and there was no one on the island who would do anything to help an American get his money back from an Aruban," Jim said. "They'd just laugh and call you stupid."

"Don't they have small claims court or some other legal means for recovering our money?"

"If you managed to hire an attorney to go after him, he'd end up doing more to protect Paul while all the time writing you hefty bills for his services. In the end, you'd be throwing good money after bad. It would be a total waste of time."

"So you think his nephews and niece are here to break your leg? Which leg should be an easy choice for those three. You've only got one left."

"I was hoping to get a step ahead of them. I assumed they were holding up at Rupert's house, but Jill told Sam it wasn't them. I can only guess they're still living in the woods by the middle of the lake."

"Wait a minute," Sharon said. "Sam was asking about your memory while you were in the woods yesterday. He said he found our tracks on the road and then again some marks in a clearing. But he said there was no hole. He didn't see a hole in the clearing."

"He must have been in a different area," Jim said.

"I told him the same thing. But he had a good point. How many places in the woods would match up like the one he saw? He said there were marks in the roadway that looked like multiple people scuffling around doing something. Like Jill and I trying to load you in the truck. Then he said he went straight towards the shoreline and found an opening with more marks. Maybe where you hit something and fell. But there was no hole. And another thing. Did you remember the doctor saying you had a bruise on the side of your head? Where did that come from?"

"I remember entering the clearing and then hearing the voice in the direction of the water. I never looked down. I just stepped forward, and that was it. I don't even remember my foot coming down. I was out cold."

"Do you think you could have hit a large tree branch that knocked you down?" Sharon asked.

"I guess anything is possible," Jim said.

"Then would it be possible that your friends from Aruba ambushed you? They were here to break a leg, and last I looked, you had one broken."

"Possibly. But I should have heard or seen them."

"Jill and Sam said the brush in the woods was so thick it was hard to see two feet in front of you."

"Yeah, there were places like that," Jim said.

"If the voice in front of you was part of the trap to get your attention, would it be possible you didn't see somebody off to the side in the thick brush?"

"Yeah."

"Does Jill know about the nephews and niece, and what they're here for?"

"She knows about them. I'm not sure how much she's put together on her own though."

"Maybe that's where we should begin," Sharon said. "Maybe she can help you with your problem."

"Funny you should say that. I was thinking the same thing."

Right. Like when he first met her.

Chapter 33

At midday, the phone rang, and Jim answered it. He had been thinking about a conversation with Jill.

"Hi, how are you feeling?" Sam asked.

"Actually, I feel good. And not just because of the medication. The cast keeps the leg comfortable, too."

"Glad to hear it. I know you'll be well soon. Look, the reason I called was to see how you were. But something else has come up I wanted to tell you about. Is it a good time to talk?"

"Yes, it is."

"Last night, when Jill and I were riding together on the way to your house, I kind of said some things to her that she didn't like."

"What things?"

"Like the reason we wanted to be friends with her in the first place. I don't know what came over me, but I felt I had to be truthful with her."

"Like maybe because you're falling in love and wanted everything out in the open?" Jim asked.

"I knew you'd understand," Sam said. "Only if it was because of love, I hadn't thought quite that far yet."

"Real love can blind a sane man. You've probably been bitten by the love bug."

"Anyway, the love bug may have flown south. I don't think we'll be seeing any more of Jill. Ever."

"Whoa now," Jim said. "This sounds more serious than you led me to believe. There must be more to it."

"Not really. She said we were using her, and she didn't like it. I also kinda blamed it on you. I'm sorry. I have a big mouth."

"I should be mad, but then again how can I be? It was my idea. But in no way did I intend it to be like using her. I honestly valued her as a real person and considered her a dear friend. We never went into details of the assault or what we found out since then. We didn't want to involve her. How are we guilty of using her?"

"She never gave me the chance to explain," Sam said. "As soon as she convinced herself she was being used, I couldn't get a word in edgewise. She shut me down and kicked me out of her car."

"Listen, Sam, I don't want to lose her as a friend. How about you?"

"Me neither. I was hoping something long-term was in the making."

"Let me talk to Sharon and have her call Jill," Jim said. "See what she has to say. I'll get back to you when they're finished talking."

"Thanks. I couldn't sleep last night thinking I ruined the one thing that was important to me. I hope Sharon can salvage our relationship."

"I hope so too. I'll call you back."

"Bye."

Sharon was sitting at the computer with an ear bent his way.

"And what did Sam have to say?" Sharon asked.

"He told me that he and Jill had a spat last night while they were driving together in her car. He's worried that she is through with us. And he has a good reason to be worried." Jim filled her in on all the details.

"I wouldn't blame her if she never wanted to lay eyes on any of us again! If I were her, I'd be furious!"

"That's why I'm counting on you to smooth things over," Jim said.

"Why would I do that? She'll probably tear my head off."

"I don't think she's like that. Didn't her friendship mean anything to you?"

"In the short time I'd known her, I was impressed with the way she handled herself. She was a quick friend."

"I think it's a friendship worth trying to mend. Call her and see what she says. Make sure you convince her to come over tonight so Sam and I can tell her how much she means to us. Blame it all on the two of us. Do what you have to so she'll show up tonight."

"I'll try. What's the number?"

Jim found it on his phone and gave it to her. He left the room so Sharon wouldn't feel uncomfortable while begging for mercy. Or maybe stabbing him in the back. But he deserved it. He never intended to use the girl, but he had made a cruel joke about it. Now it was payback time.

Ten minutes later Sharon came to the room he was in and opened the door.

"She's not coming tonight," Sharon said.

"Why not?"

"Because she feels betrayed by people she considered friends. She made it clear there aren't any hard feelings but thinks it's better to part company."

"Thanks for trying. I know you gave it your best, but I'm going to call and cry on her shoulder until she gives in."

"Good luck with that."

Jim dialed her number, but she wouldn't take the call. He asked Sharon for her phone and called again. She answered on the second ring.

"I knew who it was but figured I had to talk to you sometime," Jill said. "What's up?"

Why'd she have to say that?? What's up??

"Can you please give me time to explain what really happened?" Jim begged. *Like it's going to be way different from what Sam said.*

"I'm kind of busy here so make it quick."

He grabbed every apology he could think of and threw them at her. He begged and at one time even tried to get down on his knees to make it realistic. He challenged every remark she made. And in the end, he convinced her what she believed was right was in fact wrong.

"Please don't throw away the foundations of friendship that were being built every day by all of us," Jim said.

And then he put an arrow right through her heart. The one with Sam hanging onto the feathers.

"He wanted the relationship to begin with honesty. I'm sure he told you I was the one who was responsible, but please give me a chance to explain myself. It was more of a joke than anything else. You've got to believe me. Please?" begged pitiful Jim.

"Okay, Beanpole. See you at six." And she was gone.

"What did you think of the master while he performed his magic?" asked a beaming Jim.

"Most pathetic display of crap I've ever witnessed," Sharon spat back, "and I can't believe she bought that line. You're clearly the master of something."

"Yah, well, she's coming and nothing else matters. I told you I'd get the job done."

His next call was to Sam. He told him the news and said, "Don't be late." Then he dialed Richard's number.

"Hello?" Richard answered.

"Hi, it's Jim. How are you today?"

"Fine, thank you. What's up?"

*Something's got to change here...*Jim really hated that expression.

"Can I ask a favor of you?"

"Anything you need my friend."

"I would like to buy a gun."

"I know a person who deals in them."

"Nothing illegal or anything like that. Just a 9-millimeter handgun or a Glock. Something that will hold a few bullets in the magazine."

"I have a 9-millimeter, and it's a nice gun," Richard said. "A Smith and Wesson that holds one bullet in the chamber and twelve in the magazine. I think a Glock can hold fifteen or more."

"A 9-millimeter will be fine. Call me when I can pick it

up. And thanks for your help."
"Glad to be of service. I'll be in touch, bye."

Chapter 34

Sometime before noon, the cousins dragged themselves out of bed one by one and began moving around the house like normal people. It would be another hour before the cobwebs were completely clear from their heads, but things were looking up. Being young definitely helped.

Jose was at the kitchen table with a thermometer in his mouth. Anncherry glanced at the cup sitting in front of him and saw it was the one with the word "Rear" on it. While lying in bed, she had given long thought to why anyone would have two thermometers, and what they would have been used for. The reason came to mind when she remembered walking in on her own mother with her pants down and a thermometer inserted into her behind. It was for a "more accurate reading" she was told at the time.

"Does that thermometer taste funny?" Anncherry chuckled.

"Something about it does not seem right," Jose said, "but I do not have a temperature, so everything is good."

Anncherry turned her head as the grin on her face grew. She decided to let it go and spare her brother the details.

"We have to clean the car and then go to Burger King so we can book our flights home," Jose said.

"While you two were getting your beauty sleep, I went out in the barn to check on the car," Juan said. "It is a war zone. Even worse. But I found a wet-vac we can use to clean it and some disinfectant under the kitchen counter. With the three of us, we can be done with it fast."

All nodding, they made their way to the barn. Queasy

stomachs and all, they began the chore at hand. It was obvious the boys were struggling with the odors and sights because they were constantly dry heaving. Anncherry worked steadily and without backlash. Women just handled it better.

It was not long before they were on the road again headed for Windham. After they arrived, Anncherry and Juan went in to order food while Jose accessed the internet.

He logged on to "Cheapflights" and began his search. Before they left the house, he counted the cash that was left to spend. He figured it would be tight going.

The cheapest flights were out of Boston and were non-stop to Aruba. But he had seen articles on the internet that said getting into Boston's airport was a nightmare if you did not know your way around. So he decided on the Portland Jetport because he read it had easy access. The soonest flight they could afford was two days away. He reserved the seats and paid with the credit card, but it was again denied. Jose already planned on driving to Portland and booking the trips at the airport.

Anncherry and Juan returned with the food and the trio ate on the way to the airport. Once they got into Portland, there were big signs with airplanes on them that guided them to the airport. Even a monkey could have found his way.

The airport was not busy, and they quickly found the counter for the airline they wanted to fly on. After receiving the receipts for their booked seats, they sat in the car to think about what to do next.

Anncherry wanted to stay close by in a hotel and pass the time watching cable TV. But there was no money for that. The cousins had to make do on $45 for two more days. There were also free beds and food back in Naples. Plus three more cases of beer that needed to be drank. That was the straw that broke the camel's back, and the car was then driven in that direction.

When they arrived back in Windham, Jose said he wanted to look at a few things at the BigMart store. So they parked the car and went in to look around. Anncherry and Juan spent their time looking at DVD movies in the electronics department while Jose hung out by the jewelry counter. He watched the attendant closely as she performed her duties. When she left the counterspace unattended, probably for a bathroom break, Jose made his move.

He looked around to see if anyone was paying attention, and when he was satisfied the coast was clear, went behind the counter and selectively grabbed at jewelry from the unlocked cases. It took him less than thirty seconds to come away with what he wanted.

Jose left the jewelry department in search of the others and found them mesmerized over some videos. It was time to go and both reluctantly followed him. When they attempted to exit the building, a loud alarm sounded that stopped them in their tracks.

It did not take Jose long to realize the alarm was for them, so he told his siblings to follow him. They took off running through the parking lot when they heard voices behind them shouting, "Stop!" They did not, and ran right by their car and would not look back. After getting across the main road, the cousins ran behind a strip mall and hid in an enclosure next to a set of dumpsters.

The security personnel the store employed were top-rated and knew what they were doing. Once the two guards realized the thieves were beyond their grasp, one stayed outside to watch for them while the other went to the security office to watch video, and see if he could get a look at the vehicle they may have arrived in. He began viewing the parking area the thieves ran through thinking the car would be their first thought for leaving, but would run past it because the guards were chasing them.

It took ten minutes before the security guard said, "Gotcha!" He called a towing company and went to join the other guard so they could check out the car. The doors were locked, but the windows were left open enough so he could reach in and unlock them. He opened the door to the Impala and was assaulted by an odor he wanted nothing to do with. He slammed the door shut and would run the plates instead of getting the registration from the glove box. One security guard waited for the tow truck while the other went back to the security office and called the police.

Philip Gagnon

The tow truck came and latched onto the Impala so it could be hauled away and locked in an impound yard. They did not know it, but they were doing the cousins a huge favor.

Chapter 35

Jose was smart enough to know the Impala was a lost cause, and that a new set of wheels was in order. The cousins decided to split up and check out cars in front of the strip mall. It would amaze most people to learn not everybody took their keys out of the car and locked the doors. It took a while because they wanted to be selective as they needed an ordinary car that by itself would not draw attention. There were two to choose from that were ready to go. A white Toyota Corolla was the winning choice, so Jose jumped in, started it, and drove through the lot to pick up the others.

They would only need a thirty-minute window to make it back to Naples before somebody reported the car stolen, and Jose liked those odds. The car would be hidden in the woods until it was needed again for a quick trip to Portland so they could catch their flight. The beauty of that trip was they would travel to Portland in the early morning hours when it was dark as their plane was scheduled to leave at 6:15 in the morning.

The trio drove to Naples and came into town without incident. Just like back home, they never saw a cop. The Corolla made a left turn on Route 114 and headed home. When the property came into view, a car could be seen parked near the house. The blue lights that were mounted in the back window of the car told them it was the police. Down beside the barn was a green pickup truck with blue lights on the roof. The farmhouse was lost.

They continued along for a half mile and turned around. Passing the house, a white van with blue lights on top was turning into the driveway. The Corolla continued to the causeway and then turned down a side road that would eventually access the logging roads that surrounded the lake. Jose needed time to think. After finding familiar territory in the woods, he found a spot to hide the car and backed into it.

Anncherry desperately wanted to stay by the Portland Jetport and not travel anymore, but that option was lost also. There was no place to stay, and Portland was a city where there would be far more police to worry about. No, the cousins would make do in the woods until they had to leave for their flight. Tonight when it turned dark, they would go to a store for some food and drink. The three of them were young, and it was only a couple of days. It would be no problem.

Uh huh, OK.

Chapter 36

Jim was home watching TV when the phone rang. The tele was on, but his mind was busy dreaming of payback.

"Hi, how are you feeling?" Sam asked.

"I'm good, thanks," Jim said.

"Jill just called me and said she has to cancel tonight. She asked me to call and give you the message and was adamant it had nothing to do with what transpired last night. Apparently, her dog is very ill. After stopping home for lunch today, it became obvious something was wrong with Cuddles, her Schnauzer. She doesn't want to leave the poor thing alone."

"I don't blame her. Do you think she'd mind talking to me on the phone? I have a few important things I need to know. What I mean by that is I need her professional opinion on a few ideas. I don't want her to think I'm trying to use her."

"That's all smoothed over, and she was good about it. How about this? I suggested we get together at her house tonight so she can stay with her dog. She said that would be okay. I told her I would bring dinner so she wouldn't have to do anything. I think she's kind of excited about me seeing her house."

"Did she say that?" Jim asked.

"No, but it was implied. I think we're made for each other."

"I think so too. Are we planning on the same time?"

"If it works for you. Are you getting around okay?"

"Yes. The only thing that's different for me is I have a stiff leg. I'm getting used to it."

"Good, then I'll see you around six," Sam said.

"Okay, bye."

Jim was telling Sharon about the change of plans when a breaking story was being announced on the TV news show. It was about a robbery at the BigMart store in Windham.

"Breaking News: There was a robbery at the Windham BigMart where it's believed a group of thieves made off with almost $7000 in jewelry. Security personnel said a watch valued at more than $3000 and three rings valued at almost $4000 were missing. Security has supplied us with a video of the suspects seen entering and then leaving the store. Anyone with information regarding these suspects is urged to call the Windham Police Department at the number on the screen. An APB has been issued for the suspects."

Jim could not believe his eyes. He recognized the girl, and even though the two men had cut their hair, he could tell it was them. The same people who had assaulted him and Sam at Richard's. Paul's relatives from Aruba. He had replay on his cable box so he used it to go back to the phone number for the police. He grabbed his phone and began to dial. The call was immediately answered, and he told his story.

The policewoman who answered was nice enough but insisted on his name, address, rank in the military, etc, etc, etc, and Jim was ready to slam the phone down on her. However, she was smooth and able to convince him to give her the information. He did and she was very thankful, but Jim was left with another scar.

After hanging up, he called Richard.

"Hello?"

"Hi, Richard," Jim said. "Any luck with a gun?"

"I will have one in my hands in a half hour. I know it's what you want, so I'll pay, and you can reimburse me."

"Perfect. Can I grab it in an hour or so? And how much money should I bring?"

"$350 and that includes two magazines, a holster, and a box of ammo. This is a great deal."

"It sounds really good. Thanks for taking care of me. I'll be down to get it in about an hour."

"See you then, bye."

"Why the gun?" Sharon asked.

"I know you don't like them, but I thought it would be nice to have something of an equalizer until Paul's relatives are put away," Jim said, "and I've been thinking a lot about what's happened, and it all points to those idiots. I don't want to be left without a fighting chance."

"Don't ever go and point that thing at me. And promise you'll get rid of it after they're taken care of."

"I promise."

Really...I think.

Chapter 37

The sun had set and the cousins needed food and drink. They left the safety of their parking spot in the woods and went to the causeway. From there, it was a stone's throw to the stores with the goods. Twice on the way out of the woods, the Corolla got mired in mud, but with Juan and Jose pushing, it came out both times. It was in need of a washing, but that could wait. The trio parked in front of the Alive'n Well store first and then they would pull over to Tony's Foodland next. The idea was to grab some suds at the Alive'n Well and grub at Tony's.

Juan and Anncherry pulled off a masterful distraction on the employee at the Alive'n Well store and came out of it with a case of beer scot-free. It was easier than taking candy from a baby.

The Corolla was pulled out of the Alive'n Well parking lot and taken to Tony's where Jose would go in alone and perform his magic. He planned on coming out with two bags of groceries but would only pay for one. He could not be outdone by his crony siblings.

Chapter 38

Jim and Sharon left the house and went to Richard's. Jim called ahead and said he'd have Sharon drive around to the back of the building and asked Richard to meet them there with the gun. Once Sharon pulled up by the back door of the restaurant, she tapped the horn button to signal Richard. He emerged from the door a few minutes later with a small box in hand.

"How's the leg?"

"Not bad," Jim said. "The pain is taken care of with my meds and the cast supports it well."

"What's the coat hanger for?"

"Watch."

Jim got positioned properly in the seat and removed the straightened out coat hanger he had attached to the outside of his cast. On one end of the coat hanger was a chunk of Velcro that was adhered where a portion of metal had been rounded. He maneuvered the contraption and slid it down inside the cast for more than two feet.

"No shortage of itching. This takes care of it."

"I'll remember that. Not that I really want to. Here's your new gun."

Jim removed it from the box and was instantly impressed. He never thought he would like guns, but having it in his hand was a powerful feeling.

"Here's the money. I can't thank you enough for coming through for me."

"Always happy to help a friend," Richard said.

"Thanks again. We've got to go now."

"Bye." Richard went back inside.

Sharon drove away heading towards the road. After entering the traffic on Route 302, she headed for Jill's. A few minutes later, Jim's cell rang.

"Hello?"

"It's Jill. I've been home all afternoon with a sick dog and had some time to think. Have you got a minute?"

"Sure. We're coming your way right now."

"These people you thought were after you, if they're from a foreign country, wouldn't they have an accent of some kind?"

"A slight one, yes, because they were taught English as children."

"When I spoke to Rupert's grandson, he had a slight accent, but what I remember now was he didn't use contractions when forming his words," Jill began. "Never once when I spoke with him did he shorten any words. If he was taught English in this country, he would have said, 'I'll,' or 'It'll,' or 'couldn't.' Everything he said was full length. 'I will,' or 'It will,' or 'could not.' That guy is not American. I'll bet the girl was hiding in the house to throw me off."

"Makes perfect sense. Even though these people were taught the English language at an early age, some things get left out when you learn it in a foreign country. I think you're right. Can we call the police and tell them we think they're at the farmhouse?"

"I'd go over myself if I thought it would help. I've been stuck in my house since before noon with my sick Cuddles, and I can't leave her. I'll call it in and get back to you."

"Thanks, bye," Jim said and closed the phone. "Well, that confirms what I figured all along."

"What's that?" Sharon asked.

"They were staying at Rupert's house. And what happened to Rupert? I'm not liking this."

"Those people are serious trouble. I'm beginning to like the idea of having a weapon with us."

"No telling what else they could have done that we don't know about."

A few minutes later, Jim's cell rang again.

"Hello?"

"I called it in and they're already all over Rupert's home," Jill said. "No sign of anybody at the house."

"How did the police end up at Rupert's?"

"It was the car your friends drove. It pulled out from the farmhouse yesterday onto the road in front of an off-duty State Trooper. They pulled out in front of him without looking his way. He was going to pull them over but saw they had Massachusetts plates and that's the way everybody drives down there. Anyway, he remembered the car when it was found at BigMart today. He was able to put two and two together when he saw the report."

"We watched the BigMart video earlier today," Jim said. "I called Windham P.D. right after I saw them on it. Now the law is breathing down their necks."

"They'll get them soon," Jill said. "I feel bad all this is happening next door, and I didn't even realize it."

"We're not far now. We'll be at your place in a few minutes, and we can talk then."

"I'll be here, bye."

They were just coming into Naples, and the Naples Shopping Center was coming up on the right. Home of Tony's Foodland.

"Let's swing in and get a bottle of wine to have with dinner," Jim said. "Heck with it, let's get two. What do you think?"

"I'm sure it'll be perfect," Sharon said. "Merlot?"

"Please."

"What about your medication?"

"I'm not driving. I'll be fine."

Sharon pulled into an open space in front of the store and got out to do her shopping. Jim spent his time looking around. After a while, his eyes settled on the car next to him with two people inside. What caught his attention was the fact they were staring at the front door, like they were waiting for somebody important to come out. He could only see their profiles, and the woman had features he'd seen before. The guy in the front seat said something to the girl and half turned in Jim's direction. *Well,*

Philip Gagnon

Howdy Doody! Jim thought. *I know that guy! Short hair and all! And I know that girl! It's them for God's sake!*

There was a hat under the seat and sunglasses in the glove box. Jim put them on and tried not to stare. If only the car could be moved a few more spaces away, he would be more comfortable. *The gun. Get the gun out and load it.* While doing that he became worried about Sharon. *Would they know what she looked like?* He couldn't remember a time when they may have seen her.

He was stuck in the car with nowhere to run, but he had his gun now. The only problem was Sharon. *Would they know who she was?* The exit door from the store opened, so Jim looked the other way. If he heard the door open and shut in the car next to him, they'd all be accounted for and would then leave. He wanted to be ready and leave right after them. But at the same time, he didn't want Sharon coming out of the store yet.

The car door opened and shut, and then its motor started. It was backed away from the curbing and driven towards the road. Jim almost broke his neck when he whipped around to see what direction they were headed in. They entered the traffic going towards the causeway and ended up waiting for the light to turn green while sitting in a line of cars.

The door to the car opened and Jim came close to staining his drawers. His heart was in his mouth, and he turned and saw Sharon getting in the driver's seat.

"Start the car fast and get out to the causeway!" Jim yelled. "Now!"

Sharon was too busy finding the keys and trying to start the car to say anything. She saw the gun in Jim's lap.

"What's the problem?" Sharon asked.

"They were just parked right next to us! One of them was in the same store as you! Their car just pulled out into traffic, and we're going to follow them!"

"Why do we want to do that?"

"Because we need to see where they end up so we can tell the cops!"

"But isn't that the cops job to do?"

"They're not here right now! And I don't want them to get away!"

The light was green and traffic was moving. Jim was not a good back seat driver.

"There! There! Over there! Pass this guy! Faster! Faster! Don't you dare lose them! There! They went left on 114! Get up there quick! Go left! Go left faster! There! They're headed towards the woods! Shut off your lights and go left here! See their taillights? Keep back, but keep them in view! I'm calling the cops!"

He had his cell in hand, found the number, and hit call. The phone just gave a busy signal.

"I can't believe it!" Jim shouted. "We're already without phone service!"

"Shouldn't we turn around and call the cops?" Sharon said. "Let them take care of this?"

"No time for that! There's too much territory out here to cover! Don't you lose them!"

Jim checked the gun to be sure it was loaded. The magazine was full of bullets, and he racked the slide of the gun to load a round in the chamber. He hoped he wouldn't need it tonight but better the Arubans die than them.

The going so far was okay, but Sharon was closer to the other car than Jim wanted to be. If the Arubans hit the brakes and looked back at the same time, Sharon's car would be lit up. *Hopefully, they won't look back.*

They began slowing, and Jim told Sharon to back off a bit more. She did but ended up stopping completely as the other car was now creeping along. Jim had her use the emergency brake to slow or stop the vehicle so the brake lights would not illuminate. The two of them sat and watched as the other car slowly crept forward. It was almost in the woods as it moved forward slowly. It then moved back to the center of the road and Jim could see why they slowed down when the taillights lit up the mud puddle. The car then picked up speed and moved away from them.

"There!" Jim said. "See the mud? Straddle it like they did!"

Philip Gagnon

Sharon continued along and soon had them back on solid ground. The problem was now she couldn't see where they were going, so she stopped again.

"It's okay, I've got the gun. Turn your lights on and let's move ahead slowly. Keep your eyes peeled for their taillights or anything metallic that may shine in the light."

"What do you mean metallic?" Sharon asked.

"You know. Car metal that will reflect the light."

Off in the distance, they saw the taillights again, so Jim told her to turn her headlights off.

"Move forward slowly and I'll help looking for the road."

But it was so dark they went a few yards and stopped.

"Shut the car off and come with me," Jim said.

"You're not serious are you?" Sharon spat. "I'm not getting near those people!"

"Okay, stay here with the car. I'll be right back."

"Jim, please, listen to me. We can't do this. Let the police handle it."

"I will. I just need to see if they're stuck or parking for the night. I'll be right back."

Oh God, Sharon thought. *This isn't good.*

Sidearm in its holster and strapped to The Lone Ranger's thigh, he removed his crutches from the car and moved forward slowly, watching the taillights of the car and looking down to see what he could. His eyes adjusted quickly to the dark and that made it better. He could hear the spinning of tires and the yells and grunts of people pushing a car that must be stuck.

When Jim was thirty feet away, he had a perfect view of the situation. The two men were taking a break and facing away from him. The car was stuck pretty good. One of the men turned to open the car door and spotted Jim, crutches and all.

"What do you want?" Jose shouted. "What are you doing here?"

"I came to see where the police would find you!" Jim yelled. "Jose, Juan, and Anncherry Dalmer. They're on the way now!"

Jose motioned for Anncherry to turn the car off. She did so

Glassy Water

and got out.

"How did you get here?" Jose shouted.

"I have a car!" Jim shouted back. "I also have a gun! Stay where you are!"

"You think you can touch us? Do not be so foolish! Give me the gun, and we will not hurt you!"

"No can do, Kimosabi! Why don't the three of you put your hands behind your head and lie on the ground!"

"The ground here is all mud! We will do no such thing for you! Come and get us!"

With that said the three cousins took to the woods, and all Jim could think of was, *that's not good!*

The brush in this area was nothing like the brush closer to the lake. Two of the cousins were behind Jim within thirty seconds and Anncherry stepped out of the woods in front of him while he was trying to retreat to his car. He lifted the gun and aimed it at Anncherry.

"Don't do it!" Jim yelled. "I'm not afraid to use this! I've killed before!"

What?! A mosquito??

Anncherry was not a woman of words but a warrior of action. She knew he was relying on his crutches for stability and therefore should be easy to move off balance. She came towards him moving from side to side, quick as lightning. She saw him pull the trigger.

Jim pulled the trigger, then again, and again. *Bang, Bang, Bang,* he thought he should have heard. But the gun threw out no bullets and made no sound. Anncherry attacked and kicked him in the solar plexus. Jim went down, and she used the open palm of her hand to deliver a blow to his temple. The same temple that was bruised from the last ambush. The brothers emerged from the woods and stood over him. Anncherry reached down and picked up his gun.

"Stupid fool," Anncherry said. "The safety is on."

"Juan, go back where he came from and see if there is a car," Jose said.

Juan was gone four minutes and then a car came driving

up. Juan told Sharon to get out and walk towards the others. Anncherry and Jose had dragged Jim back away from the road, and she couldn't see him.

"Where's my husband?" Sharon demanded. "Where's Jim?"

"Worry about your own problems sister," Anncherry said.

Anncherry moved towards her and was about to deliver a blow to her solar plexus when she slipped on the roadway, and instead her foot caught Sharon's throat. Sharon's hands immediately went to her neck as blood began to ooze from her mouth while she gasped for her final breaths. She fell to the ground and was dead within a minute.

"Juan, take her car back to the store and grab two shovels and a big flashlight," Jose said. "I saw some shovels in a bucket out in front of the store. While you are gone we will move the bodies into the woods."

Juan jumped in the car and backed up slowly. He managed to get the car turned around without getting stuck and sped away. Jose and Anncherry began to move the bodies farther away from the road.

When Juan arrived at the store, there were two police cars side by side at the other end of the parking lot. He knew better than to try and steal the shovels now, so he went to shift into reverse and noticed a pocketbook wedged between the seats. He rifled through it and found $92 and change.

Grabbing two shovels from the bucket, he took them in and after finding a lantern, paid for them with his newly found inheritance. After putting the shovels and light in the back seat, he got in and drove back to the woods, careful not to speed or look suspicious. He entered the woods and drove until the Corolla was in front of him.

Juan got out of the car and grabbed the shovels from the back seat. It was then he realized his mistake.

"You idiot," Jose spat out. "That square nosed shovel will do us no good digging. At least you got one spade. Let us get to work."

The light lit the area up well, and the trio dug for what felt

Glassy Water

like hours preparing two graves to stick their victims in. The rocks were brutal so the holes would not be deep. They went to get Sharon and noticed a wolf was at her side. A wolf with red teeth. Blood covered red teeth. Anncherry had Jim's gun in her waistband and took it out. She lifted the gun and aimed it at the wolf.

"Do not fire the gun, Anncherry," Juan said. "I am afraid the wrong people will hear it and come to find us. We will move the animal away with branches. There is only one of them."

Once all three had a sizable branch in hand, they moved in on the wolf, so he turned and ran off. But not before he bared his teeth for them. When the trio went to grab Sharon, they noticed the wolf had started gnawing on her.

"Hey, they have to eat too," Jose said. "Right?"

They dragged Sharon to the hole and slid her in. While they were backfilling her grave, sirens began to wail up on the main road.

"That may or may not be for us, but I do not think we want to wait and find out," Jose said. "Let us hurry and finish so we can go deeper in the woods for the night."

While Jose and Juan were dragging Jim over to his hole, Anncherry was covering Sharon in the other one. As she moved around, she was kicking debris and leaves into Jim's grave.

"Careful, Anncherry," Jose said. "You are kicking stuff in the other hole. And they are not deep enough to begin with."

They laid Jim next to his grave while Juan tried to clean it out. But the sirens grew louder.

"Forget it," Jose said. "Let us throw him in."

And they did. Face first. Juan kicked his cast in next to the other leg and the men filled the hole fast as possible. They were grabbing at anything they could find to fill it up. Juan heard what sounded like a growling noise behind him and quickly turned. But there was nothing to be seen. He thought he was hearing things. The trio grabbed leaves and twigs to cover the freshly turned dirt and finished the job. After grabbing their shovels and light, they ran to the cars.

That was when it hit the fan. The wolves who were sizing

up the prey began their attack thinking a meal might get away. With the taste of human flesh still on their minds, the wolves were insane for more.

Juan was the first to turn and see them. He was passing by the stuck Corolla when one foot slipped in the mud and his leg went under the car. He immediately screamed for help, and both Jose and Anncherry went to grab his arms to pull him free.

They dragged Juan out in time for the closest wolf to attack him while he was still on the ground. He started squealing like a stuck pig. The more noise he made, the more violent the wolf assault became.

Anncherry and Jose left Juan and went to the other car. There were wolves on both sides of it coming their way. They both had guns and reached for them. But the wolves coming up from behind were on their backs before either knew what happened. The wolves in front attacked a few seconds later. The cousins were all devoured in six minutes. Their bones were carried away into the woods for some extra licking. The pack of wolves had their fill for the night.

If the cousins were still alive, they would probably think the sound of a gunshot would not have been such a bad idea after all. They would have gladly submitted to the police if they had known who was on the menu.

Chapter 39
Today, October 11

The following morning, Jill and Sam took the day off from work to search the woods for their friends. They went over the scenario time and again and agreed that something must have happened to bring Jim and Sharon in the woods. They checked everywhere else. The two of them were nowhere to be found. The police and wardens had been notified and were also searching the area.

Sam saw the back end of Sharon's car on the road in front of them and pulled up behind it. There was another car ahead of hers that was apparently stuck. How did they end up here trying to help someone out? Both Sam and Jill could feel something was terribly wrong as they got out of their car.

Blood was splattered all around on the ground, and they feared the worst. Two guns were lying in the roadway. What possibly could have happened here? The logging road was loaded with signs of animal prints and an obvious battle, but the scene was too confusing to determine a result. Jill said she would travel back to the main road and make the call to the police. Sam would stay with Sharon's car for now.

While Jill was gone and with tears running down his cheeks, Sam walked the road looking for any other clues about the tragedy that had befallen his friends. There were numerous imprints in the roadway from animals, but there were also dug-in shoe marks. At one place, they looked to be coming from up in the woods, so Sam went that way.

He saw in the distance a body lying on the ground. Sam moved closer while searching the area with his eyes for anyone else who might be around. The sight of Jim lying there motionless took his breath away. He reached his friend and checked for any signs of life. Sam's heart almost busted out of his chest when he found Jim was still alive. Seeing the hole next to him, he went and looked into it. Sharon was partially uncovered but obviously lying there dead. Just the sight of her made Sam start to cry uncontrollably. The love he felt for her was overwhelming. He sat on the ground and cried until the police came and helped him away.

Chapter 40

In the many days that came after Sharon died, Jim found comfort in the form of a bottle. He was mixing the booze with pills given to him for his leg. Together they helped him dream and cope. He would surely come out of his depression but needed some time alone to beat back the demons that had confronted Sharon and him. He had Sharon cremated and would soon, on a sober day, take her ashes up in their plane and scatter them around the lake.

Sam and Jill had stopped by on occasion to offer their friendship and help, but Jim wouldn't answer the door. He wanted to be left alone with his thoughts as if it were just him and Sharon. He hadn't showered in days and didn't want anybody to see him in his PJ's. He'd also shut off the phone.

Time. That's all he needed to heal, and he wanted people to forget about him. Sharon was consuming his thoughts, and that's the way it was going to be. He truly loved that girl. Nothing left now but the dreams.

Just a few more days and all would be well with him. He needed to eat some solid food. Because all of his meals were in the form of liquid, that was all that came out when he sat on the toilet. He'd eat soon. He really loved her.

A week had passed and he found the strength to go down on the dock and sit with Sharon. It was late morning and he was feeling good. Real good. Dreamland good. Jim took a bag of goods with him that also had the ash urn in it. Together, they sat and drank in the sunshine along with the liquor he brought. They dreamed of flying together in the airplane and of riding in their boat. Of enjoying each other everyday as if there would be no tomorrow.

    With that thought in mind, Jim untied the plane and stepped on the float with Sharon in his arms. He opened the cabin door, and after placing her inside, climbed up into the cockpit and got in the left seat. It took a little effort, but he managed to pull the leg with the cast into the cockpit and placed it so his foot rested on the rudder pedal. He then helped Sharon get in the right seat and fired the engine. The lake was beautiful with a glassy smooth surface. After he was clear of the dock, he set the bird for takeoff and gave it the juice.

    Within seconds, the plane was airborne and away they went up in the sky, just the two of them. At 350 feet above the lake, the engine sputtered and then stopped. Glancing at the fuel gauges confirmed the problem. Even drunk, Jim remembered Sam telling him the gas tanks were empty the last time it was flown.

    Because the plane was going 80 miles an hour, the propeller kept spinning as if the motor was still running. With the speed rapidly bleeding off, Jim slowly pulled back on the control yoke. He kept backward pressure on the yoke as the nose of the plane pointed upward. Nothing could be seen except a blue heaven. *We're headed your way,* he thought.

    The left wing fell sharply when the plane stalled in the air. With not enough wind going over the wings to give the aircraft the lift needed to fly, and Jim's hands folded in his lap, the plane went into an uncontrollable spin in the direction of earth. Now, only the sight of water filled his vision. The urn on the seat beside him spilled and ashes were flying all over the cockpit.

    One of the final things that went through Jim's mind before the plane exploded on impact with the lake's surface was at least they were still together. His last breath was an inhale of ash. His last thought was, *This isn't going to be a good landing.*

What's up??

If for any reason you did not think this book was worth reading or if you have a voice that should be heard regarding negative comments or criticisms about this novel, someone wants to hear it. Kindly proceed to the next page to begin the process of being heard. Once you start the process, the results will be instantaneous. Have your voice heard now!

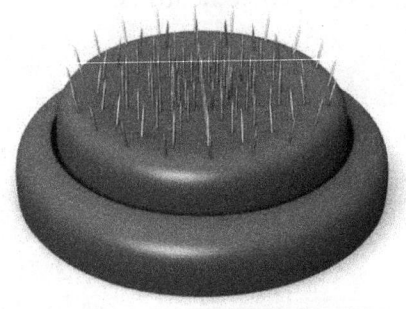

Press Button
To File Complaint

www.ingramcontent.com/pod-product-compliance
Lightning Source LLC
Chambersburg PA
CBHW022353040426
42450CB00005B/167